The Scooter
A Complete Guide

By the same author

Scooter Maintenance Complete (Out of Print)
Scootering (Out of Print)
The Sahara is Yours: A Handbook for Desert Travellers

Jon Stevens

The Scooter
A Complete Guide

Constable London

First published in Great Britain by
Constable and Company Ltd
10 Orange Street, London WC2H 7EG
Copyright © 1972 Jon Stevens

ISBN 0 09 458790 6 cloth
ISBN 0 09 458800 7 paper

Set in Monotype Bembo
printed in Great Britain by
The Anchor Press Ltd,
and bound by Wm. Brendon & Son Ltd,
both of Tiptree, Essex

Contents

5

Contents

6

Illustrations

List of Plates

List of Line Drawings

Preface

I have set out to help everybody who owns a scooter or is interested in scooters. All aspects are covered, from choosing the right machine to carrying out a planned maintenance schedule to keep the costs down, and the scooter running well and safely. The complete scooter is dealt with, showing not only how all the parts work, but also how they have reached their present form.

The advice on the problem of choosing a new scooter (Chapter 3) represents a new approach, based on the sad experience of those who have bought unwisely. Together with Chapter 4 (Initial Cost and Running Costs) it could help one to avoid making expensive mistakes.

Scooter making in Italy, Austria, France, Germany and Britain is described in detail in the opening chapters on the history of the scooter and its design. The Italians and Germans showed bold, imaginative thinking in the drawing office, machine shops and the boardroom. The staggering British failure is described in horrifying detail. Did these great motor cycle firms exhaust themselves in the attempt to make a new type of machine, or was their failure inevitable, even if the scooter had never been invented? The student anxious to write a new style thesis will find ample material in this book.

The average scooterist will find the technical sections invaluable, whether he wishes to adjust a brake cable or carry out a full decoke. All the instructions are simple and complete.

Preface

In the few cases where the work is beyond the average scooterist's knowledge or toolkit, the point is made clear.

Jon Stevens
May 1972

1 The Scooter Story

The scooter as we know it today was born in August 1945. The aircraft works of Piaggio and Co. at Pontedera had been destroyed by American bombing and the immediate problem was to get a small-scale project under way. Dr. Enrico Piaggio conceived the idea of a two-wheeled vehicle and handed the project over to his engineer, Corradino d'Ascanio. The latter had been trained and employed on the design of aircraft engines and frames. He had never worked on a two-wheeled vehicle and had very little motor cycle experience. He tackled the problem from an engineering standpoint and within a matter of weeks his first design was ready. By December it had been tested and approved. By April 1946 it was being produced in quantity. It is a tribute to his genius that today, a quarter of a century later, the design layout should have been modified only in detail, although there have been radical changes in engine design. This scooter was called the Vespa (Italian for wasp). Within ten years of its first appearance the Vespa had sold over 1,000,000. Within another five years sales had topped the 2,000,000 mark and it was being manufactured in Germany, England, France, Spain and Belgium as well as in the original Pontedera works. All these Vespas in their millions were made to a design which, fundamentally, was that laid down by d'Ascanio in 1946.

The Vespa was not the first scooter of all time. Many others had appeared, probably the best known being the Corgi folding motor cycle used by paratroopers and which continued for a time after 1945 in small-scale production. Machines described as scooters had been sold in Britain soon after 1919 and in the U.S.A. even before then; one or two, such as the Zutoped, were original in design but they had little else to commend them. The Zutoped derived directly from the child's toy scooter. It had a footboard, two wheels and a motor; steering was by means of a long handle. Curiously enough, this is one of the persistent dreams of U.S.A. inventors and every few years a new design is produced.

The other British machines which could be called scooters were based on bicycle or motor cycle designs and had a short life. They showed little originality of design. They had a mediocre performance and many disadvantages. In addition they had to compete with the products of the British motor cycle industry, and between 1919 and 1939 the British motor cycle industry was outstandingly successful. The famous names of this period cannot, for lustre and renown, be equalled in any other country – Sunbeam, Norton, A.J.S., Blackburne, New Imperial, Velocette, Triumph, Scott, Douglas, Cotton, Rudge, Excelsior – the list is endless and behind each of these names stood one or more of the British motor cycle race winners, practical men of vast experience and courage.

In trying to trace the first British scooter, historians have gone back to British machines of sixty years ago. No doubt French and German historians could claim equal foresight for their own countrymen. The question is, however, largely academic because in 1946 the word acquired a different meaning. Scooters built after that date stem directly from the first Vespa and owe more to it than they owe to any previous machine. Three things made this design distinctive:

1. The engine was totally enclosed.
2. The frame was open, with a flat footboard.
3. The wheels were carried on stub axles.

The combination of these three features in one machine was unique. When the first Vespa appeared at the 1946 Turin Show it attracted much attention and, though numerous criticisms were made, it was an instant success. It is therefore instructive to follow the inventor's reasoning. First and foremost d'Ascanio was an aircraft designer, with a lifetime's experience of air-cooled engines and stressed-skin framework construction. He settled immediately on a two-stroke air-cooled engine. He was not concerned with high speeds. Secondly he was familiar with chassis-less structures and was far ahead of his day in considering them superior to the conventional steel box or tube vehicle frame. The spot-welded frame used in all Vespas since 1946 is today common automobile practice.

The engine was enclosed because – again ahead of his day – d'Ascanio realised that owners were less and less interested in the machines they drove and were beginning to look on them more as a means of transport than as spare-time mechanical problems or hobbies. He mounted the wheels on stub axles because he had watched motor cyclists mend punctures and thereupon decided that on his scooters the wheels must be so mounted that they could be removed without difficulty and without disturbing the drive to the rear wheel. The designers of motor cycles, because they were practical men with little formal engineering training, were not able to bring their minds to this problem.

The most impressive of d'Ascanio's achievements is that he designed the Vespa from scratch, designing every component as he went along and yet he made the final assembly a practicable machine shop job and an economic sales proposition. Rarely has there been such a combination of vision and commercial acumen. By the end of 1946 some 2,500 Vespas had been sold.

Totally new was the idea of giving the rider protection from the rain. This was done by extending the sheet steel framework upwards almost to the handlebars so that the rider's legs were shielded from wind and rain alike.

In 1948 another Italian firm marketed a scooter which, like the Vespa, was an immediate success. The firm was Innocenti of Milan, noted originally for steel tubes and heavy engineering – they exported steel rolling mills to South America, for instance. They also had a working arrangement with the coachbuilding firm of Pininfarina, world-famous designers of car bodies, and there was a personal friendship between the Innocenti family and Count Trossi. The Innocenti scooter was the result of these influences and this experience. Since the Innocenti works were in the Milan suburb of Lambrate the word was used as the basis of the scooter's name – Lambretta – which, after a slow start, became internationally famous.

The triple influences – a steel tube maker, a motor car designer, an engine designer – were clear in the first Lambretta and have been responsible for the frequent changes in Lambretta designs through the years. It is interesting to compare the first Lambretta with the Vespa because, although the problems facing the designers were identical they were tackled in radically different ways. The chassis of the Lambretta was of steel tubes. The front wheel was held in a conventional fork, though the rear wheel was mounted on a stub axle. The engine was not enclosed by panelling The layout had striking points of resemblance to that of the paratrooper's folding motor cycle, afterwards continued in the British Corgi. The front legshields did not extend to the handlebars. The rear suspension problem was tackled in a new and ingenious way – another example of the fresh approach, for Innocenti (although in later years they took up the manufacture complete of the Austin A.40 and other motor cars) were not vehicle designers. One of the gadgets which must have delighted the inventor (his name, alas, is lost to history) was the foot-controlled gear-change pedal; this was linked to an indicator on the front legshield to show the rider what gear was engaged. As in the British Corgi the handlebars were extended twin tubes.

However, although the two scooter solutions were so different, they were both successful. Sales of Vespas topped 60,000 in 1950 and 90,000 in 1951. The Pontedera works were turned over completely to the production of Vespa scooters – the works had survived most of the war but were flattened by American bombing during the last months and so, although there was an interval of scraping bits and pieces together, when production machinery was finally installed it was of the latest type.

Why did these two Italian scooters succeed when so many before them had failed? Johnson launched his Max scooter in 1907 and from then until 1939 various Englishmen tackled the problem, but none with success. Failure was inevitable, primarily because the British scooters offered no advantages over conventional motor cycles – and many disadvantages. Comfort, cleanliness, a certain air of delicacy – these were the qualities most apparent in the scooter; speed, noise and a hugely obtrusive engine were offered by the motor cycle, whose riders did not want the noise, nor the dirt removed.

Other countries began to make scooters; Bernadet (France) in 1949, quickly followed by Terrot, Motobecane, Magnat-Debon and others. Both Vespa and Lambretta were made in Germany and France under licence and by 1953 the scooter was a booming market in every European country except Britain.

It is often said that the scooter met the demand for cheap transport, that it owed its success to the wartime destruction of transport and roads. Although this is to some extent true it is an explanation which has often been given to hide a more important truth; that a new thing had been created and had to a large extent made a new market.

Certainly in 1946 there was a demand for a cheap means of transport. Certainly motor cars were scarce and railways were handicapped by the wartime destruction of locomotives and tracks. Certainly some of the 1946 and 1947 scooters would be helping to make good these deficiencies, but still we have to find out why scooters were invented in Italy by two firms with no previous experience in making two-wheeled vehicles. Also we have to find out why, after 1947, when motor cars became more plentiful, as roads and railways were repaired, the demand for scooters should have increased so rapidly. Had the scooter merely served to replace things destroyed the sales would have declined as motor car production got under way. The fact that scooter sales enjoyed an all-time boom meant that a new need had been supplied, a new public created. History repeated itself when Japanese motor cycles flooded the British market, outselling every local product in years when British manufacturers were, one by one, going bankrupt.

The new scooter public grew on the things which scooters provided, on the things which they made possible. The engines were two-strokes, the simplest form of engine ever made, lacking complicated valve gear and pump lubrication. They were of small capacity, easily handled. Top speed was 35mph. Fuel consumption was 120 miles per gallon. The rider could wear ordinary town clothes since he was largely protected from the weather. His girl-friend (abroad) could sit side-saddle without having oil splashed over her legs.

The scooter was therefore the ideal casual machine for one or two people who were not interested in things mechanical. It was not built as a competitor of the motor cycle. It was built as a machine in its own right and many years passed before it competed for customers in the motor cycle market. D'Ascanio's first Vespa was aimed at a market which did not then exist.

However, a new public is more than a sales problem. It is

a symptom of change in a social organisation, of development, of expansion; it may even be a sign of decay, of poverty or of failure. It required great vision to see this social change coming in 1946. This far-sighted vision existed in Italy and founded a multi-million industry.

Ten years later the millionth Vespa had been made and sold. France and Germany shared the Italian enthusiasm for this new form of transport. British tourists in Italy saw scooters everywhere and many of them, returning home, bought a scooter for their own use. By the end of 1955 there was a foreseeable market for them in Britain and the first all-scooter magazine appeared on the bookstalls. It had a stormy passage, for these were the days of monopolistic trade associations wielding enormous powers over advertisers. The official attitude was expressed by H. M. Palin; "The industry was already adequately served by the motor cycling journals." Ironically, the scooter magazine outlived all its competitors and some of these motor cycling journals. Ironically, the words were spoken at a moment when Piaggio was welcoming the Press of the world to see the millionth Vespa made at Pontedera. The incident spotlights the peculiar difficulties of scooters in Britain where motor cycle interests were dominant.

How did this situation come about?

In 1946 the British motor cycle industry was splendidly placed. It had a reputation for workmanship and reliability. As for speed, British machines like the Norton, Velocette, Rudge and Excelsior were world-famous. In the Tourist Trophy races between 1929 and 1939 there was not one single race – Senior, Junior or Lightweight – where one of these makes did not figure in the first three home. The industry had a vast productive capacity and after six years of war every country in Europe was a seller's market for motor cycles. Many of the manufacturers were family concerns, run by technicians who had ridden, built, serviced and – in many cases

– raced their own machines. Their approach to design problems was conditioned by their practical experience and their solutions reflected this attitude. These solutions – built into machines like the Norton and the Triumph – had commanded the whole world's admiration. The designers felt justified in continuing along the same lines. Concrete examples are immediately to hand.

Power unit. The popular engine was a four-stroke. British designers and owners cared little for two-stroke engines, which they derisively called putt-putts. Dazzled by the fame and glamour which came from TT race successes these firms filled their best design posts with specialists on four-stroke engines. This was not surprising since some, if not most, of the technical directors had in their day worked on four-strokes and had built the firm's reputation on them. In 1955 one of the glittering prizes of TT racing – to be the first to win the Senior at over the ton (100mph) – was still not out of reach of the Norton concern. Amm and Brett had both averaged over 93mph in the 1953 Senior, both riding Nortons and since 1926 the string of Norton wins in the Senior had become almost monotonous. In 1955 it would have seemed only right that a Norton should carry the winner – for the first time – at over 100mph. It was an intoxicating thought, but there was not the slightest chance that the engine in the winning Norton would be the work of a two-stroke expert.

Suspension. Telescopic front forks had become the sign of a quality machine. Again, this stemmed from a racing tradition. Even where telescopics were not used – Velocette, for instance, came to them late – the front fork was adopted as a matter of course and many were the cutting remarks passed about scooters which had their wheels supported only on one side.

Transmission. British motor cycles used roller chains for the final drive. That was the end of that discussion.

Wheels. These were spoked; 16 in. diameter or bigger;

held between forks on a knock-out spindle. These details were held to be essential for safety and reliability.

In addition it was not considered necessary to enclose the engine to protect it from road dirt; nor to simplify the task of mending a puncture; nor to provide a hook for handbag or brief-case; nor to provide a saddle which could be used by a girl wearing a skirt.

These are matters of mechanical design and they would, by themselves, have been sufficient to account for the delay in scooters being produced by motor cycle firms in Britain. There was, however, an ever bigger obstacle, one which – because it was an imponderable – took even longer to overcome because its true nature was not immediately recognised. A host of objections – some of them justified – were put forward by directors of motor cycle firms when it was suggested that they should make scooters, and these objections were all too often a cloak to hide this deeper objection – which can be put very roughly as a feeling that scooters were not a good thing.

By about 1955 the teenager had come into his – or her – own. The teenage market was not only important; it was dominant, and in spite of the millions of pounds which flowed into the teenagers' pockets these young people were not buying motor cycles as they had done before the war – and just after.

For one thing, teenagers wanted colour and, while the motor cycles were finished in a utilitarian black, the scooters appeared in gay pastel shades, reflecting in their two-tone and multicolour patterns a mode of living from which much of the drabness of poverty had been removed. The new owners appeared to be frivolous. They knew little or nothing about the machines they bought and this caused a surprising amount of irritation, for the dealer who sold them the scooter was – in many cases – an ex-racing motor cyclist, brought up in the tradition that if you had a machine you should be able to look after it.

"Look," said one dealer, "here's a beauty for you. She buys a scooter for a hundred and forty quid and then she asks me where the spark comes from."

This was a new public.

A scooterist would cheerfully admit that he did not know the difference between a two-stroke and a four-stroke engine. What was more, he didn't care. Gudgeon pin and small end, pinking and crankcase compression – the average scooterist was not interested in such things. Of course there were some mechanically minded scooterists, some of whom progressed to become dealers or experts in scooter maintenance but most wanted the scooter as a means of transport, not as a hobby. The dealer was often at a loss for words when talking to scooterists, for the two groups hardly spoke the same language. In the long term this had a disastrous effect on the scooter market because many motor cycle dealers, while holding scooters in contempt, failed to realise that their maintenance called for a grasp of theory which they had never had and were unable to acquire so late in life.

Parallel with the growth of this new public was the disappearance of a public with which motor cycle manufacturers were familiar; the young men who yearned for a 500cc twin-cylinder machine that went very fast and made splendid noises. From the best, the boldest, the most fortunate of these youths came the racing drivers whose successes made British motor cycles famous through the entire world. Soon after 1946 these youths no longer came forward in their accustomed quantities to ride the big machines. Indeed, the market for big motor cycles shrank rapidly after 1950 and one manufacturer after another saw this reflected in sales figures. True, some big machines were made and some were sold but the market was small apart from police and military uses. The loss of this speed market, the disappearance of the bold youths, the falling sales of the big machines were not only a financial setback (only too often financial disaster) but marked a change in the social structure, a new outlook which the motor cycling fraternity viewed with disfavour if not with disgust. The attitude was well summed up by a motor cycling journalist who wrote of one 125cc scooter that it was light enough "for even the feeblest of females to handle and to park." When BSA launched their big scooter there was some criticism made that it was difficult to kick-start the engine. Said the BSA director: "If they can't kick the engine over they'd better go and buy something else." Neither of these remarks was intentionally offensive.

British manufacturers also felt that the scooter boom would not last. This belief started in the boardroom and was in great part the expression of a wish. Behind the wish was the hope that the old days would return, that the big machines would roar as they had done in the Golden Age, that the giants would again come into their own. This was a romantic, unselfish wish. It sprang from a yearning for a different, better type of youth and this expensive delusion – that the day of the big motor cycle would return – was long persisted in. "We shall never make scooters," said a director of Associated Motor Cycles – but very soon afterwards they ceased even to make motor cycles, joining the melancholy procession of firms liquidated, bankrupt or merely taken over.

Faulty marketing decisions do not stand alone. They powerfully affect the design staff, who feel they are ploughing the sands if they do not share the board's outlook, drawing strength and encouragement continuously from them. It was no accident – but it was close to a tragedy – that around 1955, when scooters were beginning to flood Britain, the leaders of the British motor cycle industry lost their grip not only on sales problems but on the glittering TT race honours which had seemed so firmly and rightly theirs. In that year the Norton domination of Senior and Junior TT races ended; Italian machines – Gilera, MV and Guzzi – filled first and second places. In the Senior race in 1960 two Italian MV-Agustas entered and came first and second. Both had an average speed of over 100mph for the 226-mile course. So even the "ton" victory escaped the British.

Unreasonably it was felt that the coming of the scooter was the cause of these changes, that people were buying scooters when they should have been doing something better, more manly. There thus grew up an opposition between the two forms of transport, a grouping into separate camps, one of which was better than the other, with little polite communication between the two.

This state of affairs was peculiar to Britain. In Germany, France, Italy and Austria the motor cycle manufacturers turned naturally to making scooters. To this task they brought vast resources of design originality and engine development. They made some very fine scooters.

It is necessary to make this rather long explanation because without it the late development of the scooter in Britain – and the total failure of every local effort, whether by a one-man firm or an industrial giant like BSA – is difficult to understand. The explanation is not complete. When the Velocette concern disappeared in a humiliating liquidation the reason publicly given was that it had lost £75,000 in making its Viceroy scooter – and so another famous British name vanished, but it is not reasonable to imagine that where such an error is made no others existed. The major factor in the tardiness and eventual failure of the British effort to make a successful scooter was the confusion at board level between the scooter and the social change which accompanied it.

In 1950 the Vespa was being made under licence in Germany. In the following year production began in France by ACMA and in England by the Douglas concern, a name famous in British motor cycle racing. The man responsible for this far-sighted decision was their managing director Claude McCormack who had first seen the Vespa when on holiday in Italy and who needed profitable employment for the factory's machine shops. Douglas had a fine racing history but by 1950 its production was limited and sales were dropping. To take on the manufacture of a scooter was felt by many in the trade to be financially unsound, for they hoped the future lay with motor cycles. Douglas faced an uphill task. It is possible to suggest today that they tackled it the wrong way, that they should have concentrated on importing the Vespas complete instead of making them. Their difficulties mounted one on another. To begin with, in 1950, they were so shaky financially that some British suppliers would not even quote for components. Subsequently Douglas was taken over by Westinghouse. Twenty years after the first British Vespas were made their manufacture here had ceased, the Vespa Division of Westinghouse had been hived off and all Vespas were imported direct from Italy.

When the first British Vespas were produced by Douglas in 1951 their progress was slow, their sales uncertain, even though they had the market virtually to themselves. Dealers were reluctant to stock machines. Even worse (in the long run) they were unwilling to finance the provision of service facilities, men and spares to keep the scooters going when they had been sold. Claude McCormack himself travelled the country, calling personally on dealers, trying to get them to share his enthusiasm for this new type of transport. There was no money available for a big advertising campaign and progress was snail-like for this new British-made machine.

A different technique was adopted with the Lambretta. The answer to import restrictions has always seemed to be the setting up of local factories, either to assemble from imported parts or to make under licence. In times of settled conditions this method works, although Ford have found the risks are incalculable and outside the control of the parent country. Post-war Europe rapidly tied itself up in a series of bilateral trade pacts and in these conditions Lambrettas were made in France by Lambretta SA and in Germany by NSU, a name then famous for motor cycles, later to be even more famous for its original research in engines and transmission and especially for the Wankel engine. In Britain no equivalent firm seemed anxious to lay down plant to make Lambrettas and one had not to look far for reasons. The motor cycle firms had full order books, a long list of waiting customers. Machine tools and machine-shop capacity was hard to come by. Paradoxically it was easier for a German or Italian firm to get machine tools than it was for the average British firm. Cloak and dagger tactics spilled over from commando groups to peacetime industry. One British firm ordered a lathe from USA – and also some spares for a lathe it had bought ten years earlier. It was easy to settle the delivery date for the new lathe, but in spite of repeated letters there was no news of the spares. Finally the lathe appeared, complete with an American fitter to supervise the installation. He attacked one of the lathe supports, ground off some welding and disclosed a secret compartment. Inside were hidden the spares.

Another firm had a long correspondence with a French firm about the supply of three hundred machines, but failed to get import permits for them. The French firm had its own way of dealing with that problem – all the British firm had to do was collect them from a ship which would rendezvous in mid-Channel. . . .

The early post-1945 years were far from normal and although the scooter's popularity increased very rapidly, attracting to its manufacture both large and small firms, the design, manufacture and marketing methods adopted usually owed more to expediency than to far-sighted planning. Even the giants – Vespa and Lambretta – could not follow a consistent policy. In Germany the Vespa was first made by Messerschmitt but very quickly were imported complete from Italy; while Lambrettas were made by NSU for five years and were then imported complete from Milan, while NSU went on to make its own scooter. In France the Lambretta was made locally until 1960, but after that date were imported complete.

In Britain the Vespa pattern was likewise to change. The Douglas firm of Bristol, which had made motor cycles and aircraft engines, took up the manufacture of scooters and for some years the proportion of Vespas imported by Douglas and made by Douglas fluctuated. When Douglas was taken over by Westinghouse the proportion made in Bristol increased for a strange and distressing reason. Ford had developed an automatic transmission system which was offered as an optional extra. The manufacture of the unit was a prize worth having, so Westinghouse laid down a wonderful set of precision machines to turn out some prototypes. Alas, they proved to be less than perfect and this valuable production set-up was perforce turned over to making precision parts for Vespa scooters. Plainly this was not an economic proposition. It was a hard blow for Westinghouse, doubly hard as it followed the loss of a valuable British Railways contract and it was no surprise when, in 1970, Westinghouse itself was taken over and the scooter section hived off, to become a 100% importer of Vespas.

Lambrettas in Britain have always been imported. The concession was first held by an Aldershot firm but before any considerable impact had been made it was taken over by a father and son combination which soon made Lambretta a household name throughout Britain. A. J. (father) and P. J. (son) Agg took over the agency and in 1951 imported 500 Lambrettas from Italy. They then set about selling them. It was a bold undertaking. A. J. Agg had virtually retired after a successful career in hire-purchase, motor cars and wine. To take on a completely new business called for courage and a lot of hard work, but the new firm soon showed that it had enough of both qualities. Motor cycle dealers were no more interested in Lambrettas than they had been in Vespas. To convert some of them was a matter of time, but with many of the biggest dealers it was an impossible task. Some motor cycle dealers went out of business rather than sell scooters, just as some manufacturers went out of business rather than make them.

By 1955 however some impression had been made. At the Earls Court Show that year scooters were shown by The Dayton Cycle Co. Ltd, by Douglas, by Ambassador Motor Cycles Ltd (the Bella), by DMW Motor Cycles Ltd (the Kieft), by Lambretta Concessionaires Ltd, by Mercury Industries Ltd (the Hermes), by Motor Imports Co. Ltd (the Moby) and one or two other short-lived imports. Biggest surprise of the Show was the Beeza, a scooter with a 200cc four-stroke engine made by BSA Motor Cycles Ltd and on which the President of the Board of Trade (Peter Thorneycroft) was proudly photographed after opening the Show.

Most of these scooters soon disappeared, overwhelmed by incompetence, design blunders, lack of finance and by the difficulties of a market which – while rich – was fickle and called for skilful design, skilful marketing, skilful production. Even for large firms these were difficult times. In 1956 came a wholesale reorganisation at BSA in the course of which the Beeza's designer departed and the scooter itself vanished without trace, adding nothing to the BSA reputation. Earls Court had long been noted for firms which showed motor cycles for which the exhibitor wanted someone to provide the finance (if imported) or the manufacturing capacity (if British made). Even reputable firms had shown prototypes which would only go into production if the firm got sufficient orders at the Show. If the orders or the finance did not appear nothing more was heard of the machine. It was probably the first time BSA had shown a machine and then simply pushed it down the drain. It was very unfortunate that it should have been a scooter, for the smell of failure lingered.

Other motor cycle firms heeded the warning and left scooters alone. Their caution was endorsed when the Piatti, Italian-designed but British-made, put up its brief, glorious display – and then disappeared. It was launched by Cycle-master Ltd, one of the most successful names in the motorised cycle field. Although its design was open to objections the failure had a chilling effect on other manufacturers.

Little that was new at the 1956 Earls Court Show endured. Because of one of the usual eve-of-show labour disputes the Show did not open on the first Saturday, causing serious loss and bad feeling. After that the Show was held only every other year and then left Earls Court for good.

Nevertheless, 1956 saw the tide begin to turn as far as scooters were concerned. There were suddenly a dozen makes to choose from, almost all imported, some of the imports beautifully made and backed by world-famous names like Zundapp, TWN, Peugeot, Puch, NSU, Heinkel. No British-designed scooter could stand comparison with them for design and originality. Their two-stroke engines had been developed to an incredible pitch of efficiency and reliability. Even more extraordinary, many had electric starters and were easily capable of 60mph. British makers, British designers could not compete.

There was another and less pleasant reason for the sudden appearance on the British market of these wonderful machines. In 1956 the German and Austrian scooter market suffered a severe reverse. Demand slackened. Some firms closed down, while others were taken over by the banks, especially in

Germany. Output was everywhere reduced. The very efficient sales organisations of the remaining firms made greater and more persistent efforts to capture the British market. Although results were not spectacular these firms built up a useful export trade which continued, though on a diminishing scale, to 1970. At the same time they helped to create a better attitude towards scooters because of the fine quality of the product. In this way they set a standard for comparison so that British manufacturers could not be influenced by German and Austrian achievements when they came to build their own scooters. On the other hand the plight of the German two-wheeler industry became common knowledge and did little to reassure the financial heads of British firms thinking about this new market.

Now although these factors helped to make 1956 a turning point, the most important factor of all was the enthusiasm and business acumen of A. J. and P. J. Agg, who saw that continuing sales of their Lambrettas depended on what kind of service their customers got after they had bought their scooter. That year saw the establishment of the first in a nation-wide chain of service stations. Each one had Lambretta-trained mechanics; kits of special tools; stocks of spares. At each service station was at least one mechanic who had been given a practical and theoretical course at the Wimbledon service headquarters. It was a long-term plan, calling for reserves of faith and money. It was linked to an equally courageous scheme of publicity and advertising. Success was almost immediate. The scheme assumed that the owner had little mechanical knowledge or experience. It welcomed such an owner and took care of him. Plainly this was the kind of reception the scooter buyer had long wanted. Motor cycle dealers had difficulty in understanding this new policy and were reluctant to adopt it. Most of their customers were men, usually with some considerable mechanical knowledge, who could service their own machines and who did not need telling what a carburetter was or how it functioned. If something went wrong with a motor cycle the owner was likely to diagnose the trouble, do any necessary dismantling, locate the faulty part, ask the dealer for a new spare – and fit it himself. The dealer was at home with such a man, spoke his language. He did not at once welcome the prospect of spending money on a service bay for one type of scooter, nor did he feel at home with a customer who could not tell the difference between a two-stroke and a four-stroke engine. All too often such a customer went out on his scooter and phoned the dealer in despair, asking for a rescue party to be sent out when, in fact, the trouble was very minor and would have been put right by the average motor cyclist in a few minutes. Sometimes the dealer made a charge for these services; sometimes he did not, but in both cases his opinion of scooters went down and so did his estimate of the chance that there could be a long-term, stable market with such people.

However, the Aggs persisted and their policy began to pay off in spectacular fashion. Lambretta sales in Britain not only shot up like a rocket; they eclipsed sales of Vespas. This was a tremendous achievement. In every other European country sales of Vespas were, and continued to be, far ahead of any other make. In most countries they were greater than the sales of all other makes put together. In Paris it was quite normal to see notices saying: "The parking of automobiles and Vespas here is forbidden", so dominant was their position in the market and in the public mind.

In Britain the imported Lambrettas swept the board. Even more important, they made the scooter popular, gave the trade a success story. It was no small feat. The Aggs, father and son, had had almost no advantages save their personal qualities. They had no experience of the scooter market. They had met considerable opposition from established motor cycle interests but their success was soon known throughout the whole of

Europe. In 1959 they sold over 47,000 Lambrettas in Great Britain. They not only sold their own allocation of imports from Italy – they went to France and took Lambrettas built and intended for the French market and sold them over here. It was a tale of continued success, continued expansion.

What of British-designed, British-made scooters? Their sales were increasing even if the increase was gradual. Motor cycle dealers found that they had to give more floor space to scooters than to motor cycles. At the AGM in 1958 BSA chairman J. Y. Sangster could find it possible to say that the drop in their motor cycle sales would be more than made good by their scooter sales. This was a change indeed, even though events soon made the comment look silly and ill-informed. The BSA scooters were fitted with BSA engines but not every firm had the resources of the BSA combine and the early British scooters were fitted with a standard Villiers two-stroke engine almost as a matter of course. It can fairly be said that had it not been for the forward-looking policy of the Villiers company the history of British scooters would have been different and their development, slow though it was, would have been immeasurably slower. By providing a ready-made, standard, reliable power unit Villiers solved a troublesome problem. It was possible for a small concern to design and even to fabricate a suspension system or a frame because steel tubes could be used from stock, but designing an engine was a much bigger step. The smaller firms had not the finance, the experience nor the staff to design an engine. They gladly accepted the Villiers engine and it is almost certain that without it these early British scooters could not have been built.

Since they shared a common engine the design possibilities were limited in such things as final drive to the rear wheel – which was inevitably by roller chain. This was one of the limitations which could not have been avoided but at the same time the total absence of qualified scooter designers in Britain made it likely that these imposed design features would have been included even had the makers been given a free choice. It is significant that the four best-known of these early firms were outside the motor cycle industry. One made pedal cycles (Dayton); one made three-wheeler cars (Bond); the third (Phoenix) was a small firm doing engineering sub-contracts, though its owner (Ernie Barrett) had ridden in the TT races, mostly on Nortons but for a couple of years on his own Phoenix-JAP. Ironically, his best placing was when he rode a 250 Guzzi; the fourth firm (DKR) did presswork for passenger and goods vehicles. These firms, believing in scooters, carried the load during a period of doubt.

It was a long, anxious period and was soon made darker by the Suez crisis with its acute shortage of petrol. Perhaps it was the petrol shortage which turned thoughts to scooters or it might have been a social change, but the fact is that when the 1957 sales figures were published there was consternation in the boardrooms of motor cycle makers; 75,000 motor cycles had been sold, but scooter sales were 100,000. Never before had scooters outsold motor cycles. Better face the facts, thought one firm after another and then proceeded with tentative plans to market a scooter. There was, of course, no sign of haste and onlookers could view the slow-moving elephants with amusement, though shareholders reacted differently. The 1958 figures gave a further push; in that year 60,000 motor cycles had been sold, but scooter sales were almost 75,000. There was every hope that scooter sales would continue way out ahead and so during 1959 work on British scooters was stepped up.

Although some of the new British scooters were announced earlier, the first time the general public could see the full effect of this policy change was at the 1960 Earls Court Show.

Scooters had really made their mark. The numbers on the road were:

Motor cycles   950,000
Scooters   470,000

At Earls Court there were scooters from Excelsior, Ambassador, BSA, James, Phelon and Moore Ltd, Sun, Veloce – all famous names in British motor cycling, all showing scooters designed and made in Britain. They brought the total of scooters then available to the British public up to thirty different makes and twice that number of models, ranging in size from the 70cc Capri to the 277cc Maicoletta.

The motor cycle firms were thus powerfully represented and their new policy towards scooters was very welcome. Unfortunately the new models from Veloce, Excelsior, Ambassador and James reached the market when the full effects of the 1959 hire purchase restrictions were being felt. To that extent the effort was ill-timed but, as we have seen, the beginning was made two or three years before. It can now be seen that the directors and senior executives in the motor cycle industry were living in the past and were unequal to the tasks facing them. These men formed a club, self-protecting and self perpetuating. They controlled between them enormous sums of money and their patronage was reserved almost exclusively to a charmed circle, a circle from which critics were excluded. Leading newspapers as far back as 1956 had said bitter things about British firms misjudging the appeal of the scooter. Even when a firm woke to the new market progress was slow. Between starting work on a design and having a machine ready to show to the Press a year might elapse. With some firms the time was greater. Compare this with the Vespa where, twelve months after starting on the design some 2,000 machines had been produced, delivered and sold.

There were thus ten firms making British scooters in 1960. An average year's sales would be 120,000 and of these perhaps 80,000 would be imported, leaving nothing of a mass market for ten British firms. Naturally the British firms wanted to cut into this rich market, to take over the fat slice held by foreign-made machines but in design, production equipment and sales tactics the Italians, Germans and Austrians had a long start and they were never seriously threatened. British makers depended on rugged construction and more engine power, for it was not easy in a motor cycle firm to get away from traditional design.

"What if it takes a long time to get our side panels off?" said one director. "Why do you want to take the side panels off?"

"Streamlined handlebars?" said one designer. "You can't get them in at the price."

"That hub?" said another. "We couldn't find another supplier."

These are the words of senior executives, men with vast experience of motor cycles. They show the severely practical attitude which was reflected in most British scooters, machines built for hard wear and reliability; here the equally practical difficulties of manufacture must be faced. If you can tool up for a run of 50,000 scooters you may be able to reduce your price but that is not very important since your selling price is influenced more by the prices of competitive machines than by the profit you make. The advantages lie elsewhere. You can spend more on tooling-up. You can afford transfer machines. You can buy your own presses. You can afford electrostatic paint spraying and your own plating baths. You can make your own components and so get rid of the bugs more quickly – or dictate to your suppliers because you give big orders for runs. Your finished scooter will be a nice-looking job and may have features which your rivals, with smaller sales, cannot afford.

B

These are the advantages of long-run production. They are substantial advantages. They make sales easier, which is just as well because bulk production means ruin unless there are bulk sales. More important, there must be a target sales figure. You may, for instance, plan to sell 10,000 scooters in the year. You can set out a production line for 10,000 and if you sell 10,000 you make a reasonable profit. The sensible manufacturer sets out his production line so that in March he can turn out another 1,500 if orders justify it. If he sells this extra 1,500 he will make not a reasonable profit but a fat profit. He therefore goes all out for his target figure, knowing that for the extra 1,500 he will be able to spend twice as much per machine in selling them and still make a fine profit. This calls for vision and courage.

It could be said that production figures from the Continent provided little encouragement, much to make directors cautious. Consider the figures for Germany:

	Scooters	Motor cycles
1951	18,846	318,916
1953	69,658	369,225
1955	134,159	170,549
1957	90,411	52,860
1959	67,120	48,171

These are production figures for single years. The French figures were even more depressing. In both countries the motor cycle industry had shrunk to a trickle, in Germany because prosperity made the car a status symbol; in France because the tremendous moped industry wanted no competitors. Moped sales in France hung around the 1,000,000 mark year after year. Vespa and Lambretta outsold all other scooters and these were imported, leaving no market for French scooter makers. Progressively harsh legislation drove the scooter off the market and the moped continued to sell their million per year. Thus, for two very different reasons, two big markets were closed to scooters. Sales in Britain continued high, but the story of France and Germany was daunting. British firms could have been forgiven for looking askance and deciding not to invest money in an up that might become a catastrophic down. Equally important, the motor cycle firms were being grouped into large combines and during this period of amalgamation many a bold director decided to concentrate on holding his job down.

At the same time, these directors and senior executives were no cowards. Many of them were men of rare courage, men who did not owe their position to sitting in a chair, but to racing on road and track. If they were conceited, they at least could point to past successes. If their machines were criticised, they could often take them out on the road and outpace any critic. Even if their machines failed to sell, at least they were fast, reliable and built to last. Over a period of many years they made British motor cycles famous through the entire world.

Had these men possessed vision equal to their courage they might have built a vast new industry, but their vision was blurred, their forward planning grossly in error. One firm after another faltered, disappeared. Here are two examples, one of a firm renowned in motor cycle racing and one of a firm with no such tradition.

VELOCE LTD. This firm built the Velocette motor cycles and in 1926 they started a long series of TT race successes, winning the Junior. They won it again in 1928 and 1929. Wins in the TT races meant big sales; in 1939 there were 25 Velocettes entered for the Junior. Even after the war there was magic in the name of Velocette, over 20 of their machines entering for the 1949 and 1950 Juniors. The reader will assume – rightly – that success in the Junior TT roused the firm's appetite for bigger things but the supreme award – winning the Senior TT – somehow eluded the Goodmans. Velocettes came home second or third, but never first.

When TT racing started again in 1947 it seemed that Velocette would continue winning the Junior for ever; first three in 1947, first two in 1948 and 1949 – and of course sales followed the winning names, so Veloce was riding high and was able to spend huge sums on the elusive Senior victory. Alas, the tide had already begun to turn. Italian machines began winning the Junior and the Senior. By 1955 all the winning machines were Italian or German. After that an occasional British machine would win, but first place in TT racing was almost always reserved for the Italians, the Germans or the Japanese. There would come a time when TT race successes no longer sold motor cycles and the British would be allowed to win but the foreigner had shown his superiority in design and production – his machines went faster and were more reliable on the track. For Velocette this was especially galling. Director B. J. (Bertie) Goodman, who had ridden in the TT, had set his heart on a world record – 24 hours at 100mph and shared the riding at Montlhery track for the attempt. It was a brave effort and it was successful, so Britain had a world record of some importance. Unfortunately, almost before the record was accepted the German NSU bettered the Velocette performance.

Veloce Ltd. had another product – the famous Noddy motor cycle used by many police forces; a quiet, reliable machine. It was a costly machine to produce and when one police force after another abandoned the Noddy in favour of cars there was little market for it, since it had never appealed to the public at large. Finally, Veloce tackled the scooter, turning out a heavy, massive and powerful machine which looked like a motor cycle fitted with fairings. Few girls would ever think twice of trying such a scooter. The Velocette Viceroy was a flop.

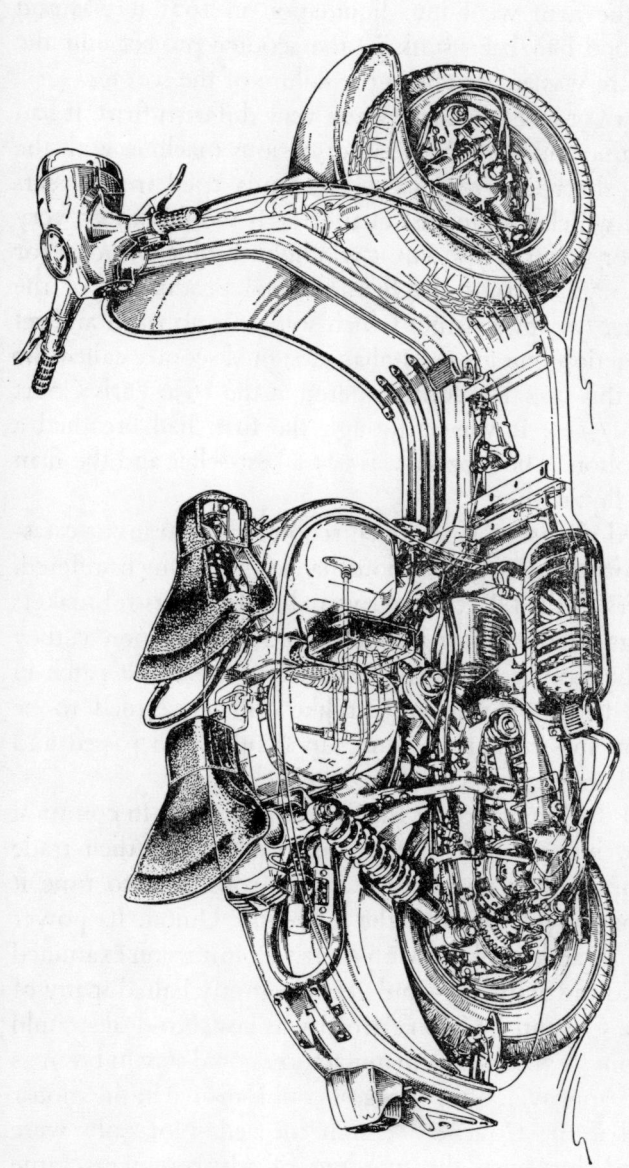

1. In the Li. Series Lambrettas aimed at the utmost standardisation of parts between the 125cc and the 150cc scooters. The complete train of gear scould be exchanged between the 125cc, the 150cc and the TV. 175cc Series II. Two separate seats are shown here, but a dual seat was fitted as standard on imports to Britain.

When the firm went into liquidation in 1971 it was said that £75,000 had been sunk in the scooter project and the firm's failure was attributed to the failure of the scooter.

CYCLEMASTER LTD. Here was a very different firm. It had built its name and fame on a rather curious machine with the engine on the rear wheel – a style Honda tried many years later – and which sold in vast quantities. It would not go very quickly, nor was it stylish but it was light, foolproof, ideal for short journeys. In 1965 the firm stopped production of the Cyclemaster (so apt a name) which sold at £30 retail and set up a production line for the Italian-designed scooter called the Piatti and this was the scooter offered at the 1956 Earls Court Show for £130. It was as though the firm had breathed a familiar poison. The scooter was not a best-seller and the firm went into liquidation.

It seemed almost as if to touch scooters was to invite catastrophe. Nor was it only the motor cycle firms which suffered. The makers of the DKR scooter were highly successful makers of pressings for the motor industry yet almost as soon as they touched the scooter business they ran into the worst patch in the firm's history. Even a giant like Villiers seemed to be touched by the scooter's plague; dividends were passed and finally Villiers were taken over complete.

Nor did the blight stop at the firms themselves. In common with many industries the motor cycle makers had their trade association. Though its name changed from time to time it will be convenient to call it the Coventry Union. Its power was immense and, until the Monopolies Commission examined its structure and activities – and very promptly halted many of them – the Coventry Union's word was law. No dealer could hope to flout its wishes. No manufacturer could stay in business without its approval. No periodical could survive in the motor cycle field if the Coventry Union sneezed. Not only were prices fixed, but even the wording of advertisements came under its steely eye. One Manchester dealer who advertised "Best exchange terms" was promptly told that he was not allowed to offer better terms than other dealers and must remove the offending words from his future advertising.

Power of this order called for a stable situation or for a group of highly sophisticated men to wield it. Until 1955 it mattered not that the industry was run by naive enthusiasts with little formal education but in that year the foreign-made scooters began flooding in and the importers of these machines found they had to join a trade association which hardly welcomed them as equals. Scooter importers were treated with barely concealed enmity and contempt and though this was tolerable in the early days there came a time when scooter sales were greater than motor cycle sales in Britain – and still the Coventry Union was dominated by the twin concepts of British and motor cycle. The industry's public image was neglected and for one vital period the Coventry Union did not have a Public Relations Officer. There can hardly be another industry of comparable size where this could happen.

Eventually – too late – the word British disappeared from the Coventry Union's title and importers were treated as equals, but by then the majority of motor cycle firms had also disappeared. So had the famous Earls Court Show which was usually opened by a Minister of the Crown. This once all-powerful trade association found itself ill at ease in its splendid, specially built Starley House headquarters. Its prestige was not increased when its director, H. M. Palin, was prosecuted – and found guilty of offences under the Restrictive Practices Act, nor could it claim to speak with authority as one member firm after another hit the headlines in the bad news section of the financial papers.

Now it is reasonable to expect that if firms in an industry suffer that industry's trade association, drawing its officers from those firms, will suffer also. Directors who are ill-informed at their own board meetings will hardly acquire wisdom merely by election to the governing board of their trade association, so perhaps a single fault has been counted twice. But what of scientists with – one would suppose – no vested interest? Were they affected by the scooter bug? It would seem so in one important case.

The Road Research Laboratory publishes a stream of papers on aspects of roads and traffic. In 1962 there appeared an RRL paper by Tanner forecasting that in 1965 there would be 2,600,000 motor cycles on British roads. Nobody whose money or livelihood was bound up with motor cycles swallowed this rubbish, but there are grounds for thinking that officials concerned with road planning took it seriously and made provision for these mythical vehicles. In 1962 there was not the slightest possibility of 2,600,000 motor cycles being on British roads in 1965 – the machine tools, the dealer network, the design staff for this vast army did not exist, nor could they be conjured out of thin air in time. Tanner appears to have calculated the rate of increase as at 1960 and to have assumed that the rate would remain constant – a somewhat unscientific method. He also said: "An increase of 100% in income would give 20% to 25% more motor cycles" and if a scientist can argue in this fashion perhaps a director will be forgiven for leading his firm into the red. The RRL vehicle forecast was revised. The new paper appeared in November 1965, forecasting the number of motor cycles in 1965 to be 1,800,000, but by that time the official figures had already been published as 1,612,000. To use Tanner's own words; "The forecasts for motor cycles are particularly inadequate . . ."

It is difficult to speak calmly about the contrast between motor cycle and scooter people. The chain of Lambretta service stations surpassed anything available to motor cyclists. The public image of the scooter was young, gay, colourful – in tune with the customers and to a large extent the market was a new one, particularly the girls, who took gaily to two wheels for the first time and brightened up not only the scooter clubs to which they belonged, but the traffic scene of which they soon became a recognised part. When the Anglo-Japanese Trade Agreement was signed another new market appeared, a market created by the Japanese firms. In 1962 some 4,270 Japanese motor cycles were imported; in 1963 it was over 50,000 and in 1964 almost 100,000. Sales of British machines in that period dropped like a stone. Neither the Italian scooters nor the Japanese motor cycles were responsible for they largely created their own markets. The defeat of the British motor cycle industry was engineered by the British firms themselves.

2 Scooter Design

Being a designer is like being in love; it is half pain, half mystery.

You look at a machine, a bridge, a building. You say – I could have done that, given the time. You look at another and say – If I were given a year of time, if I were told my life depended on it, I could never have thought of that pattern, that layout, that curve.

That is design.

Few firms can tolerate more than one designer, for he is not bound by the rules. He wants metal to curve in a new way. He wants a gloss finish that has yet to be invented. To tool up for his bits and pieces will cost money that has yet to be borrowed.

Corradino d'Ascanio was a designer. Nobody outside the firm knows what it cost to produce the first Vespa which Piaggio made but because he was a designer in a million his design still stands and a more shapely, more attractive style of scooter has yet to be discovered.

He made two mistakes. He started with a 98cc engine; and he put the front suspension unit on the near side. Both were corrected. The engine became a 125cc unit; the front suspension moved to the off-side, where it has remained ever since. A debatable point was that his design made it difficult and expensive to fit an electric starter. Nevertheless the first Vespa, made in the Spring of 1947, was a revolution in scooter design and set a pattern. It had three special features:

1. The wheels were carried on stub axles. This was common practice in car design, but motor cycle wheels were carried in forks, front and rear. Stub axles were for cars. They made it simple to get the wheel off, but even today motor cycle wheels are carried in forks.

2. The engine was totally enclosed. The critics urged that this hid a dirty engine and made it difficult to do routine maintenance. However, after a pause for breath, motor cycle designers began enclosing their engines, a process carried very far in such motor cycles as the Ariel Leader.

3. The rider had a flat platform for his feet and could sit on a saddle instead of sitting astride a petrol tank.

Attempts were early made to define a scooter because in competitive events owners introduced so many modifications that some scooters appeared looking very much like motor cycles and when the event organisers offered substantial prizes for the winners there was every reason to try to win that event by reading the small print beforehand. A running battle of wits developed between riders and organisers. In France this became absurd in the famous Bol d'Or 24-hours race. A special class was evolved for scooters and the winner of this Class gained great fame – and sales. Their scooters were soon indistinguishable from motor cycles and the Class was abandoned. In Britain the most important event was the Isle of Man Rally. One year the substantial first prize went to the rider of a Lambretta model not available to the general public at that time. In another year there was great controversy about the Puch because this had a petrol tank between handlebars and saddle, whereas the accepted definition of a scooter called for this space to be open. Finally event organisers, while accepting a general scooter definition, retain a veto in case somebody twists the rules in a quite unforeseen manner. The three points set out above are common to almost all scooters built today.

The first Lambrettas had the rear wheel in a stub axle but

the front wheel was held in a fork; they also had a flat foot-board. The engine was not enclosed and the design followed closely that of the British-made Corgi. It owes little to the Vespa design which appeared some months earlier and if this first model is compared with current production several fundamental alterations will be noticed. One of the early A models is preserved in the Innocenti works at Milan.

It has a 125cc two-stroke engine and was, from the beginning, meant to carry two people. The front wheel was carried in a fork, the rear on a stub axle; there was a flat platform in front of the rider. These are the features which have remained unchanged through all Lambretta models.

What are the differences between the early and late Lambrettas?

To begin with, the engine was not enclosed. Little weather protection was given by the front legshield. The chassis was based on the double steel tube of the Corgi. The front mud-guard was similar to that used on motor cycle sidecars. On the very earliest model the gear changing was done through a foot pedal. None of these features remain in current Lambrettas.

Although the design was different from that of the Vespa it was a great success and was substantially unchanged for about four years. Neither enclosure of the engine nor weather protection seemed to be demanded. Even more strange to British ideas, the electrical system on all early scooters was based on direct lighting, no battery being supplied. The current was taken direct from the generator and when the engine was not running there was no current, the horn could not be sounded and the headlamp was dead. There was no parking light. Details like this did little to commend the scooter to British manufacturers and it was many years before the feeble lighting system was improved. Even then the 12-volt conversion was sold as an optional extra.

The first design change in the Lambretta was in the frame. The double tube frame was replaced by the single tube system which, with modifications, is in use today. This C model also had a variant, the LC model, with the engine enclosed by side panels and with the legshield upwards to the handlebars. In the following year, 1953, came the D model, with the rear suspension changed to a torsion bar and with a choice of 125cc or 150cc engine. These were the Lambrettas which first appeared in Britain in quantity. You could thus choose between two engine sizes, and you could have them open or enclosed.

It was now that scooter design could be said to have set in the pattern we know today. Nobody knew whether an open Vespa would sell, for none were made. When the Lambrettas appeared, offering virtually the same machine in two styles (open and enclosed) there was no doubt what the customer wanted. He – and very often it was she – wanted the enclosed model. Soon the open Lambrettas went out of production. Soon, such is the perversity of fate, the enclosed Lambrettas proved to be more flexible in design. They were fitted with side panels which, with their simple fastening, have been excelled by no other scooter maker. Removing these panels made the whole engine accessible for inspection, for routine maintenance – including thorough decarbonisation – or for riding in scrambles and such like events where side panels could be taken off to prevent them being damaged in a slight spill.

The two Italian makes were now running along the same lines. They both had 125cc and 150cc models. They were all enclosed. They were roughly equal in performance largely because the machines had been designed as social or useful transport and no thought had been given to their use in sport. The next stage was forced on both firms, owing nothing to design or production necessities, but owing everything to human nature. People had become used to scooters and had come to take their sturdiness and reliability for granted. They now wanted something more and this something was being provided by the German manufacturers who, having a fondness for the more powerful engines, were turning out the Heinkel, Zundapp Bella, TWN Contessa, Progress and others, all with bigger engines and with speeds well up into the sixties, against the Italians with a modest 40 or 45mph. In reply Vespa produced the GS model with a 150cc engine, four gears and a top speed of about 60mph. Very soon Lambretta produced their TV.175 with a comparable top speed. Both these models had 10-inch wheels and here again was a design change of some importance. Motor cyclists have always been contemptuous of the scooter's 8-inch wheels and it is possible that this single feature was responsible for much of the ill-feeling which the early scooters aroused. The German scooters almost always had bigger wheels and their advertising made great play with this as a safety feature just as some Lambretta advertising hinted slyly that a centrally-mounted engine (Lambretta) was more stable than one mounted off-centre (Vespa).

The love of big wheels may be a national characteristic, varying between countries. The desire for a bigger engine, however, was common to all countries where scooters were sold, and by 1957 it was rare to find a range which did not include at least one 150cc engined scooter. From Germany also came the urge towards electric starters. Bella, NSU Prima and Contessa had them as a matter of course, the first two not being fitted with a kickstart pedal at all. The electric starter was a complication and for Vespa it was an almost insoluble problem but it had one tremendous advantage – it brought improved lighting and a reserve of current sufficient for such things as winking indicators, stop lights fitted to the brake pedal, and fog lamps. At the same time the combination of bigger engine, bigger batteries and electric starter meant heavier, much heavier machines. Soon scooters were weighing 3 cwt – twice the weight of a D type Lambretta.

Soon after 1957 it is fair to say that the scooter consolidated itself. There was only one major change – the introduction of the two per cent mixture engine and we will deal with that in some detail later, along with its stable-mate, the engine in which oil and petrol are mixed automatically. By 1957 many experiments had been tried and had been abandoned. One of them was automatic transmission. In 1952 the French Bernadet scooter was marketed with an ingenious but complicated solution to this well-known problem. It was not completely automatic in the way the Uher system was. Indeed, it was almost two systems, with a lever which switched from one to the other. Very few of these complicated Bernadet scooters were made. Another solution was the Ducati and in 1951 the Ducati Cruiser appeared at the Milan Show. This had a genuine automatic transmission with a 175cc engine, four gears and power transmitted through an oil-driven turbine. As is well known, if a fan revolves in air or liquid it will cause an adjacent fan to revolve. If the fan (or turbine wheel) revolves in a chamber through which oil is circulated power may be transmitted to another turbine. This simple principle was adopted in the Ducati and, combined with an electric starter, gave a smooth transmission and a silence of operation hitherto unknown in scooters. Unfortunately it was not a commercial success and did not go into quantity production though for years afterwards there were continuous reports of one of these Ducati Cruisers being seen in Rome, Milan or Frankfurt, gliding along like some shapely ghost. A similar system was tried out by NSU. Here again a splendid machine was developed and some examples, mostly limited to NSU personnel, are said to be giving good service still. The NSU automatic transmission scooter was not put into production because the maintenance of the engine called for a standard of skill and workmanship not found everywhere.

The most successful automatic transmission to appear in a

standard production scooter was adopted by the DKW concern for their 98cc Hobby scooter. The Uher system of V-belt and expanding pulleys was used. Both driver and driven pulleys are free to expand against powerful springs. The higher the road speed the smaller becomes the effective diameter of the driven pulley and the smaller (in effect) the gear ratio. The first reaction of the engineer to this scheme is that since there is considerable belt-slip the belt must require replacing frequently. Theoretically this is so, the friction being considerable, but in practice the belts have a long life and the Uher system has proved to be remarkably trouble-free. It has not been more widely adopted perhaps because for practical purposes the engine size is kept below 100cc; also it is difficult to get brisk acceleration from this system. Speed is built up gradually however suddenly the throttle is opened, for the two pulleys must move in step as their effective diameters vary. When the Hobby rider starts from traffic lights he is usually left behind by machines which have the conventional gearbox and final chain drive – or the direct drive used on Vespas and Lambrettas.

Automatic transmission for two-wheelers is still a dream which haunts designers. It is not an insoluble problem, nor is the present halt in its development due to lack of technical skill. Japanese scooters with automatic transmission have been in production since 1960. One of the first was the Silver Pigeon, with its 125cc four-stroke overhead valve engine, transmission being through expanding pulleys and V-belt. Another and bigger scooter was the Rabbit, in a quite different class. It had a 250cc side-valve engine with transmission through the Superflow torque converter, a fully automatic scooter of impressive performance and smoothness. The Rabbit Superflow was a beautifully designed and built scooter. It had an electric starter as well as a kickstart pedal. Winking indicators were standard equipment. The filler cap had a brass chain so that it could not be lost. It was in fact a luxury scooter and this quality was reflected in its weight – some 330 lbs. The Super-flow was one of a series of Rabbits, the others having smaller engines and the centrifugal clutch which had been adopted by the French in so many mopeds. Strangely enough, Fuji Heavy Industries, who made the Rabbits, made their first scooter in 1946, at about the time Piaggio began. Sales were considerable in Japan, and fair in the United States, but although the Fuji executives visited Britain to explore the market the Rabbit scooters were never marketed here, though its technical superiority was outstanding.

Why was such an apparent advance left to the Japanese? British designers had a poor opinion of the Rabbit – as they had of scooters in general – but probably the strongest argument against it was that the British market wanted more speed, more powerful acceleration, better fuel consumption. Although the Ducati had appeared the Italian designers ignored trans-mission, being dominated by the direct drive system which broke away so successfully from conventional motor cycle practice. French scooter designers – even giants life Peugeot – had produced machines but no sales, so that fresh finance was hard to come by, while in Germany the NSU concern, having made one scooter with automatic transmission, but no pro-duction line for it, first of all doubted that automatic trans-mission had a future and then abandoned two-wheelers completely, though efforts to conceal this fact were strenuous and varied.

It was in Britain that automatic transmission had some of its most faithful friends. Perhaps they were not good friends, but they certainly spoke up strongly. Edward Turner of BSA publicly said that the ideal transmission system was automatic, and his firm had more than forty years of practice in this field. It is true that when the BSA scooters appeared they had a final chain drive, but later there appeared the Tina, with 100cc engine and automatic drive by belt and expanding pulleys. The Tina had, to put it mildly, certain defects and was quickly followed by the T.10 Automatic in which some old defects were remedied and some new ones built in, but the BSA bias towards the belt and expanding pulleys drive system (and the poor sales of these two models) meant a halt in any thinking about torque converters for scooters.

Applied to two-stroke engines the transmission of power through fluids (oil) presents special problems because of the two-stroke's low-speed torque characteristics. The mechanism is simplicity itself. The water wheel is the simplest form of turbine. Water drops on paddles fixed to the wheel, the wheel turns. We can go a stage further by enclosing the paddle wheel inside an annulus and have the water forced through jets in the latter. Finally we can make a fluid coupling in which a vaned shaft is driven in an oil-filled housing and thus drives a vaned, but not connected, member to which a shaft may be fitted. This is a substitute for a mechanical clutch, to be more accurate. The other two systems are genuine automatic transmission systems.

The belt and expanding pulley system has a long history, going back at least to 1902, when a Rudge motor cycle was fitted with a leather belt and expanding pulley. This was a case of designers not waiting for suitable materials to be produced. The success of the infinitely variable belt and pulley drive had to wait on the development of V-belts which were both accurate and long-lasting.

At the Motor Show of 1933 a BSA was shown fitted with an hydraulic coupling and preselector gearbox. Very few of these were made and even fewer of them found customers. The experiment was not repeated but there is little doubt that the notion of automatic transmission had taken up residence at BSA and now and then nudged their designers into producing something tangible.

Hydraulic transmission thus remained one of the scooter problems to be solved. Although it has been called the ideal system it has serious disadvantages for the small engine, the chief being that, with the machine stationary but the engine ticking over, a certain slip is required – or some kind of brake applied – to prevent the machine creeping slowly forward. The problem was solved in motor car engines by accepting this small power loss, but in an engine developing only 5bhp such a loss cannot be tolerated. There were also some safety problems for the inexperinced scooter owner. With the Tina, the machine started moving briskly forward when the throttle was opened and many a Tina owner, idly blipping the throttle, found the Tina getting away from him (or her) to the surprise of those in the immediate vicinity. This was met in the later model by fitting a safety lever under the saddle. In theory you could open the throttle but the scooter would not move off until the rider was in the saddle. Unfortunately, some owners (or their friends) tended to apply a heavy hand to the saddle and so short-circuit this well-meant device. Beyond these technical considerations is the fact that the scooter-buying public has no preference for an automatic transmission system and will not pay a higher price for a scooter so fitted. The demand is for a brisk performance, for good acceleration, which is not surprising since in heavy town traffic a scooter with sluggish acceleration is at a disadvantage.

Three other systems have been used:

Shaft drive. This was adopted by Lambrettas from the beginning and was maintained until the Li Series of machines was introduced in 1958. Shaft drive was also used by NSU and since they had made Lambrettas in Germany under licence for five years, and since their NSU motor cycles used shaft drive, they can be said to have had enormous experience of the system, so it is not surprising that when NSU began making their own scooters they should have adopted shaft drive, with straight spur and spiral bevel gears. In their later scooters NSU mounted the engine transversely with the gearbox in unit with the engine. Primary drive was by straight spur gears on a shaft. The final drive was direct to the rear axle through spiral bevel gears. They can fairly be said to have attacked the problems of shaft drive from most angles without committing themselves to any as the best solution. In this they were in sharp contrast to the steady, successful and single-minded BMW firm whose big motor cycles – all with shaft drive – set a European standard.

Chain drive. This is traditional motor cycle practice and though motor cycle rear wheels were carried in forks, so that to change a rear wheel where chain drive was fitted could never be less than a dirty nuisance, it was a simple, practical system of great strength. Roller chains, either single or duplex, are used and although the development of present-day roller chains has given an incredible increase in efficiency the chain drive system worked very well without them. Two serious disadvantages were accepted as inevitable, even with the most efficient roller chains. Firstly, the rear wheel pivoted about a point distant from the centre of the driving sprocket. Secondly, the chain stretched with wear and the chain centres had periodically to be altered.

Since 1945 the swinging-arm rear suspension system has been used in almost all motor cycles and scooters with conventional chain drive. The rear wheel thus has considerable upward and downward movement along the arc of a circle whose centre is at the pivot point. When the machine is driven under constant load on good surfaces it is possible to have the chain almost ideally adjusted for tension, so that the chain wear will be almost negligible. On rough surfaces, however, and especially if the machine is sometimes ridden solo and sometimes carries a passenger, the movement of the rear wheel is appreciable and varied and there may be rapid wear on the chain. Frequent adjustments will be needed and, eventually, the chain will have stretched so much that it is a link too long. At this point replacement of the chain should be considered. Wear would be greatly reduced if pivot centre and drive sprocket centre were on the same axis but crankcase castings make this difficult, if not impossible. With the development of bonded rubber (or synthetic rubber) bushes for use in such oscillating members the winds of change may blow and if this happens the roller chains will have longer satisfactory life.

Changes there have been. There are new types of chain adjusters on some scooters. The conventional practice was to have the rear-fork tubes flattened and a slot machined in each to take the spindle with a pierced and threaded adjuster on either side. Although this system was widely – almost universally – used on British motor cycles some scooter designers who employed a rear fork have tried to improve on it, as in the case of the DKR Capella. Earlier French scooters such as the Peugeot had the adjustment taken up by a small cam, a very simple and robust method which the Velocette designers used for their motor cycle front brake – and with their Viceroy scooter. Some makers have kept the chain centres fixed and have relied on a slipper to take up any chain slack. This method was much used in motor car design and was adopted in the BSA/Triumph and Lambretta scooters although, because of space restrictions this brought some serious disadvantages.

In practice a slipper is useful where little adjustment is required, usually where the chain is totally enclosed and runs in oil, as in timing gears. Few final-drive chains were so enclosed in British designs, the motor cycle having set the pattern of open chains with sheet steel covers. On imported scooters such as the Diana and some French models the chaincase was a robust casting, acting as a chassis member. Chain lubrication here was therefore simple, and wear was reduced because dirt was excluded. Chain adjustment could therefore be by means of an externally mounted eccentric. The necessity for fitting a tensioner is one of the serious handicaps of chain drive and on the Vespa, Lambretta and NSU this method has either not been used at all or was replaced by making the final drive direct or through spur and bevel gears. In the Lambrettas designed for the sporting and competitive rider, however, provision was made in production models for sundry modifications – sometimes minor but sometimes completely altering the engine and gears; here the advantages of chain drive became clear, chiefly the flexibility. With the Lambretta Vega, for instance, it was possible to run it as a standard 75cc or to buy standard modification parts to turn it into a 125cc scooter and since the Vega weighed about 170 lbs the owner had a clear advantage over a standard 125cc Lambretta perhaps weighing 240 lbs.

Direct drive. This brings us to the third method of transmission, where the gears are mounted alongside the rear hub, a method peculiarly suitable for scooters. There have been many objections raised to this method, but it has stood the test of time and it has become standard on most scooters throughout the world. It is sometimes forgotten that, if we judge solely by the number of scooters, then direct drive is and has always been the most popular transmission system of them all. Even more important, if we exclude British designers (whose models failed for other reasons) those makers who have tried shafts for their final drives have one by one abandoned shafts and have in their later models standardised on direct drive, though it must be said that the NSU Prima D continued with its original shaft drive until NSU abandoned the scooter market altogether.

The most obvious disadvantage of direct drive is that the engine must be located off-centre and close to the rear wheel, two things which conventional designers do not like. Motor cycle engines are placed centrally so that the machine is in static balance and their designers do not like carrying big metal masses away from the central axis. It would be wrong to say they have never had the chance of seeing an engine mounted alongside the rear wheel for this has been done on various machines, including the very successful Cyclemaster, but they could not take seriously a design such as the Vespa, where the entire engine was set alongside the rear wheel. They were sceptical when the first Vespa appeared. They were surprised, but still sceptical, when the millionth appeared. Today, when most British motor cycle designers have had to find other jobs, they remain unconvinced. They look on the system as something that works, but shouldn't, something beyond understanding or control, something that happens once only and is not to be copied. What they did not realise was that the 1946 Vespa direct drive system was a masterpiece of original design, calling for a new way of thought about the problem. It was a technical advance surpassing any British advance since 1945.

This type of drive made it easy to obtain a compact engine layout and great rigidity in engine and transmission components. It was also easy to make the transmission into a chassis member and combine this with a chaincase. A pleasing example of this was the TV.175 Lambretta, where a duplex chain was used to the gearshift, with direct final drive. The crankcase, transmission and rear hub form a single unit, rigid and totally enclosed.

In reviewing design since 1946 we have dealt so far with outward appearance and with transmission. This is not an accident. The first rough sketch of a scooter sets a pattern which becomes rigid. Major alterations to it are not easily made, and at an early stage everybody connected with the project acquires a vested interest in what has already been decided. Especially is this the case with the external shape.

Decided by someone in the top echelon, this will not be varied without difficulty.

But perhaps the design did not start that way. Perhaps there was a senior director who (substantially) left design to look after itself. Such a man will concentrate on either engine or transmission and if his firm is big enough to design its own engines it is the transmission which will have the biggest influence on what the scooter is going to be like when it is in production. Alternatively, if the engine is of an awkward or clumsy shape the problem of fitting it into an attractive body will be solved by making the body fit – and to hell with shape. If Villiers in their palmy days had marketed a scooter it is unlikely that they would have fitted an Italian engine, whether their own engines were superior or not. It was equally unlikely that they would change their engine design for the sake of a streamlined body. When Veloce launched their Viceroy scooter it had a snail-cam front brake adjuster which had disadvantages for the novice scooterist who could not, by inspection, tell whether his brake shoe adjustment was nearly all taken up. The big advantage of the adjuster for Veloce was that its design had been tested on their motor cycles.

Having decided on engine and transmission the designer has a limited freedom of movement. If he is not allowed to design his own engine (or is not competent to do so) and must buy this out he cannot be said to have chosen the form of transmission, which will be dictated by the engine, and in Britain will almost certainly be by roller chain. Designers have to be practical. They may put off the evil day but, sooner or later, the design must leave the drawing board and go to the toolroom, the machine shop and even – dreadful thought – assembly line; after this the sales staff will start their own war. Disaster or failure at any of these points is a serious matter. It was a great misfortune that the designers of British scooters (with one notable exception) were men who had shown themselves competent in other spheres many years previously. They had proved themselves in sales, in production, in engine design and sometimes on difficult, dangerous race tracks. Designing a scooter was never their sole nor even their main preoccupation, for they had duties in sales, production or finance which tended to limit their scope and to weigh their decisions in favour of the obviously possible. Thus, having at hand a well-tried chain drive, there was a tendency to accept this uncritically for the scooter. Against this background it can be seen that the BSA/Triumph scooter transmission unit was a considerable step forward and, accompanied by the stub-axle wheel, shows much originality of thought. It is also an example of a designer settling on chain drive when other methods were open to him. British manufacturers are wholeheartedly in favour of a roller chain for the final drive. They like the chain. They have great experience with it. They assume that the scooterist, like the motor cyclist, will attend to its servicing and adjustment.

Suspension. If the wheels and the frame are not separated by some kind of shock absorber the rider will have an uncomfortable time on bad road surfaces. In addition the vibration may set up rapid metal fatigue. Frame members will then tend to fail at bends, joints and changes of section more quickly than the designer had expected. To offset this he may, in the absence of good shock absorbers, make the frame members unduly heavy and may even fit a bigger engine. This process can continue indefinitely and is a policy of despair.

Suspension is a question of money and of good design, but if we look at the variety of ways in which scooter wheels are carried and sprung we quickly see that differences of opinion were many and fundamental. Racing experience with motor cycles has taught that both wheels should be sprung and this method is followed in scooters. Occasionally a designer has omitted suspension on one or two wheels, as with the small

Laverda, but this is a rare exception. The most popular suspension is the coiled spring, either with or without hydraulic dampers. Vespa (after the first model) fitted the front wheel with a simple coil spring and hydraulic damper on the off-side. This highly unorthodox system has been modified in detail, but only in detail. In spite of its small size it is clear that this stems from aircraft practice where designers would tolerate considerable forward displacement of the frame relative to the wheel when absorbing landing shocks.

British designers could not take this type of suspension seriously. Steeped in a racing tradition they had difficulty in accepting this considerable relative movement as good practice and perhaps this was why – with one or two minor exceptions – the front suspensions of motor cycles became a stereotyped front fork with double shock absorbers. This applies equally to small and to large machines; whether 200cc or 750cc; whether racing machines or runabouts. There were exceptions, such as the Ariel and the Cotton, but they were very few. One result was that the front end of British motor cycles followed a pattern. Style variations were confined to matters of detail.

Judged by such standards there was excessive dipping on the Vespa front suspension. Not to put too fine a point on it, the Vespa front suspension was treated with contempt, as a design blunder. Its very great advantages were overlooked and today it continues successful and unique. Corradino d'Ascanio anchored the front damper – and in later models the spring – to the mudguard, a highly unorthodox arrangement which has not been copied by others. Over rough ground there is considerable dipping of the front end of the Vespa, a thing quite alien to motor cycle practice but this soft springing is common to Italian-designed scooters in general.

On machines like the Vespa and Iso Milano the steering head carries the suspension units externally on welded lugs, offset to carry the wheel. Very different is the Lambretta front suspension, for the wheel is carried in a trailing-link system, using a conventional fork. Springs are carried inside the fork arms, and are fitted with a solid cup-ended guide to prevent deflection or rattling. The complete suspension unit is a sealed box containing the spring ends, the right and left reaction levers and the spring buffers. The trailing link fits externally on the splined ends of the reaction levers, its open end fitting on the front spindle. This method allows the front wheel to be taken out without removing the front spindle, but carrying a wheel in an open-ended front fork was very far from being standard practice. Again it must be said that, whatever its theoretical disadvantages, it works. This method was used with small variations throughout the Lambretta D and LD models. In the later Lambrettas the same principle was used but the reaction levers were merged into the trailing links, a great simplification. Beginning with the TV.175 an additional hydraulic shock absorber was fitted and this is perhaps a defect of design for with the Vespa no extra was needed for the bigger scooters, merely to scale the units up.

The NSU concern originally used this trailing-link system but with their III.KL and Prima V scooters they began mounting the front wheel in a pivoted fork with a combined coil spring and hydraulic damper on the near side only. A somewhat similar system was used in the later Zundapp Bellas; in both cases the damper was anchored to the horizontal member behind the front spindle. In the earlier Zundapp Bellas the front wheel was held in telescopic forks, the front spindle being shaped like a high-tensile steel bolt, threaded at one end only. When the R.150 and R.200 Bellas were first marketed the owner could choose which of these types of suspension he would have on his scooter, a somewhat unusual choice.

The pivoted-fork system was very popular. It was used on

the Moby, Puch, NSU and Zundapp Bellas abroad; by many British manufacturers such as DKR, Excelsior, Sun and Ambassador. It is to be noted that the NSU and Zundapp scooters had a suspension unit on one side only. All the others have two. The James scooter used a pivoted-fork system though this was not obvious at first glance. The fork was a horizontal U-tube carrying the wheel at the open end on a conventional spindle – two vertical members from the steering column pivoting on this tube so far back that they were hidden by the mudguard; a coil spring and a separate hydraulic damper were fixed behind this.

A third type of suspension system was taken almost unchanged from motor cycle practice. This had been found after long use in racing and touring alike to be both rugged and reliable. This was the double telescopic fork as used by Heinkel, Maicoletta and Velocette. A variation was the BSA/Triumph use of the single telescopic damper with the front wheel mounted on one side.

There was a much greater variety of front suspensions among scooters than among motor cycles. Usually suspension was on the soft side, which was to be expected from scooters built for moderate speeds and of modest weight to be used in the sunny climate of Mediterranean countries. Scooters built in Britain, Germany and Austria, however, were with very few exceptions equipped with much harder suspension systems, since the scooters themselves were built on very different lines from those designed in Italy. With British scooters this was partly due to the fact that manufacturers had to buy their suspension systems from a closed circle of suppliers; partly, too, it was due to the overwhelming motor cycle influence.

In the case of Germany and Austria the cause was almost solely the very strong motor cycle traditions of the leading firms. Apart from the originality of the Italian designs, the most interesting and unusual solutions came from France, where the Dolina and the Moby adopted methods which have not been followed. Mention should also be made of the TWN Tessy's complicated but effective layout.

For the scooter owner the main difference he notices is that some types suspension make it easy to get the wheel off. With some others it is a difficult and dirty job. If you have to remove the driving chain when you have a punctured rear tyre – well, you ought to realise that before you buy the machine. There was one scooter where this was particularly awkward. You could get the rear wheel off right enough but you had to get a couple of bricks to support the frame when you had done this. This is faulty design. There was also a scooter stand that worked splendidly on level ground. If you parked on a hill you had to be careful to point the scooter uphill, otherwise the wind from a passing car would be quite enough to upset the scooter's delicate balance on the stand. On another scooter you had to remove the engine if you wanted to adjust the contact breaker points, which reminds one of the old Sunbeam cars where you started to adjust the clutch by unshipping the rear axle.

Once you have settled wheel size, weight distribution, type of final drive and selling price the rest of the scooter designs itself. In Britain, and particularly in small British firms, a designer would have little freedom of choice. They had to include whatever components the firm can buy in the open market. They usually had to accept standard components and adapt their design to them. For many years you could tell a Villiers-engined scooter by the strangler lever on the handle-bars – there was no getting away from it. This was not because Villiers were obstinate. Indeed, there was a long period during which there would have been no British scooter had it not been for Villiers. It was a matter of economics. You can hardly afford to tinker with a mass-production assembly line.

It was not always impossible for a designer to arrange for small alterations to be made to standard components but he was likely to wait a long time for delivery, so we must not be too hard on him if the finished product looked like an ill-assorted jumble of components we have seen elsewhere and perhaps in happier surroundings – for this is very likely the best he could do in the time. He may hate that front fork as much as you do, but there just wasn't another to be had at the price.

In Britain the tendency is to use standard parts and accept the awkwardness of the resulting design. In France more ingenuity is employed in getting changes made. To the outsider it seems that the French job looks nicer, but the English job stays in production for a bit longer.

It is not easy to point to any design development in scooters which has not some compensating disadvantage. One obvious improvement is in the handlebar unit. The style first used by Vespa and followed by Lambretta, Iso Milano, DKR and many others is a thing of beauty. It is elegant, streamlined and (since the headlamp is built into it) cornering in the dark is simpler and safer. However, many an owner has asked plaintively how he can get at the cables, and some owners have found it impossible for them to get the handlebar cowling off. On earlier scooters the clutch, gear and brake cables looped around in the open.

Engines, as we have seen, became bigger. Speeds rose. This applied to almost all makes because this was what the customer wanted. It brought design complications since it was accompanied by a demand for a sleeker, more streamlined bodywork and to fit the bigger engine and other components in seriously reduced the accessibility (for maintenance) which had been one of the attractions of the first scooters.

Gear changing. Each manufacturer tends to stick to his original method. French and Italian scooters usually had handlebar controls. British and German machines had foot changes – again showing the motor cycle influence. However, Lambretta started with foot change and then switched to handlebar control. The Rumi had foot change for their Tipo Sport but changed to handlebar control for their later, more streamlined scooters. Vespa and Puch – who were faithful to the handlebar control – started with a series of jointed rods, but changed to cables. Here again it can be said that there has been no design improvement, but that mechanical details are better arranged.

Lighting. In France and Italy it was not necessary to have lights on scooters parked at night and parking lights were therefore not fitted as standard equipment in the first scooters exported to Britain. Even if a battery was fitted the light from it had little magnitude or staying power. Current for the head-lamp – usually 25 watts – was direct from the flywheel magneto. The faster the flywheel turned the brighter the light. If you came to a bad corner you could go round quickly with a good headlamp beam or you could slow down and manage with a tired glow. When the engine failed, from a whiskered plug perhaps, the engine immediately cut out and left you without lights. In later years the lighting, particularly on the Italian scooter, improved considerably but this was because the British market demanded it. Indeed, when the Italians were slow to respond, the British scooterist went ahead himself – a reader of the magazine *Scooter World* in 1960 worked out a practicable system of converting the Lambretta 6-volt lighting to 12-volt and this 12-volt conversion proved so popular that it soon became a standard accessory. For the first time it was possible to fit winking indicators, stop light, fog lamp and a host of other electrical gadgets without overloading the battery. It was usual to fit two 6-volt batteries with this conversion, which enabled the scooterist to go touring by night with a headlamp of constant brilliance. The British-made scooters followed the motor cycle tradition, using parts developed for motor cycles, and almost without exception they had excellent lighting. The little BSA Dandy, for all that it had but a 70cc engine, had better lights than the majority of Italian-made scooters in 1956.

Machines with electric starters tend to have powerful lighting because they are fitted with 12-volt batteries as standard. This term is used for convenience, rather than for its correctness – in fact scooters with 12-volt electrics had two 6-volt batteries since it was simpler to stow two small ones than one large one. The German Diana, Maico and Bella normally had electric starters while very few Lambrettas had one and Vespa did not fit one at all because of its curious engine layout. It was no isolated accident that the German machines had electric starters. It was rather a sign of the overall difference running through the whole machine – the German machines having bigger engines, greater speed and weight, ignition switches, headlamp flashers and so on; more elaborate equipment all round. It should here be said that 6-volt lighting is not necessarily inferior to 12-volt. For many years 6-volt electrics were standard on motor cars, but a 12-volt system has a bigger reserve of stored power (for parking and spot lights, etc.) and smaller diameter wiring can be used without the risk of an appreciable power loss. The current required for a scooter electric starter was, however, so great that the 12-volt system was used except in the Maico pendulum starter where a 6-volt system was adequate. This was a most ingenious device and will be dealt with in some detail later. From a design point of view its use was fortuitous, and was another example of the designer accepting a ready-made solution. The starter was designed by Bosch and there happened to be a very close link between Maico and Bosch. No other scooter adopted it.

Starting. This is and always has been a point of great importance to the scooterist, especially to the feminine half. The usual method was by a kickstart pedal, geared to the crankshaft. The series of events – in theory – was that by pushing on the pedal the engine was turned over, mixture was drawn into the cylinder, current was generated and after the first spark at the plug points the engine fired automatically and continued to fire. The kickstart gear disengaged and the owner drives off. This was the theoretical sequence and is one field where great progress might have been expected. Few motor car developments are so spectacular as the present-day ease of starting. There may have been good reasons connected with batteries and ignition systems to account for it but probably the most important reason of all was that many women drive cars and they would not tolerate a car which had to be cranked by hand. Therefore on most cars a starting handle is not even fitted and the starter simply has to work well.

There was no corresponding improvement in scooters. Much research into starting problems was done by Vespa at Pontedera but certain of the early two per cent Vespas were erratic in starting and after them there was a noticeable improvement. The German solution was to fit electric starters, often without fitting a kickstart pedal at all. In Britain, unfortunately, the motor cycle tradition spilled over into scooters and the attitude was that all you needed was a hefty kick at the pedal. If you couldn't kick hard enough you were a cissy – a somewhat dubious consolation for the girl wearing light shoes. Very few motor cycles have electric starters and the tradition of the hefty kick dies hard. There were two curious exceptions – on the Veloce Noddy machine you pulled on a starting lever. On the DKW Hobby you pulled a starter cord, as with marine outboard motors.

To get a good spark with the standard scooter ignition system something between 7kV and 10kV were required. To produce this voltage the crankshaft must turn at a speed which varies with the machine; on some it is as low as 200rpm whereas one firm is quite happy with an engine which must turn over at about 500rpm to get 10kV. Where a scooter manufacturer buys his engines from an outside supplier he is not greatly interested in such problems, which he feels are the responsibility of the engine maker, and the latter would not alter his engine design merely for a pack of light-footed scooterists. The stock answer to complaints about starting is that the engine will start easily if it is properly maintained.

Two final points on which little progress in design were made – weather protection and the carrying of luggage, including the spare wheel.

Motor cycles and the earlier scooters paid no attention to the problem of weather protection with the notable exception of Vespa, where the pressed steel chassis extended almost to the handlebars. Soon after 1947 almost all scooters had this form of protection but the logical extension – a windscreen – was usually made and sold as a separate item. Windscreens were rarely designed at the same time as the scooter. Usually a production model was borrowed and the windscreen was then made to fit. The result might have been expected – windscreens which looked like stuck-on bits rather than an integral part of the scooter. This was bad enough when scooters had open handlebars, with tubes of uniform section, but when streamlined handlebars became general the windscreen had to be fitted to a tapering member and some very unhappy windscreens flopped about the country. The problem could easily have been solved at the design stage and this was done with great success in some Vespa models, while the Lambretta solution, though highly efficient, used a fabric flap to close the gap between screen and legshield. Both Vespa and Lambretta later left the problem to others. In the Czech Manet 100cc scooter – a miracle of complete and harmonious design – the windscreen fits direct to the legshield; with the German

Maicomobil – a huge and ungainly 277cc scooter – a similar, but larger, solution was found. Both these continued as standard equipment as long as the scooters themselves were produced and they are rare examples of integrated design. British scooter designers appeared to have no energy left over for windscreens.

In the same way the problem of carrying luggage on the scooter was tackled after the scooter had been built, usually by a different firm. In general there were two types – a chromium plated tubular steel platform to which rucksack or suitcase could be strapped or a specially made frame supplied with pannier bags complete. In one neat variation of the latter the pannier bags were styled so that they could be used as normal pieces of luggage. In all cases it was necessary to fix the framework to an already finished bodywork. The drilled holes added nothing to the scooter's appearance and became focal points for rust. Rarely was the sheet steel bodywork strong enough for these carriers, which sometimes incorporated a slot for a heavy spare wheel. Since the luggage was thus carried at the rear a scooter carrying a pillionist in addition had a disproportionately heavy rear end, which meant light – too light – steering. In the James scooter the low-mounted engine left room below the dual seat for a fair amount of luggage and the French-built Peugeot in the early models had a luggage compartment built in above the front wheel. These were rare examples to the general rule that the carrying of luggage was regarded by scooter designers as somebody else's problem. Bound up with this was the spare wheel – to fit one or not? The early Puch RLA.126 had a spare wheel as standard equipment, fitted very neatly at the rear. The big Vespa which was a 160cc in 1963 had become a 180cc scooter by 1965 and carried a spare wheel tucked away inside the near-side blister, a most ingenious arrangement. But generally the spare wheel was abandoned. The BSA scooters had a shapely rear end, but adapting it to take a spare wheel or luggage was complicated and where the bodywork was split it was necessary to remove luggage and dismantle the carrier before even starting on the panelling – on a wet night with a rear wheel to change this was misery.

3 Choosing a Scooter

The most costly scooter is the one you buy, only to find that it is not what you wanted. It looked good in the showroom. Your friend has one, but you found it too heavy, too fast – or perhaps not fast enough. You might even have found that it was sluggish to start and sluggish even when on the move.

It is unfortunately very easy to choose the wrong machine. A high speed touring scooter is at its best on the open road. When the GS Vespas and the TV Lambrettas first appeared these powerful scooters attracted many buyers who could not use them to advantage and blamed the scooters when they should have blamed themselves. If you do most of your scootering in a built-up area you will rarely use top gear or if you use top gear you will be wrecking the big engine. Again, if a sidecar was to be fitted these high speed touring machines were not truly suitable, a fact not always made clear by dealers with them in stock. On the other hand, if you want at some future time to fit a sidecar, you don't want to buy an 80cc scooter, however suitable that might be for your present purposes. A third consideration is weather protection – if you want this avoid the sporting machine which has extremely small legshields. If you intend to keep your scooter for three or four years you do not want to start with a model which has been out of production for two years.

Your dealer can help you if you start by helping him. This

means having in your own mind a clear idea of what you want to do on the scooter – and telling him. Take two examples:

A girl goes into the shop: "I want a scooter costing not more than £200. Which is the best?"

A man says: "I have a car, but I can't afford car rallies. I'd like to do some scooter rallies and hill climbs. What's best for me?"

In the first case the dealer would hardly be able to answer without a lot more information, because there is no single best scooter. In the second case the man might be happy with something like the Lambretta Vega or the Vespa 90 – or with one of the out-of-production British Villiers-engined scooters, for here with some mechanical ingenuity and hard work he could build up a very potent rallying scooter at low cost. Scooter magazine readers continually write in for advice and we can quote three:

1. "I want a scooter chiefly for going to and from work as the buses are not frequent round here. This means sixteen miles each way and I live in a hilly district. I should like to take it abroad also for holidays with my girl-friend, so it would have to be up to its work."

In such a case the temptation is to suggest a light scooter, bearing in mind the daily journeys. It would be low in first cost, economical to run. Why buy the bigger engine and higher speed, since most of your running would be done without a passenger and at moderate speeds? However, the best machine for solo riding to and from work may not be the best machine for two people with luggage heading for Switzerland or Germany. It is not easy to recommend one scooter for two such different purposes.

2. "We have a car for long journeys, but inside London I find it so awkward that I am seriously thinking of buying a scooter for getting to the office and doing occasional shopping. Outside London, I think I would still use the car."

This is a much easier problem. No pillion passenger; moderate speeds, short journeys – a big scooter would be expensive and would have few compensating advantages. Any of the 125cc standard scooters would serve, but so also would the under-100cc models and these would be cheaper to run. They are not mopeds, but they are almost as economical. They are ideal for short journeys ridden solo. The engine starts easily. The kickstart pedal does not hurt your feet even if you wear light shoes. These small engines will take a lot of ill-treatment before they pack up. What is even more remarkable is that some of these under-100cc scooters are made to carry two people. This does not mean that they should normally carry two. You would find their speed cut down considerably but for short journeys a passenger can be carried without harming the engine or transmission. Therefore, for shopping and visiting, for a spare machine, for short journeys in heavy traffic a lightweight scooter is the answer.

3. "I am a motor cyclist and have been a club member for some years. I would like to get a scooter because I like going about with a club but I don't care any more for the scrambles and mud-plugs you get with our club. Still, I don't want to potter along at thirty miles an hour. Is there a high-performance scooter for me and some club events I could enjoy? I want a scooter with a motor cycle performance."

This again in fact is simple. There are several high-speed scooters. The Maico, for instance, which has covered over 1,000 miles in 24 hours round the TT course. You might still find an odd DKR or James tucked away in some dealer's yard. The DKR Manx did 500 miles in 500 minutes on the Silverstone circuit. And though there are no true 80mph scooters some of the 200cc Lambrettas can be tuned to give tremendous performance and something very close to this speed.

Scooters like the Heinkel, the Zundapp Bella, the Progress and Maico had much in common with motor cycles, as did almost all the British scooters – even the BSA/Triumph models, in spite of their sleek lines, were plainly built by a motor cycle firm. They were not as adaptable as the Lambrettas for sporting events and except in long-distance runs they have had little success in competition work except for odd events where the good big engine beat the good little one. This reader who wanted a scooter with motor cycle performance had many types to choose from but he might need a second machine for rallies and track events.

The three letters quoted above are typical of many other written by people who wondered whether a scooter was quite what they wanted. Many such letters merely asked for the name of the best scooter and these it was impossible to answer for in spite of the advertisements the best of anything simply does not exist. Every customer wants the best carpet, refrigerator, car and scooter; and salesmen spend much time explaining why there is no such thing. Good salesmen, that is.

The question of best has nothing to do with mechanical layout, reliability or cost. There are beautifully designed scooters, made by first-class firms and yet one would hesitate before recommending them in every case. Here are examples of scooters which proved unsatisfactory – though it was not the scooter's fault.

Too heavy. Here is a superb machine, made in Germany; very powerful, very reliable. When it was loaded with luggage (rear carrier) the girl owner had a struggle to get the machine on its stand for parking.

Too fast. An Italian machine, made for high speed solo riding. A too-keen salesman sold it to a youth as his first machine. Result – continual first and second gear work was needed in crowded traffic. Being nervous, the learner-driver tried to ride in top gear at low speed. This is a common fault. The engine noise in the lower gears is disconcerting to the beginner. In the present case the engine never reached a reasonable working temperature and considerable damage was done to engine and transmission during the first 500 miles. Here was a lovely machine, one of the best in its class, but it was put to the wrong use.

Too small. A young man, rather heavy for his age, wanted a cheap scooter. He bought – or was sold – an Italian machine with a 70cc engine. From the start he usually carried a passenger as heavy as himself, even during the running-in period. The engine did not fail but the clutch had a short life and the brakes were inadequate for such a load.

Out of production. Not until he had bought the machine did the owner find that the makers had ceased production two years before and were now making typewriters. This did not matter at first but spares became difficult and getting service impossible since dealers had no staff trained in that make. Soon it was not even possible to get comprehensive insurance at normal rates. In this particular case the scooter was a good bargain, for nothing went wrong and it was sold a year later for a good price, but some who have bought scooters not in production have been less fortunate. When a machine breaks down it is no better than the service that can be obtained for it.

The examples are taken from actual incidents. The owner of the high speed machine found himself in the middle of the Birmingham evening traffic rush. The clutch cable became stiff to operate. He finished with a badly swollen wrist and a numb left hand. The heavily built youth lived in a hilly district and his 70cc machine was quite unsuitable for his purpose. It is easier to choose a car than a scooter. You have an effective price ceiling with cars and this eliminates many of them – some of them good, some merely expensive. With scooters there is not such a wide range. Almost the whole list is within your reach and though this makes selection difficult it means that you can afford the scooter best suited to your purpose.

Having decided to buy a scooter you will make up a short

list of possibles, from those you have seen on the road, or advertised, or perhaps you have been offered a machine at a bargain rate. If you have seen "your" machine in the showroom half the job is done but you may only have seen it on paper. The ideal shop window is one where you can see every type but with the Earls Court Show gone there is no such thing nowadays. It has its compensations for at Earls Court there were always a few rogue scooters, shown as a gesture, to get financial backing for manufacture or to book sufficient orders to make importation profitable. The machines were samples and if sufficient financial support appeared they would soon be on the market in quantity; without backing, no more would be heard of them. You might thus be badly stung.

In this respect, the Show was like any other shop window and not many shop windows carry warning signs. Things are displayed with the idea of selling them. Now, since you want to see before you buy, you run into the first risk, of buying not what you want but what someone wants to sell you, and a dealer may want to sell a machine for several reasons. Take an example:

Dealer A gets a letter from the importers of the Blank scooter, made in France. Sales have dropped. Production is to cease. No more machines will be available after the end of the year. Dealer A is in a quandary. He has five of these scooters in stock and naturally wants to get rid of them as quickly as he can. He is even ready to make a small loss now rather than wait for a big loss after the year's end. Once word gets round that production has stopped not every customer will want the machine. For a little time, therefore, when Dealer A is talking to a prospect he may dwell on the virtues of the Blank scooter with more insistence than he would have done before he got the news.

This position hardly obtains with motor cars where, apart from the specialised journals, there is a national Press ready to publish such news. It was unfortunately possible for a scooter to go out of production with barely a mention in the scooter Press. It has even happened that a magazine has published a road test report of a new scooter, the Piatti, after the editor knew that the makers had gone into liquidation and there was no possibility of the new model ever going into production. Or take the Dutch-made Bitri. Optimistic reports were published, accompanied by paid advertising and a few Bitris were imported, but no service or spares section was even thought of over here and this left Bitri buyers somewhat exposed. There has been little critical writing about motor cycles and scooters. In the field of engine design the third port; and in the field of production methods the shell-moulding system – these are two cases where British firms were woefully beaten by the Germans and the Japanese yet these firms knew that the technical press would protect them from criticism. Not until the Hondas appeared in Britain did the finish of British motor cycle parts improve. Not only production methods but production figures were kept from the British public. At the Paris or Frankfurt Shows you could learn the exact figures for individual makes produced but British makers have always been coy about giving these figures. There is much to be said in favour of publication. The inefficient or the unlucky firm becomes the centre of public discussion and as a rule either the luck or the management changes.

The reticence here stems from dependence on a limited number of major advertisers and the utter dependence of the specialised press on this advertising. The monopolistic character of the British motor cycle industry was absolute until the passing of the Restrictive Trade Practices Act, but at least there was a wide scattering of small firms, and if you fell out with one you could perhaps get advertising from another. But first with accessories and then with major components the small firms disappeared or were merged and soon the major advertising contracts were in the gift of a handful of individuals. The editor of a famous motor cycling journal was only half joking when he said: "If I published that about BSA how long do you think I'd hold my own job?" There was no doubt in his mind whether advertising affected the editorial contents.

News of new machines seemed to be written by enthusiastic copywriters from the makers themselves rather than by journalists possessed of a critical sense and a duty to the reader. No doubt the editor, the managing director and the sales manager derive great pleasure from optimistic write-ups but in the long run they have done harm and the editors of such journals carry a grave responsibility, as do the directors concerned. In America boards of directors are open to public criticism and comment, a system which can work unfairly but if the Press names names the shareholders can be awakened and take action to protect their investment. The new directors may perhaps be no better than their predecessors, but at least they make a profit for the shareholders. This rarely happens in Britain, where the rights of shareholders are not often exercised in this way. One reason was that the British shareholder was not given the production figures which are considered the natural right of the American equivalent.

Not every reader is a shareholder. Not every reader wants to change the board of directors but it cannot be denied that more and better information, published regularly, would have weeded out many incompetent officials and would have removed some of the pitfalls scattered around the prospective scooter customer, whose first inclination might be to buy a scooter on cost alone. Apart from price there are two basic questions which you should consider:

1. Do you want a small scooter or a large one?
2. Do you want one of the popular makes, or will you take a chance on one that is out of production – or soon will be?

The German scooters, for instance, are mostly out of production though the Maico and Heinkel continue, the latter with a big sale in the Netherlands. They are big machines, as were many British scooters, but the big machines have been in decline for some years.

Do not accept too readily that the small scooter is not strong enough. There has been a tremendous swing in favour of the small capacity engine and the Laverda with a 50cc engine was designed to carry two people. Small scooters have their limitations. They have a top speed of around 33mph. Their hill climbing is steady rather than pushing. Some of them are lightly built but they are splendid value for the money and you should ask yourself what you want from your scooter before you dismiss them out of hand. The Vespa 90cc and the Lambretta Vega 75cc machines offered astounding performance. Put it this way – if you find that three-quarters of your scootering consists of journeys in built-up areas, going shopping or to and from work, to club meetings, dances and socials and so on, why not have a light scooter? Suppose you travel seven miles each way every day on it. That makes 14 miles a day, about 80 per week and something like 4,000 miles in a year. If you do 40 miles of pottering per week you have a grand total of 6,000 miles every year of scooter travel at fairly low speeds. If this is your kind of scootering, seriously consider a small scooter.

The big scooter does not like this low speed work. The engine has no chance to warm up. At speeds below 30mph a big scooter is running at one-third efficiency and is expensive on fuel. Many a big two-stroke engine has been ruined by a series of short runs at low speeds.

However, if you like fast touring and make a habit of going out twice a week for a decent run and if you take the scooter abroad each year, or on a really long tour in Britain – well, a big scooter is the obvious answer. It will master any gradient. You will never have to get off and walk, nor will your passenger, however steep the hill. You will have a big radius of travel and the better suspension will enable you to enjoy roads which inconvenience the rider of the small machine.

So when you are looking through a list of scooters, have these two categories in mind and decide for yourself on which side of the 100cc mark your choice will lie.

(a) Buying a new scooter

Having decided whether big or small, you want to know where to buy your scooter. With Vespa and Lambretta you will find firms who sell little else. Some Vespa dealers do not touch Lambrettas, and vice versa. Some dealers handle mopeds and motor cycles as well as any type of scooter.

The advantages of the one-make dealer are tremendous. He will have a wide experience of that make and will usually have good spares and service facilities. His mechanics, busy every day servicing that make, will often spot what is wrong with your machine as you ride it into the workshop. There will be spares for the asking. If a repair has to be done, the dealer will have the special tools required. Often his mechanics will have been trained at the factory. These are solid advantages, both of the specialist dealer and the specialist repairer. The dealer who handles several different makes can hardly maintain full spares and service facilities and tools for them all. It used to be said that if you bought a British-made scooter you could at least get spares even if it meant going along to Villiers or the accessory maker in person. Unhappily, time showed that British makers disappeared very rapidly and it was easier to get spares for the Jawa Manet, made in Czechoslovakia, than for the Phoenix, made in London.

Having selected your dealer, you can now approach him. You would be well advised to ask first for a leaflet about the scooter you have in mind and then, if you are seriously interested, ask for a look at the instruction book which should be given free with the scooter when you buy it. Many owners ask where they can get an instruction book. Usually one was promised when they bought the machine but has not come through. It is sadly true that if you had difficulty in getting an instruction book before you bought the scooter you will find it almost impossible to get one after you have paid up. If a manufacturer is serious about his scooter there will be an instruction book – and in English. There will also, as a rule, be a leaflet giving details of the model in which you are interested. Have a look at both and, if they do not exist, you might – to put it mildly – ask yourself questions. If the scooter breaks down when you are far from home, the mechanic will ask for the instruction book if it is an unfamiliar make, and if you cannot even explain the wiring circuit, how is he expected to put things right?

If your machine (you are already calling it that) passes these very simple tests you will sit on it and test for size – one or two scooters are not comfortable for the long-legged. Test the controls. To change gear on some scooters you turn a twist-grip on the handlebars. With others you press foot pedals. A girl with a small hand might find the twist-grip lever awkward when there are four gears because the lever will have a long travel. With a foot gearchange, think what shoes you will wear.

Have a look at the lights. Are you being offered a scooter without a battery? This would mean no parking lights. Test the kickstarter – you might as well see now whether you can operate it with your present shoes. There was one scooter where the kickstart pedal wore a hole in a man's heavy rubber-soled shoes. Wheel the machine about and put it on its stand. You may be awkward at first but this will give you an idea of its weight and balance. One or two scooters need a bit of a heave-ho when you have luggage on the back.

You will have found out the price of the scooter but be

sure what this price includes. You may find the cost of insurance is included also. This means that you are in effect borrowing the insurance premium and of course you are paying a high rate of interest on it. Most dealers insist that scooters bought on hire purchase terms shall be covered by a comprehensive insurance policy and if you are under 21 years of age you may find this costly. You might be able to get the same cover at a lower rate by paying the premium in cash with another insurance company. As for hire purchase – once there was no alternative, but with the increasingly competitive style of the leading banks it might be possible to borrow the purchase price on decidedly advantageous terms. The bank might ask for repayment in a shorter time than a finance company would, but this might in fact be a further advantage. After all, presumably you would use the scooter to go to and from work and your saving in fares would go far towards paying for the machine. Since the repayment period would be shortened this would automatically mean lower interest and as the bank might be more flexible in its approach you should certainly consider this angle.

Finally, you should give some thought to the maintenance of the machine after you have bought it. Whether you are mechanically minded or not, some of this you should do yourself. On some machines it is easier than on others. Try to find out. There are, however, three things which you may have to know how to do and you should find out about these before you buy.

How to remove front and rear wheels. Even the best of scooterists may have a puncture. If you have no spare wheel fitted you may prefer to remove punctured tyre and wheel, take them along to a garage and let them do the job while you have tea. A necessary preliminary of course is to remove the wheel. With the NSU you put the machine on its stand, unscrewed three nuts and off came the wheel. With the Vespa you put the machine over on its side. With the Li Lambrettas you needed a little stand from the toolkit. With the Diana you would need to have the operation described in detail. With the Raleigh Roma there was an easy and a hard way with the rear wheel. In all scooters removing the front wheel is simpler but you should find out about both in good time.

How to change a plug. Again, this may be forced on you and you may have to do it in the dark and in the rain for even the best of plugs may whisker or become oiled. This is one of the almost inevitable jobs on a scooter and although you would hardly choose one scooter because it's easy to change its plug you might think that if this job is simple the designer has probably given a bit of thought all round. Where the plug has to be lifted vertically the copper washer on some types may drop off. In the BSA/Triumph scooters you might have to remove the panels to get at a dropped washer and on a wet, dark night you could spend forty minutes just getting them off and back again. On Vespas and Lambrettas you get the panel off in two seconds flat. On the Velocette Viceroy and the James you didn't have to remove anything – the plug was there in view.

How to adjust the driving chain. Where you have a final drive by roller chain you will need to adjust the tension from time to time and it was more difficult on some makes than on others. The BSA had a very simple adjuster. The James and Raleigh Roma had the conventional cycle-type adjusters. Vespa and Lambretta had no final chain drive. Do find out how chain adjustment is arranged before you buy.

One other question – Is this scooter, this model, in production? You may find some difficulty in getting a clear-cut answer since dealers are shy with their answers and you are unlikely to get a reply from the makers if you cannot get one from the dealer. There are still scooters being produced abroad which are available in job lots and are picked up by British importers. Sometimes these can be real bargains, where the manufacturer is reputable. Sometimes they can be traps, where the maker never was reputable, or is now bankrupt and after this batch there will be no more scooters of that make, no spares, no service and it is difficult to give firm advice. A vigilant press could help, but there has been more discretion than vigilance about the scooter magazines. Take the case of the Diana. One magazine bravely published the news that production had ceased, but the importers, having some Dianas still to be sold, asked for a little camouflage to be applied to the announcement. The magazine, to its credit, refused. Or take the NSU – where the same magazine discovered that the firm had abandoned all two-wheelers and published the news. A solicitor's letter arrived very promptly and again the magazine, to its credit, refused to withdraw even though it was pointed out that NSU were showing at the next Amsterdam Show. Some keen detective work disclosed that the NSU machines had been made under licence in Yugoslavia, though the fact was not publicly announced. These two examples will show how difficult it is to find out whether a scooter is still in production. For years after the Diana and NSU had gone out of production their machines were still included in lists published by the press of Britain – along with advertisements for them.

Here the instruction book may not help you, though it may give you an idea of the maker's importance and resources. Here is where a reputable dealer may help and it is always worth while to ask point blank and to stay for an answer.

Finally and perhaps most help of all, you can get first-rate advice from members of a scooter club. Vespa and Lambretta clubs flourish, even if in diminished numbers. One or other member will have a specimen of almost every model the firm put out during the last five years and you can thus see them all in action if you go out on a run with the club. The owners will be very glad to talk at length about them. There is also a group of clubs catering for scooters of all makes and at any of these you will get valuable advice. Here you can talk to poeple who have actually ridden the scooters, testing them against road and weather. You will get great pleasure from a club after you have bought your scooter but even before buying you will find the local club ready to help you – and perhaps it will save you a lot of money.

(b) Buying a secondhand scooter

You may not wish to buy a new scooter.

If you find a good used scooter you have the chance of a fine bargain. There is a big and continuing trade in them because scooterists have become fashion-conscious and like to buy the new model, handing their present one in part exchange. There are two main classes which you will meet:

1. Guaranteed. This is a scooter, not a box of trouble. Only the bigger dealers handle them. When the scooter was taken in part exchange it was handed over to the mechanics who stripped it down, checked piston, crankshaft, bearings, etc. If any of these were outside the maker's limits of wear they were replaced. Clutch and brakes have been inspected and parts replaced as necessary. The scooter, after re-assembly, has been road tested and is almost like a new machine. This is a first-class buy.

2. As is as was. This is the machine that was taken in part exchange at a low figure. It is three or four years old. It has been casually checked over but the engine has not been stripped down. This is the average secondhand machine, pretty much as it was taken over, and it is with this type that a little advice about checking will help most. Most dealers take scooters in on part-exchange purchases and offer them for sale without any real check or overhaul. With a car costing £1,000 the dealer can afford to spend money on an overhaul but with

a scooter there is no margin for this. Attempts were made particularly by Lambretta to get a secondhand guarantee scheme going but dealers were less than keen on it and as the cost of skilled labour rocketed the chance of such a scheme enduring vanished. This is merely economic pressure. The customer hates to pay extra for the guarantee.

You as a customer have only a certain amount to spend. You want to get something tangible for it. Or you want the scooter only for occasional use. Or you may be the mechanical type, able to do the overhaul yourself. You look at the two types and you work out the price differential. You may think the extra worth while; in your first year with the scooter if you have to fit oil seals, crankshaft bearings and new tyres you may have paid something like this price differential – and you cannot get repairs done on hire purchase terms. So if you can find a guaranteed secondhand scooter you may decide to pay the extra for it. This is absolutely within your own discretion.

AGE. This is most important. If it is three years old it is probably no longer in production. At five years it almost certainly is not in production. With Vespa and Lambretta, BSA/Triumph and Capri and a few others you can still get spares, even if you have to wait. With most other makes the spares situation is so difficult that you will even have to pay a higher insurance premium. If you crash a modern Vespa you may get a £75 repair bill settled by the insurance company but if you crash a Velocette Viceroy or a DKR you may find the machine written off and be left with a derisory cheque – the estimated current value of your beloved scooter. Always find out the year of manufacture of any scooter offered to you. If in any doubt, get the engine and frame number and write to the maker or the importer.

MILEAGE. Do not trust the speedometer reading blindly. Speedometer heads are easily replaced on scooters. The dealer will usually refuse to guarantee that the mileage shown is correct. Perhaps even the previous owner could not guarantee it. A scooter may do anything between 4,000 and 10,000 miles a year. Tyres might last two years at this rate.

Especially with a two-stroke engine the low mileage scooter is not always the best buy. The owner who has done only 2,000 miles in the year has hardly used the engine. He will have been making small runs, with the engine hardly working and, if the engine is over 125cc, hardly ever reaching its best working temperature.

Against this is the Vespa which in six months had done 30,000 miles. It was owned by an American who had visited both Canada and Patagonia on it. He had run through two sets of tyres but the machine was still in excellent condition. Hard work never killed a scooter, though neglect and bad driving may – quickly.

You will get a good idea of the scooter's true mileage from the tyres, from the sloppiness (or not) of the handlebar controls, from the overall appearance. If the mileage claimed is much below the average, ask yourself why.

PREVIOUS OWNER. It is always helpful to find out who had owned the scooter and how it was used. A rent collector or an insurance salesman, for instance, might have made thousands of small journeys and such usage is hard on a two-stroke engine.

ACCESSORIES. These give a clue to the previous owner and the pride he took in the scooter. Winking indicators and stop lights, fitted as extras, show more than average care. A windscreen, neatly fitted and not cracked, is a good sign.

TOOLKIT. Some owners empty the toolkit before they hand the scooter over, which might leave you unable to remove the rear wheel. Have a look at the tools. If they are complete, clean and neatly packed the previous owner was probably a careful person who looked after the scooter properly.

TYRES. Examine the treads, of course; front and rear

wheels, and spare if fitted. Examine the tyre sidewalls for cracks or cuts. Are the tyres remoulds? Tyres can only be remoulded once. Having the law in mind, how soon will you need new ones? With some scooters, check that the size is one still in production.

PANELLING. Look at the bodywork all over. If the previous owner has kept it clean and polished that is a good sign. Look particularly at the legshields with the light at an angle. This may reveal a serious dent or fold – relic of a bad crash.

WHEELS. With the machine on its stand spin both front and rear wheels separately. See that they run freely. With an old scooter you may find considerable play and this may mean new hub bearings are an early need. This is expensive and with some older makes the bearings may be difficult to get hold of and this would be serious.

CHAIN. If there is one, is it worn? Is there excessive play? The lower half is the slack side and if there is more than half an inch of movement in this the odds are that the chain is worn. You will easily get a new length of chain, but if you fit one you should fit new sprockets – and these may be very, very difficult to get hold of. A clean chain, well greased, with some adjustment still to be taken up – good signs.

BRAKES. Spin the wheels and apply the brakes slowly. If the handlebar lever can come right back to the handlebars, or if the footbrake pedal goes right down to the footboard, the brakes are badly worn and new shoes will soon be required. Look at the cam operating lever. If this goes back beyond the vertical further adjustment will be useless and new shoes must be fitted. At the same time this is not a difficult job for the average scooterist. Having new brake shoes fitted is costly; fitting new ones yourself is not.

CLUTCH. If the clutch needs overhaul it will be a costly job. Test the clutch. Put the machine on its stand, ignition and fuel switched off, and press the kickstart pedal down slowly and repeatedly, meanwhile squeezing the clutch lever. You will feel the kickstart pedal begin to move more easily. This should be when the clutch lever is about one-third through its travel; the kickstart pedal should move quite freely when the clutch lever is two-thirds way through its travel. If this happens you can assume that the clutch is in good condition. It will tell you nothing about the condition of the clutch bell or housing – this can only be checked by visual inspection.

STEERING. With the machine on its stand, move the handlebars through their full lock. The motion should be smooth. If you feel a snatch or hear an odd crackle then suspect a damaged steering head – either the ball bearings or the race. This could be a costly thing to put right. It should not be possible to move the front wheel relative to the steering column or handlebars.

CONTROLS. The handlebars, and the clutch, throttle and brake levers will give you valuable clues to the amount of use the scooter has had. Very slack and worn levers on a machine supposed to have been little used suggests that something is wrong. The control cables should be clean and greased at the ends. The cable ends, which are held in brass nipples, should be undamaged. If the cable is frayed, or the nipples obviously soldered by the previous owner, it suggests that the cables have given trouble and may give you trouble. Some scooters have cable trouble; others do not.

ELECTRICS. Some scooters, especially the earlier models, have direct lighting, which means no parking lights. If there is a battery see that the terminals are not corroded. A careful owner will have smeared them with Vaseline or some other suitable grease. Check that all the lights – and the horn – work when the engine is running. Check the lighting switch in all positions and look at the wiring. If the leads are frayed or obviously patched up this is a sign of neglect which may have extended to the other parts of the scooter. Have a look at the fuse box. If the fuses are there, covered with a light film of dust, all is well. If there is a bright clean fuse there, surrounded by dust, wonder to yourself why a new fuse had to be fitted.

You may be offered a scooter with modified electrics – perhaps one fitted with a 12-volt conversion. This is one of the most popular modifications possible and if it has been done well you are in luck. Conversion kits have long been available but the stator plate must be modified and this is not a job for the unskilled. Thus you may have a 12-volt conversion that is badly fitted. You may even find a conversion fudged up by the owner and not bought as a kit.

A modification which was popular – but led to a lot of trouble – increased the charge rate by shorting out the impedance. Although popular, this was not a good idea and would quickly wreck the battery. You cannot detect this merely by inspection but in such cases the owner has usually added winking indicators or a brake stop light to a circuit not made for such accessories. Look for this. You might think that they add to the value of the scooter, but not if they wreck the battery.

TYRES. Have a look at the treads for you can learn much from them. They should be worn evenly. If they are worn on one side more than on the other you should wonder why. Perhaps the wheels are out of alignment? Uneven tyre wear of this kind is usually a sign of something seriously wrong. The steering head may be bent, the front fork twisted or the scooter frame itself awry, perhaps the result of a smash. Tyres with excessive centre wear indicate continual use at too high pressure. Cracked walls may be due to running at too low pressure – or with too great a load.

ENGINE. This is left to the last because it is the simplest. The mechanic can start the engine up and learn a lot from the noise it makes. Not so the beginner, who should concentrate on piston, bearings and oil seals. If these need replacing the bill will be large. The manufacturer has laid down dimensions for these and if wear has put these parts outside the maker's tolerances they are unserviceable and should be replaced. You want to know whether piston and bearings are within the maker's tolerances and we suggest you ask the dealer just that, and prepare your questions in advance. Set them out in a table with a space for the answers. The dealer does not need to put a micrometer on the piston, etc. – he can check them all inside ten minutes, though the average owner is advised not to try them.

Have the following been checked and found to be within the tolerance set by the manufacturer:—	
Little end bearing	
Big end bearing	
Play at mainshaft bearing	
Piston	

There is one further and important point about the engine which is not simple. Since 1966 there has been an enormous interest in engine conversions, usually to increase the engine capacity by 25cc or even by 50cc. This stemmed from rallies and track events where the extra capacity might bring an extra placing. At first manufacturers adopted a see-nothing attitude and scooterists had to find the bigger pistons, etc., themselves. Often the parts they found were not satisfactory and these converted engines blew up with expensive regularity. However, so great was the demand that enthusiasts started small businesses supplying these conversion kits; high compression heads, racing big bore exhausts and carburetters, competition clutch plates and springs, compression plates, racing pistons – and a host of others. Soon the makers, notably Lambrettas, catered for this growing demand and marketed tested and proved conversion kits. They even marketed the 75cc Vega with a standard conversion kit to make it a 125cc.

The scooter you are offered may have been converted to a bigger capacity and you must check this. Conversions are usually done by owners who enter competitive events and thrash the scooter unmercifully. They may also be done by scooterists who simply want to be in the fashion, in which case the conversion may be a failure, giving you bad starting and an unreliable engine. Most important of all, if you buy a scooter with an engine conversion the fact may not have been reflected in the insurance; a scooter insured as a 150cc may have a 175cc piston and barrel, in which case the insurance may be invalid even though a premium is paid. You should watch this point very carefully. Owners are reluctant to tell insurance companies about changes to their scooters because usually the insurance company puts an automatic increase on the premium, even if you have only changed the colour of the panels, but if you buy a scooter and insure it as a 150cc you will be out on a limb if anything goes wrong and you have actually been owning a 175cc. Do not take the chance.

Finally, look at the scooter as a whole. Does it give the impression that it has been looked after? Are nuts rusted on? What about the chrome plating? Has that been regularly cleaned and protected? Even without any mechanical knowledge you can get a reliable impression if you look closely at the scooter. It is, after all, a used scooter and you must not expect showroom condition, but you would be better off with a scooter that has been cared for than with one that has been badly neglected. Quite apart from the state of the frame and engine, what about the hire purchase situation? Who is the registered owner? Have a look at the log book, though this may not show the name of the legal owner. Is the scooter still officially the property of a finance company? If so, how much is still owing? Your dealer can easily find this out and must tell you if you ask him.

Do not underestimate the dealer. If anything goes wrong he is the man who can get you out of trouble. He is more important to you than the manufacturer. It is not too much to say that choosing a good dealer is more important than choosing a good scooter. The average scooter is sturdy and reliable, so you need have little fear on that score, but you do need helpful advice so that you buy the scooter best fitted to your purpose and you may some day be in urgent need of after-sales service.

You will naturally ask how you can recognise a good dealer.

There is no certain method. It is a good sign if you see scooterists coming to the shop, not scooter buyers but scooter users and especially if they ask for spares and get them. Another good sign is a notice saying the dealer's shop is the headquarters of a scooter club. This does not mean that other dealers must be worse, but if a dealer is the semi-official repairer to a scooter club he probably gives excellent service. In some cases he is still a club member. In rare cases the club members, for a small fee, have the use of his workshop and his special tools. Mention has been made of the help scooter clubs can give you when considering a new scooter. This help could be vital when buying a secondhand machine. You could become an honorary or temporary member or in some other way be able to go along with the club members. Their business meetings are their own concern but they may have open meetings where you would be welcomed. Some clubs run a maintenance meeting every month. If you get in at one of these you can see what troubles the scooterists come up against and how easy – or not – it is to put them right. Talk to the members and you will learn much. They have experience that may soon be yours. Will it be happy?

Best of all, get an invitation to a club run. This may not be easy, for you will need transport, but on a run you will get a good idea of what the scooters can do and whether you would be quite suited by one. In this way you will have met some nice people and may have saved yourself trouble and money. The method is not infallible. There may be no club near your home. In a mixed club you may see only one scooter of the make you fancy and that may not be a good specimen but at least you can get honest advice, based on personal experience.

4 Initial Cost and Running Costs

The three biggest items in any scooterist's budget are:—

> Hire purchase charges
> Depreciation
> Fuel and maintenance

The first two may equal the third but will usually be much greater. Your depreciation cannot be given as a fixed percentage per year which will apply to all machines every year, but one thing can be said – your mileage has comparatively little effect on the figure. A five-year-old machine is five years old and with two-stroke engines the low-mileage job has often had the hardest wear. If you do 3,000 miles per year your engine will have been working cold for a fair proportion of its life. If you do 10,000 miles in the year your engine will probably have been working under best conditions. This is not always appreciated. As fuel prices rise you may think the cost per mile will be a bigger proportion, but somehow if fuel prices rise the prices of scooters will rise in sympathy.

However, this line of reasoning must not be carried too far. With motor cars there is a line drawn round about the 20,000 miles a year mark. Over that line the trade-in price takes a sudden drop. Something of the kind happens with scooters at the point in their life when bearings, pistons and cylinders have to be replaced.

Is it possible, then, to set a figure for depreciation? Within limits, yes. The figure will be somewhere around the 25% per year mark. Allow 5% either way. Also limit it to a reasonably new scooter. If you keep a scooter for a year or two you will find the figure fairly reliable for all but the smallest machines – and for some of these even it will be a good guide.

There are notable exceptions. The price-drop of a machine which goes out of production soon after you have bought it will be heavy. Such a machine may lie in the dealer's show-room for six months before a customer is found for it. It is very unfortunate that during the whole of this time, when it has not run a single mile, the machine has been steadily shedding pounds from its value and the fact that the maker has changed the design in the meantime will not help. There may be reasons, good reasons, for the change but the better the reasons the lower will fall the price you can get for the old model that was improved on. If you point out to a designer that his creation has such-and-such a fault he will usually say a hundred other people have mentioned it and it will be put right as from machine No. so-and-so. What he does not stress is that the manufacturer keeps quiet about this improvement in design until he has unloaded his stocks on the unwary dealer. The customer comes last in this chain.

Depreciation figures will also be unusual after a bad season. When scooters were few, sales were clear sales. In some parts of London and in other cities where crowds of Jamaicans took up residence, for instance, there was an instant rush to the dealers in search of bright new scooters and mopeds, preferably those which made a brisk noise. All these sales were clear sales. The customers appeared, put down the cash, and drove the machines off. There was no question of the dealer taking another scooter in part exchange and of course this was often too good to be true for the customer who bought on hire purchase terms and then sold it down the road before the burden of payment became unduly onerous – but then you cannot have everything. Later the average customer proved to have a machine he wanted to hand over in part exchange and the market had to expand not only to absorb new production but also to take these secondhand scooters safely out of the dealers' showrooms. Where the market does not expand to this extent the general level of trade-in prices will fall steadily.

This steady fall will become headlong after a bad season. This happened during 1960. At the end of that year you could pick up exceedingly good bargains, often at one-third below the price of an equivalent machine twelve months earlier. Where a machine had gone off the market, and during 1960 several well-known makes such as Dayton, Peugeot and Terrot disappeared, the fall was even more severe. This is quite reasonable. When you buy a scooter you should know how long you want to keep it and you should have an idea of the price you will get then. If you buy one that is not in production your chance of selling at a good price three years hence is not bright.

Similar drops in secondhand prices may also be due to social changes. Since 1967 the demand for scooters dropped, following the demand that crash hats be worn, that pillion insurance should be compulsory and that the minimum age for riding a scooter be raised to 17. These demands were accompanied by apparently concerted propaganda stressing the dangers of scooter riding and although some of this propaganda was blatantly ridiculous it was effective, in great part because of the ineptness of the counter-propaganda but also because gangs of motor cyclists created disturbances which inclined parents to forbid any two-wheeled vehicle in the house. To such parents any law which restricted two-wheelers was good law. In 1971 police stopped a scooter club outing from entering Blackpool, not because the scooterists were rowdy or troublesome but because Blackpool was infested by rowdy (and presumably uncontrollable) gangs of motor cyclists who might have attacked the scooterists. Prudent parents could hardly be blamed if they warned their offspring to have nothing to do with scooters. No doubt the motor cyclists' parents had different views. As for the police, no doubt they found it simpler to control a few law-abiding scooterists than to tackle unruly law-breakers.

If you buy one of the big scooters you will pay more new, but depreciation will not be very different from that of a small scooter. You will usually have bought a better finish, more robust construction, better electrical wiring, etc., and the bigger engine will last longer. If the scooter stays in production and if you can get spares and service for it, the resale value will be high and over a period of four years you may find it is a better bargain.

If you buy one of the small scooters you will pay less initially, but small scooters are not economical if you ill-treat them – with an engine of less than 100cc you overload it at your peril. You may find that in three years it is almost unsaleable so that the entire purchase price has to be written off unless you want another scooter, in which case you will get a token allowance. With a 50cc moped costing £75 you may write off £25 per year in depreciation.

You see now important it is to know your intentions before buying?

These depreciation figures are based on the price you would get if you wanted to sell. If you don't sell the figures mean nothing. There are many seven-year-old scooters on the road giving excellent service. These do not depreciate by £20 per year, nor anything near it because their cost has already been written off. If a scooter cost £200 seven years ago you can say it has cost £30 a year in depreciation – its resale value today will be almost nil yet it is still running about and giving

Signor Corradino d'Ascanio, Vespa designer, with the original 1946 Vespa and, in the background, a 1961 model. The resemblance between the two machines is a tribute to the advanced nature of his original thinking about the scooter.

One of the early Vespas. Apart from the handlebar layout it is strikingly similar to current Vespas.

The D type Lambretta. This retained the general layout of the original but the frame became a single tube, not a twin tube; the foot-pedal gearchange has also disappeared.

no trouble. If the owner does not wish to sell it, the fact that nobody will buy it means nothing to him except that different people have different ideas about the value of things.

Depreciation figures are thus misleading. They may also mislead in a different direction because if you calculate depreciation as a percentage you will over-value your machine. You would be wiser to budget on a fixed fall in value per year. With few exceptions a three-year-old scooter is no longer in production. The make exists but the model is vastly altered. Take the Vespa GS. This was first introduced in 1955 but though following models of the GS were improvements – the engine went up to 160cc – it was replaced in 1964 by the SS model with a 180cc engine and at once all GS.160 Vespas were devalued. When the first TV.175 Lambretta appeared it was very much the odd one out of the range and was hastily followed by the Series II TV.175 which had engine parts interchangeable with others in the Li range. This in turn was followed by the SX series and the GT.200; each development putting the previous range in the shade. Secondhand prices for the TV.175 Series I fell like a stone in one year, with depreciation more than £80. The Triumph Tina suddenly acquired a give-away price when the T.10 replaced it. In cases like this depreciation may fluctuate wildly.

Hire purchase charges. Although many scooterists pay cash on the nail, many more use hire purchase facilities of one kind or another. Naturally you pay for this credit. Remember that few dealers finance their own hire purchase deals. They have an agreement with one finance company or another so that all deals go through the same channel and there is no competition either about risks or rates. Often also the dealer is linked to a particular insurance company, which may be convenient but has its dangers, since the dealer becomes the insurance agent and draws commission on the deal. As a rule the cost of Road Fund tax and insurance will be included in

D

the total price on which hire purchase charges are made. If so, you may care to work out the items separately. You are not likely to get a Road Fund Licence at a cut rate but the same cannot be said about insurance. Shopping around costs you little but time and effort. If you shop around you must keep your eyes open. Between 1960 and 1970 some apparently sound insurance companies went suddenly out of business, leaving a trail of debts and many thousands of people without insurance cover. It is sometimes said that if you choose a member-firm of the British Insurance Association you will be guarded against this kind of catastrophe, but when you take out insurance you do not get this in writing. You are sometimes also advised to deal through an insurance broker, but here again brokers are no better than the firms they deal with. Certainly your scooter dealer will be unlikely to have advance information about the soundness of the insurance he can offer you and until vehicle insurance is handled direct by the state the risks will continue and perhaps grow.

Running costs. Having bought the scooter – and begun to pay for it – what can you expect to pay for running it? The answer depends on whether you want the cost per mile or the cost per year. At one time Lambrettas made great play in their advertising with the cost per mile of a Lambretta as compared with a bus and as bus fares continue to rise this can still be argued, although if the scooterist wants to work out his total costs he will have to do a somewhat involved calculation. He should also cut his oil costs drastically. He can do nothing about buying petrol in bulk, but he can save a wad of money if he buys his oil by the gallon and measures out his own oil when refuelling. Some scooter clubs go further and buy oil in five-gallon drums, with members buying by the gallon. In this way the cost of oil may be cut by as much as 50 percent. Another cut in running costs comes from the scooters which run on a petroil mixture containing only 2% of oil. This is a great advance, for the first scooters had engines calling for a 6% oil content in the mixture. Where you have a scooter – both Lambretta and Vespa have them – running on a 2% mixture but with the oil in a separate tank and mixed automatically in the engine you do not have to measure the oil yourself – just keep the oil tank topped up. The fairly high cost of oil is often forgotten by both scooterists and motor cyclists, the latter in particular if they have four-stroke engines although the two types spend roughly the same amount of money per mile for oil. Because the motor cycle will have a four-stroke engine running on petrol the cost of oil is passed over; but you have merely to look at the exhaust of these machines to see that the four-stroke may burn even more oil than the two-stroke engine.

Scooterists usually claim a higher mileage per gallon than they get. With all seriousness they say their claim must be correct because after putting one gallon in they did 120, 140 – or more – miles; more likely they say they travelled from A to B, which is 120 miles so they must be doing that per gallon. Some manufacturers make specific claims for their scooters. These claims are accurate – there is no doubt of this – but they refer to performance under particular conditions in the same way that the bhp developed by an engine refers to special conditions. The German DIN figure refers to an engine complete with air cleaner and exhaust; the Italian CUNA figure is for an engine minus these parts. For the SAE figure even more parts are removed. With fuel consumption figures the speed, gradient, weight of rider, wind and so on are all specified and given these conditions the maker's claim can be justified. So please accept the claim and realise that if you do not get something close to it the fault lies in yourself or in a defective scooter.

One scooterist who kept records over 20,000 miles found that the fuel consumption varied through the year by as much as 20%. It was best of all during his holiday period when he toured Scotland and had some long-distance runs. Long runs are cheaper per mile in both fuel and maintenance. Your style of driving, as well as the length of run, will greatly affect the cost per mile.

Tyres. The average scooterist may do something between 7,000 and 8,000 miles per year. Your style of driving affects tyre length even more profoundly, so it is not easy to say how long the average tyre will last. A fair figure is two years with a total of 16,000 miles. Correct pressures, moderate acceleration and braking; these extend tyre life. Since scooter wheels are interchangeable, you should switch wheels round since the rear tyre will wear more rapidly than the front one. If your scooter has an odd size in tyres you may find replacements difficult and costly.

Maintenance. This is a major item with some, covering a multitude of expenses from a fresh plug to fitting new main bearings. During your first year you should need to spend very little on a new scooter under this heading. Because less oil is used – both Vespa and Lambretta have engines needing only 2% of oil – the engine is kept much cleaner than in the past and decarbonising, which some makers used to call for every 1,250 miles, may not be necessary until you have done 5,000 miles or even more. However, do not think that your scooter can dispense with regular maintenance.

In some – but not many – cases there will be set charges for servicing. Lambretta in particular tried hard to get their service dealers to keep fixed prices for routine servicing but it was impossible to get the average dealer to stick to them. His view was that he always lost money on service, so sticks a bit on where he could. Today there are not many places where you can get the VW-style servicing, but ask your dealer about this before you buy. Then you will perhaps know how much your first year of running will cost in maintenance, apart from accidents. If you do your own maintenance you will spend more time than money on it but be sure you know what you are doing. Detail improvements and modifications are continually being made by the maker and these are notified to the dealer, so if the dealer replaces a part he will use the improved version and perhaps clear his stock of the earlier type to keen scooterists who do their own servicing. This has been known to happen. Here is where joining a club can save you money, especially a club where one evening a month is set aside for maintenance. Some clubs have bought the special tools necessary, tools ranging from simple Allen keys to complicated and costly items such as Fluxmeters for the magnets in flywheels. If the club does not actually own them it might be able to borrow them for these evenings. What more could you ask?

The major cost of any repair has always been the cost of labour and the proportion of cost due to labour seems likely to increase still further. A new ball race may cost you a pound, but fitting it may cost several times as much. The cost of a new oil seal may be a few shillings but will call for the complete dismantling of the engine – a major repair. Many owners defer these small attentions so that if you buy a secondhand machine and have no mechanical experience you will almost certainly have maintenance costs to meet in your first year and these will be out of all proportion to the cost of the new parts. On some secondhand scooters a small end bush was almost always required within the first year and fitting the new solid bush meant two special tools and some knowledge. This job is not required so often today because needle roller small ends are the rule and these last much longer than bronze bushes.

A further point. How long will you keep the scooter? If you buy a new scooter and plan to exchange it in a year you will have few maintenance costs because neither tyres nor battery will need replacing and at the end of the year you will have a scooter in first-class condition to bargain with. This is an important consideration when you do not intend to be a long-term scooterist, so to speak. In many ways this is the best way of buying. You always have a modern machine. You never have trouble getting spares. True, you have to run in a new scooter every year but apart from that dull period you will have scootering that is all pleasure. It is worth considering and it is largely governed by the crucial question – how long do you intend keeping your machine? Also, if you want transport but cannot afford a car, consider buying a scooter, keeping it for a year and offering it to the car dealer in exchange. He may puff and snort but in car dealing there is latitude for compromise and the profit margin on cars can be cut by the dealer wanting to sell a car. You may find a scooter dealer who bluntly refuses to take your tattered scooter in part exchange – the profit margin on the scooter he offers may be slight; but it would be a rare car dealer who so refused. Indeed more than one man, anxious to buy his first car, has had an allowance made on the scooter he handed in which allowed him a small profit.

Keeping a scooter for only one year works well with the larger machines, of 125cc and over. There may be exceptions but it is usually the most economical way of scootering. It is not so satisfactory with some smaller machines which are not so sturdy and whose equipment is not up to the same standard. Below 100cc weight is a critical factor. Many parts are made on the light side with a low safety factor and these may show signs of wear in twelve months of normal use. The smaller machines may lose half their original cost price during the first year. After two years most of the 50cc machines can be written off, though you may be offered more than the average if you wish to part-exchange for a 150cc scooter. The dealer is then sharing his profit with you. Or you may get an excellent price from a private buyer who wants just that model. We are not considering this – we assume that you will go to a dealer.

This is one of the disadvantages of the smaller machines but it should be taken into account when you are working out your costs. The scooter may be invaluable to you, the apple of your eye, the envy of the neighbours – it may have given no trouble at all for two years, but to the dealer it is just another model that went out of production, with a worn-out engine and dubious bearings, which will need a replace engine and then might stand around his showroom for six months waiting for a buyer. We mention fitting a new engine because this sometimes pays. Both Vespas and Lambretta launched service exchange schemes for engines and other parts. Hand the old engine in and receive one which has been factory overhauled. This suits the dealer because if he has an overhaul done in his own shop he may have to pay his men weekly. If he buys a service exchange engine he can keep the supplier waiting. Truly, the dealer has many things with which to occupy his mind.

So we come to the crux of the problem of working out costs. In a situation with so many variables we have tried to isolate those you can pin down. We will not give concrete figures for any item since prices continue to rise but since the rises are fairly uniform you can use the proportions to settle the actual amount; thus you might well pay, for each mile:—

Purchase price	?
Hire purchase	2
Fuel	3
Maintenance	1
Depreciation	3

and of these costs the only one you can control at will is the cost of fuel. Purchase price might be between 6 and 10 per mile. If you do more than 8,000 miles in a year your fuel cost per mile will remain constant but the others will drop because the above figures are based on an average of 8,000 miles a year. Do not think that this means you are saving money by travelling further. Your total expenditure will have increased but you will be getting better value for your money, more miles per unit cost. The hire purchase figure includes insurance as this is often negotiated by the dealer. After two years you will have paid for your machine and the first two items drop from your budget, much to your relief.

Is this a sensible way of working out costs? It has serious defects, for if you cover 15,000 miles in the year the cost per mile is drastically cut. If you cover only 4,000 miles the cost per mile goes up though your total outlay does not. If you pay £150 for your scooter when you might have paid £250 the depreciation cost may not vary greatly (remember that the lighter scooter is not so rugged as its big brother) but the hire purchase charge per mile will alter. So will the fuel cost per mile.

What these figures can do is to help you to work out the cost of having a first-class scooter and keeping it like that – first-class. You will find owners who boast that their scooters cost nothing to maintain. Such people spend many hours on maintenance, and you can follow their good example, but no matter how good your workshop, you will have to buy out such items as plugs, tyres and cables.

The major costs are for depreciation and hire purchase charges. These are outside your control once you have made your purchase. You can ignore them, but you can hardly cancel them out. If you keep a scooter for five years you can, for all practical purposes, write it off. That means writing off between £20 and £50 per year for depreciation. In practice you reach a level – varying with the model, but always a modest figure – below which the machine's value will not fall because you will get this allowed when you buy another machine. If you keep a scooter beyond two years and it still goes well you start on the bonus years, for then you have neither hire purchase nor depreciation to worry about. The total cost of your scootering will genuinely be the cost of fuel and maintenance, tax and insurance. You can further save money by insuring only for third party, fire and theft since the insurance company will refuse to pay any substantial sum even if the machine is badly damaged.

The notion that you can run a scooter for a penny – or any other figure – per mile is widespread but it has its dangers. The true cost is high; not so high, not nearly so high as even the smallest car, but high. You would be wise to face this fact. If you refuse, you may find that after three months you cannot afford to run a scooter for which you must continue to pay. Settle first how long you want to keep the scooter and at least then you can begin to work out the cost, if you wish. Fortunately for scooter makers people do not wish to work out in advance the cost of a scooter. They see one they like. They buy it and then they work out how they are to keep it running. This curious system, for all its illogicality, works excellently, as does the scooter.

Is a light scooter – in the £100 class – very much less expensive to run? It is certainly less expensive, but not as much less as you might imagine. First of all, you will normally ride alone. Many forget this point but if you are comparing one form of transport with another it is crucial. The scooter may not save the cost of bus fares for a solo rider, but it will show a handsome saving for two people. Secondly, your small machine depreciation per year may be very close to that of a big scooter. If you mostly ride solo the small machine is excellent and there is a strong trend towards them but when they are made to carry two people with luggage, they are unfairly stressed and their life is shortened. It is foolish to save a little on fuel if you are to waste more in depreciation or maintenance charges.

The question most often asked in connection with costs is – how many miles to the gallon? At the risk of offending some manufacturers who claim better figures, here are some averages:

70cc	130mpg
125cc	100–110mpg
150cc	80–90mpg
200cc	75–80mpg

On a works machine, on tests arranged by the manufacturer or concessionaire, these figures can be improved and we have mentioned the DIN and CUNA figures earlier on. Not only can these figures be improved, but the true figure you get from your own scooter can be improved. If you complained that your scooter was too greedy for fuel it would only require that the carburation and exhaust, the timing and engine condition be improved for your consumption to show a marked improvement – for very few scooters are maintained so as to give best performance.

However, the figures given above are workaday averages, using the fuel you have to pay for this year – and next year. The better claims made for scooters can be substantiated even when they are made by owners, not dealers. If you ran up and down a motorway you might get wonderful consumption figures but what the scooterist wants to know is at what intervals during the week he will have to buy another gallon of fuel.

Although this is the most commonly asked question you will see, if you look at the breakdown of total costs per mile, what a small percentage is accounted for by fuel. Some people buy one scooter rather than another on the score of fuel consumption alone and some makers go along with them by concentrating on it in their advertising. Is this wise? The biggest item in your running costs bill is depreciation and in the long run this can be your biggest extravagance. Look at it this way. Suppose you do 8,000 miles a year. Suppose your fuel costs come to £35 if you do 80mpg; and £27 if you do 100mpg. That is, by setting it out;

at 100mpg	Fuel costs £27	
80mpg	„ „ £35	
	Saving £8	

It looks more convincing if you set the figures out like that. By getting 20mpg more from one scooter you have saved £8 per year. You may say that this is a saving worth having and since you have to pay cash for fuel you can almost feel the saving week by week. Sadly we have to say that you should abandon any idea that two scooters of the same power and performance vary in fuel consumption by anything like 20mpg. This fact means that in practice you cannot, repeat cannot, save £8 in fuel per year by choosing one 150cc scooter rather than another. A saving of this order is not easily made.

With depreciation you can get differences very much greater than this, and very easily. Suppose you had bought a Peugeot scooter. This was a fine machine in the medium price range – reliable, well made, robust. You could reckon its depreciation per year at normal rates, something like £25 or £30 per year. Now the moment it went out of production the second-hand value dropped at once and you might easily have found your Peugeot had lost £30 of value overnight. You could buy a lot of fuel for that money.

There are few subjects about which more – shall we call it nonsense? – is talked when scooterists get together. Many and wonderful are the suggestions for getting another 5mpg and great is the harm done to some machines in the search. In this respect the makers are ahead of the customers. The former used to headline fuel economy and some scooters were sold on this claim alone. Today the makers have dropped many of their claims and there is a more mature attitude to the market, with sales campaigns stressing safety and reliability.

A similar state of affairs exists among gardeners. Weird and wonderful are the products sold under the claim that their use will increase yields by astronomical percentages. Each year some new marvel appears and each year the claims are more fantastic. Reading them you really wonder whether anybody believes them. Certainly the farmers do not for they conspicuously do not use these wonder substances either because they do not work or because the added cost would be greater than the added yield. Perhaps gardeners will in time follow the scooter people and concentrate on some other aspect. With scooters and fuel consumption, of course, the change has to be linked with the falling value of money, rather than a conscious effort by the makers to appear more rational. Reliability and safety are more popular today.

Buy a scooter for pleasure or for hard work. It will be splendid for both, but keep fuel economy in its proper place. Do not allow this single factor to decide your choice of scooter.

Other costs than those we have mentioned will present themselves. You may need accessories such as crash helmet, gloves and perhaps a special scooter coat. You may also need shelter for your machine – a wooden hut, a corner of your parents' garage, or simply a polythene sheet tied round, though here you are likely to come up against a big rust problem through condensation. You may go shopping for windscreen, extra lamps and luggage carriers.

These accessories are optional and the total you spend on them is within your personal control. Many of them are ideal for secondhand buying, though a secondhand crash helmet may be dangerous and is never a good idea.

There you have something said about the costs of your scootering. You will decide on your machine according to your own ideas, your own pocket, but do remember the two big items – hire purchase charges and depreciation. You should settle these before you buy and you cannot do this unless you know how long you intend to keep your scooter.

5 Driving and the Driving Test

Scooter riding cannot be taught from a book. It is amusing to hear one's friends explaining how they learned. After all, there was a point at which they went to the dealer's shop and took delivery of their first scooter – and drove it home. There must have been some eventful rides home. Some dealers have been heard to say that all they wanted was to see the scooter clear of his premises. On the other hand one or two dealers have set up instruction classes, with a road circuit laid out on nearby waste land complete with traffic junctions and other road signs. On this course the learner was taken by qualified instructors and on hired machines. The lessons were graded and after attending a given number the pupil was competent to handle the scooter on public roads. This was some advance on the average motoring school which sent learners out in the driving seat before they knew how to handle steering wheel or gear changes.

Unfortunately, with the decline in scooter sales and the continued apathy of local councils, the new scooterist may find it difficult to get instruction from qualified people. One or two education committees run classes, some dealers interest themselves, some scooter clubs have members who are on local safety councils and so can get instruction courses arranged, but the greater part of the burden is shouldered by the RAC/ACU driver-instruction organisation which has built up a network of centres throughout the country where adequate instruction is given. This scheme has always suffered from a lack of enthusiasm and practical help from successive governments.

Regardless of the system by means of which you become a safe, courteous scooterist you should start with good habits in starting the engine, changing gear and braking.

Starting the engine. Almost all scooters today have kick-start pedals. There is a right and a wrong way of operating these. The wrong way is to lift your foot and jab it suddenly and fiercely down.

This is definitely and harmfully wrong. If your foot slips you may bang your ankle and hurt yourself. If your aim is correct you will place a sudden and unnecessary load on pedal and kickstart mechanism. On most scooters the crankshaft is turned in two stages:

1. The pedal is pushed downwards a couple of inches. This moves a ratchet or quadrant into engagement with the first gear wheel. This should be done gently.

2. Having thus engaged the gear, press the pedal down firmly and briskly.

If you aim vicious jabs at the pedal the ratchet will be moving at some speed before it engages and it will tend to grind its teeth away. Once it is firmly engaged you can safely exert as much pressure as you like and no damage will be done, but many kickstart mechanisms were destroyed by sudden jabs at the kickstart pedal.

Changing gear. This is the correct sequence of operations when you change to a higher gear:

Accelerate briskly, then close the throttle.
Declutch.
Operate the gear-change lever.
Release the clutch lever slowly.
Accelerate.

There is also a correct sequence when changing to a lower gear:

> Declutch by pressing the clutch lever.
> Accelerate briskly, then close the throttle.
> Quickly engage the next lower gear.
> Release the clutch lever.
> Accelerate.

You can take your time about changing to a higher gear but you should get into the habit of changing briskly to a lower gear. The critical moment is when you are snicking the gear in. At this moment you should not be accelerating. It is not necessary to close the throttle completely when changing to a lower gear – just accelerate quickly and then turn the throttle twist-grip the other way. There was a fashion at one time for changing gears without using the clutch. This can be done. On some scooters you can change to a higher gear by accelerating and then giving the gear lever on the handlebars a sharp knock; and you can repeat this for every gear including top. It is not a good system, and if you are learning to ride a scooter you should go through the gear change drill until it becomes second nature. The same system is used for all scooters, regardless of the kind of gearbox or engine.

Braking. Correct braking is the heart of good driving. The less you have to use your brake the better driver you will be. Occasionally some other road user will make it necessary for you to brake (and perhaps to brake sharply) but you will find that the longer you have been driving the fewer brake linings you will wear out. The beginner drives from one crisis to the next. He uses accelerator and brake alternately to cancel each other out, whereas the experienced driver maintains a smooth progress, without sudden changes either way.

When you first drive your scooter you should operate the controls – all of them – as often as possible. Change gear frequently, both upwards and downwards. Where you have a clear road, use the brake frequently so that you become accustomed to the scooter's behaviour under varying conditions. Do not look at the controls. If you do, you may miss something interesting on the road, to say nothing of losing control altogether. It is dangerous to look at the handlebars when braking or changing gear. It is a habit to which many scooterists are prone.

On the question of braking you will hear contradictory advice, especially with regard to the brake you should use. There has grown up a school of thought which can be briefly described as – Front brake good, back brake bad. You will even hear this advice given in dogmatic form, such as: "The front brake has more stopping power than the rear brake" or that "The sign of a good rider is that the front linings of the machine's brakes are worn more than the rear."

If the manufacturer wanted you to use the front brake as a matter of course he would fit a stop light to it. No production scooter has a stop light coupled to the front brake. Where a stop light is fitted as standard it is coupled to the rear brake.

Again, consider the sizes of brake drums and linings. Many scooters have front and rear brake drums – and linings – of identical sizes. Where the two differ the front brake linings have a smaller area than those at the rear.

Finally, one of the dangers always present when braking is a skid. A rear wheel skid will often be unpleasant but not dangerous. A front-wheel skid is out of control almost as soon as it begins.

It is difficult to account for the emphasis which has been put on the use of the front brake when so much evidence points the other way. A likely explanation is that it has spilled over from motor cycle racing, where a footbrake is very much of a nuisance. A great deal of braking is done for corners, where it is essential to go down through the gears and up again as quickly as possible. It is not to be thought of that at 100mph one foot should be operating a brake and the other a gear-change. A brake with control on the handlebar is the only solution. However, at these high speeds the angle between the steering column and the ground must be maintained almost constant and so the springing at the front is made stiff.

On a scooter conditions are very different. The front springing is soft. There is considerable movement of the frame relative to the front wheel and the rear brake is the instinctive choice. The beginner's instinct here is sound. The beginner, left to his own devices, will almost always use the rear brake. However, if you buy a scooter where the bigger brake lining is on the front wheel or where the brake warning light is coupled to the front brake – well, you have come across the first scooter so equipped and the manufacturer might have meant you to use the front brake in preference to the rear brake. He might also have done something about front-wheel skids so you should ask about this.

Gear changing and braking are linked and both can be used to reduce your speed. One school of thought argues that it is better driving to use the gears than to use brakes. Others argue that it is cheaper to fit new brake linings than to replace worn gears. If you reduce speed by changing to a lower gear your overall travelling time may be longer, as you lose speed more slowly. However, if you are in top gear and you brake suddenly you will almost always have to change to a lower gear. There is not much pull in some top gears and with the big Vespas and Lambrettas, for instance, top gear is almost like an over-drive, which makes these machines not absolutely made for sidecar fitting.

This is important, especially with a new machine. If you have to brake and you lose more than about 7mph you should almost always change to a lower gear. The higher your engine revs the more power your two-stroke engine develops and this is quite independent of the gear engaged. When you are learning to ride, your instructor will tell you this many times, but the engine can make a fierce noise in the intermediate gears and this disturbs many learners who tend to rush along into top gear with a sigh of relief because it sounds quieter that way. It is a good thing to get used to the noise of the first and second gears and to realise that by means of clutch and throttle you have the engine under control, whatever noise it makes.

Gear changing with a handlebar control is easy. You can either hear or feel the gear going home – there is a nice positive feel about it. You find neutral without difficulty and there is no tendency to slide past the gear you are trying to find. This is one of the great advantages of handlebar controlled gear changing and the only difficulty you are likely to encounter is in getting out of gear if you stall the engine. This sometimes happens. The gears slide easily in and out of engagement when the engine is running but if you turn to the chapter on gears you will see why, with the engine not functioning, you may have difficulty getting in and out of gear. You are not meant to change gear with the engine stopped. In bad cases you may have to declutch and start the engine. Then the gear can be disengaged at once. If you struggle with the gear lever you may merely damage the control. Usually the gear will come free if you rock the machine back and forth and then try again.

The constant-mesh gears usually fitted to scooters make gear changing quiet and you will rarely clash them unless you forget to declutch at the proper time. If you have a foot control pedal for the gears you may find them not so positive in engagement and here it is even more important not to struggle to get gears into and out of engagement when the engine is not running. If you try you may bend one of the control rods and then you may have difficulty with all the gears. With this type of control you are advised to check that you actually are in neutral when you halt the machine, as at traffic lights, and you can do this easily by releasing the clutch lever very gently, for if the engine begins to pull away you are still in gear and you will have to try again. On one or two of the earlier scooters there was a neutral finder, and this was an infallible gadget. On scooters like the Rumi where there was a heel-and-toe gear change which was far from being infallible, it sometimes took a little time and experiment for you to locate neutral beyond a doubt.

Whatever system you have on your scooter it should become completely familiar to you so that you could change gear blindfold if necessary. On the Heinkel and the Peugeot there was a little handlebar indicator to tell you what gear you were in. This was a useful gadget, but if you came to rely on it you would find yourself adrift during a night ride. With some of the British scooters where you had four gears and foot change, it was not always easy to remember what gear you were in. With most crash hats you get so much wind noise that you cannot hear the engine at all and cannot tell when it is over-revving. You had to solve this problem yourself. One thing to remember though, if you change to a lower gear the effect may be as though you had suddenly put your brake on, so if you want to test what gear you are in it is usually better to try changing to a higher gear than risk this sudden braking effect.

You will be given much excellent advice about braking. Some of this advice presupposes that you will only use the brakes in ideal road conditions – when you have plenty of space around your machine, when you are upright and are travelling in a straight line. This is the ideal position and one you should try to keep even when the road is neither clear nor straight. If you have to brake and change gear for a corner you should do it before you start turning. This is not difficult except that there may be other vehicles on the road going into the same corner and since your speed may be less than theirs you may be overtaken by them rapidly and find them braking across the line you have chosen. This is always disconcerting. It may throw you off your line. It may lead you to think that their method of cornering is better than yours.

But if you cannot keep to your line, keep to your opinion. Yours is the correct way of cornering. You should never need to brake or to change gear after you start going round the corner. If you stand at a busy roundabout, one on a fairly fast road, you will see how badly people drive and how much better the average rider on two wheels is than the average motorist – to say nothing of lorry drivers. Watch the stop lights glow. With motorists you will see the lights on and the car half-way through a turn. The motorist is turning and braking at the same time. Still with his car turning he will change gear, sometimes keeping the brake on and sliding the car round as he imagines racing drivers do. The rider on two wheels has no need for such silly tactics except in a sudden emergency – as when he meets one of these motorists – and then he may have to brake and swerve. Under normal conditions you brake, change gear, go into the corner, accelerate through it and out, and then change to a higher gear when you are travelling in a straight line again.

You should accelerate going round the corner because you have better control over your scooter that way. Never idle round corners. Get into a lower gear and accelerate round. Many road bends can be taken in top gear but a fairly severe corner calls for a lower gear. Generally speaking, go into a corner wider than you come out of it. You will see many riders keeping well into the correct side until half-way round a corner – then they begin to swing out. Perhaps they are excellent riders. More usually they have just begun to lose a little control. They have taken the corner just a little too quickly or misjudged camber and road surface. If you do any competition riding you will sooner or later misjudge a corner. It is frightening. It may not be your fault because you may be forced off your line by another rider but you see the corner stretching ahead. You know you are heading for the bank. If you are lucky, you will be able to pick a soft landing spot. It can be terrifying.

The path you take round a corner is called a line, and if you pick the right line you will find it is a single sweeping curve; for left hand bends it starts a little wide of the kerb and goes out of the bend close to the kerb; for right-hand bends, with the camber against you, it starts further from the kerb still. You may pick a different line when racing, but for normal riding a good line finishes nearer the kerb than it starts. In other words, swing into a bend. The art of cornering is not to be learned in a day. It requires that you have confidence in your machine and familiarity with it. You will find there is pleasure in cornering properly, and great safety.

Sooner or later you will have a skid. If you are prepared for it you may correct it instinctively and no damage will be done to you or your scooter. If a skid suddenly creeps up on you and you know nothing about what causes skids you may react instantly and make matters worse. You can skid with front wheel, rear wheel, or both.

When you are riding your scooter in a straight line, self and machine vertical, you have maximum adhesion to the road. All your weight is acting vertically. At this point in any explanation of skids it is customary to refer to the parallelogram of forces and to draw one. However, you do not need the diagram and in any case you would need one for each wheel. If, when riding like this you apply one or both brakes you will in theory come smoothly to a halt in a straight line.

This theory must be applied with caution. The wheels may

be mounted off-centre. The brake linings may pull to one side. Your weight may not be equally distributed – and so on. Sudden braking at high speed may, therefore, be disastrous. You will now begin to see why some manufacturers did not like scooters. A certain number of people who bought the Dayton scooter found out very late that the frame was two inches out of alignment. The makers knew about it as soon as the frames were welded but the cost of scrapping them was considered too great and the scooters were built on these faulty frames. You could not expect the theory to hold there, perhaps.

Roughly speaking, the reason you slow when you apply the brakes is that the brake lining grips the drum and since drum and tyre move together the tyre has two forces acting on it. The scooter's weight is pressing down holding it to grip the road whereas the brake drum is trying to make it slip on the road. Since tyres are well designed they have a firm grip on the road and do not slip. If the brake pressure is too fierce the tyre will stop revolving and will slide on the road instead of gripping it. The brakes are then said to have locked the wheel. It is generally accepted that you get maximum stopping effect just before the wheel locks and that the moment the wheel locks the stopping effect is dramatically reduced.

When you are not travelling in a straight line you are not exerting as much downward pressure. It is rather as if you were leaning against a wall and most schoolboys know that in such a position the feet are more easily kicked from under one. On the road there is a certain safe maximum angle of lean which depends on your speed and on the grip of the wheels. This angle varies for various surfaces, from the rough to the very slippery. If you exceed the safe angle the scooter will slide because as you go round the bend a certain amount of centrifugal force will be acting horizontally, tending to push the scooter sideways. Your angle of lean will not of itself increase the centrifugal force but the further you lean the more effect the same amount of centrifugal force will have.

If you apply the brake as you are going round a bend some of the centrifugal force will be there as before but there will be added the sliding effect of the brake acting on the front wheel – not all of it, but a proportion and if you add to the front wheel sufficient sliding effect of braking, your front wheel will tend to slide from under you. The rear wheel will then continue on its normal path and if the front wheel behaves itself (that is if it tends to slide but does not actually slide) nothing unfortunate will happen. If by some misfortune the front wheel does slide a sideways force will suddenly be applied to the rear wheel and that will slide also. If this happens there is very little – if anything – that you can do. A front-wheel skid becomes uncontrollable almost at once. It is in the highest degree dangerous to apply the front brake when going round a bend. There is little chance of you recovering from such a skid and a fall is almost inevitable. Expert drivers will know on what occasions and on what machines they can safely use the front brake when cornering.

A rear-wheel skid is not nearly so dangerous. The rear wheel will swing to one side but you have an excellent chance of recovering without a fall if you steer into the skid; that is, turn the handlebars to face the direction in which the rear wheel is trying to go. This is known as applying a restoring couple. Even quite severe rear-wheel skids can occur without causing you to fall.

These two skids may occur when the wheels are locked or when they are revolving. A locked-wheel skid dangerous. If your front wheel locks and skids you have little chance of avoiding a fall. Indeed, if your front wheel locks you will almost certainly skid. If both wheels lock and skid the machine is at once uncontrollable and you will certainly crash. If your rear wheel locks it may skid but if it does your chance of avoiding a fall is considerable and depends largely on your speed and angle.

Since front-wheel skids are so dangerous you should avoid them as you would the plague. If you are a good rider you will never have one on the road and if you are not a good rider a front-wheel skid will mean a crash. Rear-wheel skids are different and you would be well advised to practise them, though not on public roads. Choose a flat, open space with a good surface and apply the rear brake so fiercely that the wheel locks and swings round. If you take this slowly to begin with you will soon build up confidence. You will find that a rear-wheel skid can quickly be brought under control and need have no unpleasant consequences. The secret is to release the brake at once and steer into the skid. If you do not release the brake the skid will continue until the scooter comes to rest.

When the road surface is slippery from oil, rain, frost or loose sand you will do well to leave the front brake severely alone as when descending very steep hills. One or two scooters will hardly hold the machine on the front brake alone on a very steep, long hill. Very steep hills often have bad surfaces – all the more reason for leaving the front wheel free for steering.

You should descend hills in the gear you would use for their ascent. Beware of too high a gear. Change down too soon rather than too late. If your engine stalls when going up a steep hill you may find it difficult to get going again; set the rear wheel against the kerb or against a hefty stone, with the machine angled at about half-way. The hill may be so steep that the stand will not hold the scooter while you kickstart it, and you may have to hold it on the handbrake and operate the throttle at the same time. It is useful to practice this before you need it. You should be able to hold the handbrake on and rev the engine, but it is a knack to be learned.

When there is ice on the roads your scooter should be off the roads. On the Continent there is ice and snow for weeks at a time and riders get used to it. In Britain few riders have time to acquire the skill needed for riding on ice. You are best off the roads then. Snow driving is fairly simple – largely a matter of confidence – but there is no useful tip for the beginner who meets ice except that throttle, brakes and gears are all likely to lead to bad skids. All mean changes of speed, changes of sideways thrust on the wheels. It is often forgotten that a skid can be started by opening the throttle. In the fog the scooterist has great advantages over the motorist and should be able to make reasonable progress even in a quite thick fog. Some headlamps throw a lot of light back at the rider and for such machines there are standard cowls which cut off much of this glare.

When you come to take your driving test, remember that a good rider who cannot answer set questions on the Highway Code has no chance of passing. You may be a brilliant rider, very safe, very fast – but if you do not know what the yellow lines mean, or what shape a STOP sign is you might just as well start booking your next test right away. Therefore, get the answers right. Here, according to a senior police official is a typical one:

"Before riding your motor cycle on the road there are some points which you should REMEMBER. What are they?"

The specimen answer includes: "Children require special attention. Old people should be given consideration. The blind also need help. Only ride when you are fit. Alcohol makes you less safe. Vehicles should be maintained frequently. Protective helmets should be worn."

Intelligence is not necessary to concoct answers of this kind – they must be learned by rote. It is going too far to say that when taking a driving test you should leave your brains outside, but please make limited use of both intelligence and commonsense. A case in point is the left turn. Some authorities feel that in most cases the scooter rider is wasting time signalling a left turn, but in a driving test you should abide by the rules.

Have your scooter in good order on the day. Above all, get it ticking over nicely. It is awkward if you have the engine stall two or three times during the test run and it is liable to fluster you. You should wear sufficient to keep you warm, but do avoid wearing a new pair of gloves. You will be more comfortable in that old pair. Although goggles are not compulsory you should wear them but, if you have just borrowed a pair, test them beforehand. Some goggles leave the rider blind at the side, and the fewer surprises the more likely you are to put up a good show. Give yourself every possible chance on the test.

Since this is not a test to see whether you are a good rider you should make hand signals which may not be strictly necessary. A good rider will glance back and then decide whether a hand signal is necessary before changing direction. If a signal is not needed he will not give one. You are taking a driving test, however, so do not omit signals merely because there is nobody to see them. The examiner may be watching. Here the subject of winking indicators pops up. If you have them on the scooter you will gain no advantage from using them. They are not considered a substitute for hand signals from the scooterist. If you use the indicators you still have to make hand signals and since there is the risk of you leaving them flashing you may wish to put them out of action – or simply not use them.

Road signs and signals from police, traffic wardens, etc., should be scrupulously observed, as should pedestrian crossings – and that means what it says. You may be unlucky and meet a pedestrian who stops half-way over a crossing and smilingly waves you on. Do not accept this invitation. The law says the pedestrian has precedence, which means he goes first. A judicial ruling some years ago left this in doubt, but the learned judge has since been politely corrected. Many people use their commonsense about pedestrian crossings and you are unlikely to be prosecuted if someone waves you on, but you will certainly fail your driving test if you accept the invitation.

The most difficult part of the driving test is probably the turn to the right, from a main road, where you have two streams of traffic. This may be very awkward indeed and if you are on a very busy road it may be almost impossible to get across the stream to the middle of the road, either because you are not bold enough or because there is a sudden rush of vehicles moving at a goodly rate. There may be no other course open to you but to pull in to the kerb and wait. This is better than coming to a wobbling halt with vehicles rushing past you on either side. However, if you choose your moment you should be able to move over towards the centre of the road, having looked behind and given a hand signal. Be quite happy about coming to a halt there and waiting, but continue your hand signal so that traffic approaching you will know your intentions. Allow plenty of room on your near side for traffic to pass and be patient. When the scooter is at rest do not try to put both feet on the ground. This is awkward on some scooters and unnecessary on all. Put your left foot on the ground and lean the machine over that way. You then have the right foot ready for the brake or gear-change pedal.

There are two problems connected with overtaking. It often happens that you can trickle to the head of a line of traffic without hindering any other road user. Alas, this scooter habit infuriates the motorist who, in his little tin box, has to wait. It also seems to infuriate driving test examiners who perhaps feel tenderly towards the motorist's blood pressure. This filtering is often done on the near side of other vehicles – sometimes sensibly, sometimes not quite so. When taking your driving test do not trickle through traffic on either side.

Confidence is useful during the driving test but scrupulous attention to the wording of the Highway Code is better. Try to drive some distance ahead – think out your next move and be ready for it. You may have to make a crash-stop, or to start off up a hill, or to make a narrow turn. You should have had some practice in them all beforehand. Turn up punctually for the test and have driving licence and insurance cover note ready. Finally, remember that the examiner is human and is there to do a job, not to trip you up. Usually he wants to pass you – if he can – so in addition to giving yourself every chance give him every chance too.

6 Social and Sporting

Scooterists have always been social animals, gregarious and convivial. They formed local, national and international clubs. They have run every kind of scooter event from rallies which were purely social gatherings of a dozen or so to an International Rally which took scooterists from fifteen countries on a journey from Venice to Istanbul and back through Brindisi; competitive events ranging from a Saturday afternoon hill climb at Lydd to a 24-hour timed run over the Manx TT course. Two members of a local Lambretta Club rode their scooter from Singapore to London; members of the Malta Scooter Club successfully organised a ten-day non-stop scooter run in the island. There seems no end to the new ideas scooter club members think up.

Club life and organisation differ widely from country to country. In Italy the clubs were primarily social affairs and a typical rally there would consist of a reception, a procession through the town, a dinner and perhaps a dance. There may be accompanying gymkhana events, but these would be strictly optional. However, one of the biggest scooter races, The Three Seas, took place in Italy and during its five days competitors covered over 1,800km. It was limited to Vespas and the winning rider was almost always an Italian. It was a most exciting event, taking in most of Italy south of Naples where winding roads and great heat made the test severe; it also covered Sicily from Messina to Palermo.

Social and Sporting

In Britain there developed a well-organised club life with its own distinctive features. At one time there were over 300 scooter clubs and while many were small, some had over 200 active members, one or two clubs becoming so large that they had to suspend further recruitment. There are weekly social meetings, whether at the club's own premises or in a hired room, and a run each weekend is normal, though most clubs cut down on them during the winter months. These runs are planned well in advance. One club had its own programme settled and printed for six months in advance, with times and destinations set out for each weekend run. Most clubs used to organise local rallies and though these were basically social affairs there was almost always a road trial, a treasure hunt or a series of gymkhana events.

It was unfortunate that from 1960 onwards the nuisance created by motor car rallies rapidly increased and led to legislation to curb both the number and the type of rally. This legislation also covered motor cycles, whose riders had been cutting up sundry moorland tracks – but it also overwhelmed scooterists, whose rallies were very little nuisance to anybody except the hard-worked organisers. The immediate result was a decline in the number of scooter rallies and many clubs which had concentrated on rallying found themselves short of events and short of members. Curiously enough, some events were automatically exempt from the rally regulations and one of these was to Esso Scoot to Scotland in which each year hundreds of scooterists took part, along with a dozen or so motorists. After 1967 the Esso Scoot first failed to attract scooterists and then disappeared altogether from the scooter calendar. The new regulations proved so intricate, and the procedure for obtaining a permit so tedious and complicated that scooter clubs in general abandoned the attempt to run rallies on public roads. It is to this ill-directed piece of legislation that scooter track events largely owe their popularity.

Vespa clubs had, right from the start, a strongly individualistic character. Membership was restricted to owners of Vespas, a point on which almost every other club suffered. The original conception sprang from Dr. Enrico Piaggio's interest in social problems, an interest which accounted for the well-run community life of Pontedera where the Vespas were made. Vespa clubs were directly financed by the national Vespa concerns (in Britain from the Douglas firm of Bristol) in such matters as rallies, equipment and subsidised tours, although generally the clubs paid affiliation fees to the central committee. The Vespa Club of Britain (VCB) was started by the late W. M. Bond who, on the point of retirement, suggested the idea to the Bristol firm, an idea taken up with enthusiasm. He soon became known throughout British Vespa circles as Bill Bond, becoming successively secretary and president of the VCB and, at the same time, a vice-president of the Vespa Club of Europe.

The Vespa one-make-only policy was followed strictly. When the National Scooter Association was formed Vespa decided to remain outside it, preferring to be completely self-governing. This attitude was maintained until 1960 when the European Vespa Rally, held in a different country each year, was organised by VCB at Cheltenham and a very strange position developed – or at least was revealed. A series of eliminating trials had been held for the European Championship finals to be held at Rome at the same time as the Olympic Games there. The last eliminating round was to be contested at the Cheltenham Rally, with competitors from all over Europe taking part. Somewhat late in the day it was discovered that unless VCB was a member of some body affiliated to the FIM none of the riders from Spain, France, Italy, Germany etc. (all of whom belonged to an FIM-affiliated body) would be allowed to compete. The Vespa policy was, force majeure, reversed and VCB became a member of the National Scooter

The 1957 Peugeot. It carried a spare wheel at the rear, but was built to carry most of the luggage above the front wheel.

The 60cc Laverda. Although it had such a tiny engine this was a four-stroke of intricate design.

A three-wheeled Vespa scooter made in Spain. It was specially made for a scooterist injured in the Civil War.

The German-made 250cc Maico scooter in action, a rare example of a top motor cycle firm producing a top scooter.

Association. It has, however, continued with its policy of limiting membership to Vespa owners. A separate body, Friends of the Vespa, was formed to include Vespa owners who had changed over to cars but still wished to retain their interest in the movement. It might seem that these two things showed the policy of VCB to be wrong or at least outmoded but this is hardly correct. The National Scooter Association had aims and methods widely at variance with VCB and the alliance between the two was uneasy at best. Soon the internal stresses of the NSA tore it apart and VCB continued strong and refreshed and when the subsequent Federation of British Scooter Clubs was formed VCB found itself with more congenial company to work alongside.

The corresponding organisation for Lambretta owners was the British Lambretta Owners' Association (BLOA) which, run from the Croydon headquarters, made a distinctive feature of the Lambretta shade of blue in its uniform. The different conditions under which the two makes of scooter were produced had its influence on the patterns of the clubs. Pontedera was a small community of 20,000 people with the Piaggio works a dominant factor in the employment market and the Piaggio family with great social responsibilities. The firm not only provides jobs, but a complete social environment – houses, communal services and a financial framework for the employees. The Vespa Club shared some of this background whereas the Lambrettas were made in Milan, the financial and industrial centre of North Italy in which employers did not incline towards paternalism. The Lambretta Club was therefore an extension of the advertising and publicity surrounding the scooters and in Britain between 1960 and 1968 it acquired an increasing bias towards competitive events for the sales value which victories brought. Here it had an advantage over the Vespa Club. Sporting events were more exciting than social meetings. The Lambretta engine

E

was more adaptable to track racing and the administration of the club, first under Derek Guy and then under Robert K. Wilkinson, was a model of efficiency.

It was early recognised that it was not necessary to own or ride a Lambretta in order to belong to one of the clubs. True, there were Five-Star Lambretta Clubs, where membership was strictly for Lambretta owners, but this covered only a proportion and was at once a guard against valuable prizes being won by riders of BSA or Vespa scooters but paid for by the Lambretta concern – and a reasonable effort to canalise Lambretta subsidies and staff-work to the benefit of Lambretta owners. In the event the scheme was not wholly successful and did not of course survive the time when Lambretta clubs ceased to be directly controlled, financed and administered by Lambretta officials.

There were clubs for other makes, notably Bella, Capri, Rumi, Diana and Heinkel all of which received more or less support from the importers of the machines; they suffered the handicap of having to provide their own administration and depended on a few keen enthusiasts whose disappearance often meant the disappearance of the club. Rather different was the NSU Prima club, which was directly sponsored by the NSU concern and was truly international, with its own holiday complex near Venice to which all NSU club members had the right of admission. Also different was the Maico club, which for many years ran an exemplary club magazine and maintained close touch with the factory in Germany. It became a clearing house for Maico information, and often took the lead in supplying spare parts and technical assistance. Finally there were scores of clubs whose members merely had to own a scooter. These again were started by enthusiasts who provided their own organisation, funds and headquarters. Meetings were usually held in private rooms at pubs. These scooter clubs were entirely self-financed and, unlike the one-make clubs, got money only from their own members and well-wishers. It was a matter for regret that local authorities who could provide funds for youth activities ranging from knitting to mountaineering, missed a notable opportunity of canalising the immense reserve of energy which these scooter clubs represented. Designers of community centres did not accept any responsibility for helping scooterists to learn to ride their machines, for example, whereas on the Continent such training grounds are numerous.

In spite of this neglect some of the all-makes clubs were amongst the biggest in the country, with an elaborate organisation and a capacity for large-scale sustained effort. They were entirely self-governing, membership being based on local residence. Occasionally this had amusing results. In one town, two separate scooter clubs were organised, each unknown to the other. By an extraordinary coincidence they met in the same building. By an even stranger chance they met within an hour of each other. The custom grew of one club poaching members from the other (a two-way process) which raised problems only solved by the amicable amalgamation of two clubs into one. It was not unknown for a town to contain two clubs which ran side by side for a long period without conflict but usually outside London there will be only one local scooter club, though an exclusively Vespa club may exist alongside.

Members of scooter clubs are not alone in disliking organisation and the routine of club management, nor are they alone in finding it difficult to elect keen and efficient officers. This dislike has gone so far that clubs have been formed which declared they had no rules, no idea of a constitution, no officials, no regular meetings – and nowhere to meet even if they had wanted to. They were merely a group of enthusiastic competition riders with a common aim. Apart from the name there was no sign of the club apart from its few members. However, experience showed that for a club to live long a fairly tight organisation was needed. Without a fixed headquarters, a keen set of officials and a well thought out book of rules few scooter clubs managed to live long.

The organisation of a scooter club differs very little from that of any other club, though the way in which the clubs express themselves may vary. A club may centre round a nucleus of twenty or thirty members with fifteen turning out for a Sunday run. At times the club seems to be two different units; one part goes on runs while the other concentrates on social activities during the week. Or a group in the club may spend its time on sporting events, which raises the problem that these members will spend their weekend racing or tuning their machines and will take little part in the social life of the club or of its organisation. Because scooterists marry, move to another town, or sell their scooters, the younger side of club membership changes rapidly. The club officials may crystallise into a small group who alone are willing to bind themselves to the routine of organisation. Some clubs solve this by the compulsory retirement of officials, and occasionally a small club will devote a disproportionate amount of time and effort in organising its own local rally, holiday programme, dance or other event. When support is not forthcoming the organisers feel out of touch, or feel that members are ungrateful or lazy. There may then follow from the club chairman a protest such as this:

"Your social secretary has taken great trouble in arranging visits to interesting places – factories, offices etc. – but these visits have been very poorly attended with not more than three people turning up. So frankly I ask you: Do you wish to have more visits of this type arranged or are you more interested in cinema and theatre shows?"

Another club organised – with immense labour – a Road

Safety Rally. This required many officials and the club was strained to provide them, but managed. On the fatal day the local Road Safety Officer phoned to say he would be attending and would bring with him three local councillors. There was consternation among the club officials, raised to fever pitch when it seemed that only three contestants would struggle for the prize. By rapidly shifting officials from one place to another and making them contestants as well, a semblance of popular support was given to the councillors, but the club organised no more rallies.

These problems occur in other clubs, but scooter clubs feel them with particular keenness because the movement is attracting members who would not normally join a club, and also because membership is with many a passing phase, lasting perhaps two years, after which the scooter is sold and other interests call for attention. With some clubs the rapid change in membership means that new faces are in the majority. It is thus impossible to observe one of the golden rules of club life – that members should know each other. The bigger a club becomes the further away is this ideal and many scooter clubs had to choose between limiting the number of members and starting a waiting list. The moment the suggestion was made there was another – that some present (but apathetic) members should be replaced by the keen types. At least one club met the problem by splitting itself into separate clubs, one sporting, one social.

The financial position of the clubs was often precarious. True, some of the bigger clubs became property owners, even landlords. A South African scooter club built its own club house, furnished this with a hard-drinks bar and ran a dance band which accepted outside engagements, but many clubs, some of them among the happiest and most active, just about made ends meet. They organised rallies and lost money on them. The situation could be saved by the manufacturer or importer who donated articles which were used as Tombola prizes – from which a profit was certain.

The major expense for one club may be the rent of a club-room and garage. With another club the production of a club magazine may account for two-thirds of its annual expenditure. In one sense a club defines itself by the nature of its major expenses. As one member pointed out;

> "Has the club ever stated that it meant to make money out of its rally? Has any member ever stood up at a meeting and said so? If so, to what use would the money be put? There does not seem to be any policy for encouraging the younger – and less well paid – trials or rally rider; no plan to set out and get club premises of our own; in fact, no venture in the offing that requires cash. So why the Midas act?"

There were clubs where the young trials enthusiast would feel very much at home, clubs which own their own trials machines. These clubs devoted most of their time and energy – and cash – to preparing scooters for hill-climbs, road trials and for the track events which became so popular from 1965 onwards. Their members were more interested in engines than in theatres. They did their own maintenance and in many cases had a second scooter for everyday use. One or two clubs organised a display team – highly skilled riders who put on a show of trick-riding at rallies all over the country and through these shows raised a considerable amount of money for charities. There was simply no limit to the variety of clubs.

A difficulty shared by most scooter clubs was that of the pillion passenger. The scooter owner might be a member, the pillionist not, but both would want to go on club outings and to join in the various social events. One solution was to have an associate membership for pillionists at half the standard rate, the sub being paid by the pillionist. Alternatively the scooterist might have a kind of floating associate membership which will cover the pillionist, even though the latter's name may vary from time to time. As a result, such clubs contained an element with comparatively little interest in scooters, membership of a scooter club being almost accidental. The question soon arose – should such members have voting power? In practice the problem was left alone and solved itself for, after a promising start, girls rarely took up membership and soon clubs were appealing to girls to join them on almost any terms. A similar problem arises when members of a one-make club buy scooters of a different make or perhaps buy cars. In both cases there is the chance that one member in three may have no direct interest in scooters. In the clubs ostensibly devoted to golf, motoring, hockey and other sports there is no such problem. Not all members of golf clubs play golf regularly; not all members of climbing clubs climb even once a month, but with a scooter club it is usual for all members to own or ride scooters. When many keen Vespa Club members moved on to car ownership but retained their interest in the club a special branch, Friends of the Vespa, was formed. The necessity for such a club highlights one of the peculiar difficulties of scooter clubs in general.

Most scooter clubs have nicknames – The Poachers, Vulcans, Black Knights, The Sutton Snipes. One of the largest and most famous was called The Bats. Another was The Lucky 13. Members often wear the club badge on their scooters along with a collection of plaques and transfers gathered on runs at home or abroad. Some clubs had gay sashes in three or four colours, which were draped across the legshields and looked very gay in a parade. The club showing these signs of membership gives a most attractive picture of scootering when it is out on a club run. In some countries the signs of membership are carried to the point of special uniforms. This was so in

New Zealand and in South Africa – in the latter country crash helmets often cannot be worn because of the extreme heat. A later development in Britain was to have the owner's name in coloured metallic tape on windscreen or side panel; often this was accompanied by the pillionist's name, which was varied as necessary.

As with most groups, there are solid practical advantages attached to membership of a scooter club; discounts on spares or repair bills at specified service stations; or the secretary can negotiate special terms for holidays, whether in this country or abroad. Many clubs were started and continue to be supported by dealers, with the weekly meeting being held on his premises, which overcomes one of the major obstacles

The dealer hopes that new machines, when needed, will be bought through him but in the meantime the club has free headquarters, sometimes the use of the garage, and in general is provided the framework without which few clubs can long survive. Particularly is such help valuable to the club which has no national organisation to call on and which must finance itself completely. With Vespa and Lambretta the national organisation was efficient and highly developed but owners of other machines who wished to start an all-makes club considered themselves fortunate if they could get a local dealer interested to this extent in their scheme.

Without a meeting place a club can hardly be said to exist and, as would-be organisers of other clubs have found, the possibilities are often limited to public houses and political clubs of one complexion or another. The advantage of meetings in the home of one of the members are soon exhaused, though that is how several clubs began. Another sign of stability is the club magazine. This may vary in size and format from a four-page affair run off on the office duplicator in someone's lunch hour to an almost professional affair complete with paid advertisements. In their pages were to be found much humour, much enthusiasm and occasionally a gem of good writing. The authors had been given their head – or had taken it – and wrote with a candour and a directness which compelled several emotions, including admiration. The sins of dealers, motorists and dogs; the sloth and ingratitude of other members – and of other clubs; there was little beyond the reach of writers in club magazines and they faithfully reflected the keenness, the impatience, the energy of scooterists in general. There were three quite distinct types of scooter club magazines. The first was the official organ of the makers or importers. Both Vespa and Lambretta ran one each and filled it with news and views about their respective machines and the activities of their own branch clubs. They reflected the official attitudes and between 1968 and 1969 they (if unintentionally) faithfully reflected the growing official uncertainty about the principles on which the two clubs had been built and which has sustained them for so many years. The second type of magazine was the expression of the average club's happy and enthusiastic scootering – a bubbling up of youth and fun. It contained little that was deep, nothing that was ponderous. Crammed with platitudes, cliches and chestnuts, this type of magazine survived by a miracle of endeavour, constantly supplied from a membership which changed almost every year. Occasionally these magazines contained gems – witty or informed. Occasionally they contained views about certain scooters which could hardly have been published elsewhere. Sometimes the magazines had a long and useful life – the issue of *Cheetahs' Chatter* which celebrated that club's tenth year of existence contained fifty pages. These magazines depended entirely on voluntary help. A third was typified by one called *Maico Awheel*, published by the Surrey Maico Owners' Club. This was a first-class magazine, full of useful technical articles for Maico owners and its production, taking into account the very small number of Maico owners in Britain, was a considerable achievement.

One problem which faced all three types was whether the magazine should be paid for or counted as part of the facilities covered by the subscription.

Linked with scooter clubs is the matter of rallies, racing and competitive events in general. The rallies started as purely social affairs, an excuse for a colourful get-together of scooterists and spectators. They were immensely successful – at the St. Albans rally in 1959 there were nearly 2,000 scooters and the rally was sponsored by the *Daily Mirror*. The Esso Scoot to Scotland was a 24-hour event and drew over 300 scooters. Neither in these nor in other rallies that year were there prizes of any value and big national rallies of this kind continued as mainly social affairs for some time. It was a rare scooter club that did not organise at least one rally per year, with a parade, gymkhana events and a happy, informal atmosphere. The value of rally successes for advertising had already been realised, mainly by the Lambretta importers, and there began the long string of events where Lambretta machines figured with marked success. In the 1959 Scottish Six-Days Trial, for instance, three Lambrettas were entered and all three finished with awards. However, the accent then, and for a few years to come, was still on the social side of the many rallies. For instance in the most important rally of the year, the Isle of Man Rally which started in 1957, the events were still fought out as between one rider and another or between one club and another. The winners overall had ridden various machines – 1957 Lambretta; 1958 Maico; 1959 Diana; 1960 Maico; 1961 Lambretta and 1962 Vespa.

After that year it can be said that the competitive element increased not only in the Manx Rally, but in rallies generally, and soon a few event winners were riding what were practically works-supported machines. Nor did the support come only from the importers, for dealers realised that winning machines could also increase their own sales. Some of these dealers were also riders. Some riders, after a string of successes, set up business first as engine tuners and then as machine dealers. Clubs followed the trend and social events suffered because the keenest members were racing or tuning their machines. As the gentle, social road rallies had been driven off public roads many clubs found themselves compelled to lend support to the track events. In this way, heavy emphasis on competitive riding exaggerated its scale and distorted the picture because so much effort was spent in promoting a few events of limited interest and located in a small section of the country. The lesson of France, where scooter racing had flared and burned itself out so quickly, was not heeded. The situation was further complicated because although events were run on racing circuits – Snetterton and Brands Hatch – the word "racing" was avoided. To call an event "a race" would mean that riders would have to wear leathers and special helmets, while the organisers would have to observe a host of complicated and costly safety measures. The solution was to announce a Regularity Trial in which set times were specified for set distances, or average speeds were set over a given number of laps.

Each year the difficulties grew. The Goodwood circuit closed. The Oulton Park circuit became unavailable in 1967 and the cost of Brands Hatch for a day rose to £200, which would mean entrance fees well above £4 per rider even to cover the cost of the organisation, leaving nothing for future items. Nor was it easy to settle on a national authority to control these and other events. Between 1961 and 1966 there were endless discussions, mostly fruitless. The National Scooter Association commanded little support and then collapsed. For a short period the Vespa and Lambretta importers shared the responsibility but in October 1969 an agreement was signed between the Federation of British Scooter Clubs and the ACU giving scooterists, through the Federation Management Committee, full control over organised scooter sport in Britain.

In spite of these difficulties scooter sport flourished; the Mallory Park, Lydden Hill and Snetterton circuits continued to be used. Most encouraging of all, the Association which organised the Mallory Park events could even show a profit, a rare feat of skill. The Isle of Man Rally also continued its triumphant progress, drawing hundreds of scooterists each year to the Island for a full week's sporting and social fun. The rally had included the Manx 400, run on the TT course, but the deciding event for the overall trophy had always been the Druidale events, part of which was run on closed roads. The popularity of this stimulated the organisers to stage a series of free-for-all races on the hard dry sand and these drew such crowds that it was only a tiny step to organising a separate speed event on closed roads, where the riders could use the experience they had acquired on British racing tracks.

The Manx Rally has generated not only enthusiasm, but heat. In few other events have scooterists attacked organisers and other riders with such venom. Protests have flown thick and fast, and on one occasion a gibbet was set up outside the office of the respected Clerk of The Course. In 1959 almost every scooter maker or importer – as well as the tyres, petrol and oil companies – gave the rally lavish support. One importer was said to have spent £10,000 on it, and many of the machines entered were almost works entries. Factory experts came over with trucks full of spares and pit work was excellent – one rider had a new front fork fitted and was off again in two minutes. Feelings grew keener as the week unfolded its events. The rivalry between two makes in particular led to some unhappy incidents – supporters went round the Island pulling down banners advertising the "other make" and tempers became very strained. It was a wonder that more serious trouble did not occur, but the senior officials on both sides were patient and understanding. Looking back on it now the 1959 Manx Rally had its amusing side. It certainly taught the organisers a sharp lesson and the bad feeling never again came to the surface. In the following year official support was not evident and not until 1967 was the surface slightly rippled. In that year three top Italian riders came over to compete on 125cc Lambrettas of a special type not available generally in Britain. Rather naturally they won the Team Prize with ease, while John Ronald won the Overall Award, together with a handsome £100 cheque from the importers. This caused a great stir and can be called the beginning of the non-standard scooter. Other riders were eager to obtain these special machines, to modify standard parts, to fit special pistons or exhausts. The organisers of events reacted slowly to this move, but soon competing machines were classified according to engine capacity – with a rag-bag section for specials, as these non-standard machines were called. Very soon riders abandoned the idea of riding their scooter to an event. Apart from being modified so that it could not be ridden on public roads the scooter was often too precious to risk there as well as being the devil to start and impossible at slow speeds.

7   The Engine

(a)   The two-stroke engine
With very few exceptions scooters have two-stroke engines. This is an innovation in itself since the two-stroke has never been popular in Britain in spite of the numbers sold. It has been under a cloud, as a device that worked but was hardly sporting – like shooting foxes.

The engine runs on a mixture of petrol, oil and air. It would run on many other substances such as hydrogen, marsh gas or even turpentine. You could use oxygen though this might lead to your engine dissolving in one shattering explosion. When engines are run on the test-bed coal gas, straight from the town supply, is often used because of its advantages – the consumer has not to pay for it being stored in the mains; and not so much care is called for in handling it as with petrol. In France quite a few cars run on methane and even in Britain there are not lacking engineers who consider that petrol is wholly unsuitable for motor cars and that steam is the ideal. In view of the speed and economy of steam cars built in 1900 it can be argued that if one-quarter of the effort put into petrol engines had been given to steam power we should have better motor cars today along with a noticeable improvement in the air we breathe. Steam engines are slow-revving and do not require gears. The steam engine has a fatal fascination for British engineers and the world homage paid to the early pioneers in steam may be in part responsible for our tardiness in electrification of the railways and also for over-weighting engineering students with steam-engine lore. Certainly it led to a preference for slow-revving engines, a preference reinforced by the fame which W. O. Bentley gained, a preference which led to British designers being overtaken by foreign-designed multi-cylinder engines which were comfortable at 9,500rpm.

The two-stroke engine is mechanically simple. It has only three moving parts and there is nothing for the average scooterist to adjust. About all he can do is to alter the plug and contact-breaker points gap – and interfere with the carburation. Perhaps that is its greatest drawback, one that will never be overcome.

There is some dispute about the inventor. A Frenchman, de Rochas, described it in 1862 and by some he is held to be the inventor. The Germans support the claims of Dr. Otto who, in 1876, built the first four-stroke engine that worked. A year or two later Sir Dugald Clerk tackled the problem of the two-stroke engine and between then and 1930 the two types were developed side by side in motor cars, motor cycles and even in aeroplanes. A fascinating social study has yet to be made of the ways in which, after that date, the four-stroke stole the limelight and became the object of something like hero worship. Whatever the social or economic reasons may be – and they are not so much in dispute as waiting to be discovered – the fact is that fame and glory attached themselves to the four-stroke during the period 1925–1939. During that period the design plums – and the sales plums – went mostly in one direction. Several legends were created and fostered during that period, the most powerful being: the two-stroke ran hot, had poor fuel consumption figures, was inefficient as an engine and used too much oil.

In spite of its design limitations the two-stroke has an ideal efficiency equal to that of the four-stroke. The type of engine chosen on a particular occasion would in theory depend on the comparative efficiency but in practice would be decided by the early training of the engineer, the working conditions of the engine, the firm's technical resources and so on. Up to about 1930 the choice would be made as between equals, one of which happened on that occasion to be more suitable. After that date the feeling in British design offices crystallised into a conviction that the two-stroke was a kind of poor relation. This stemmed from a variety of causes, some of which we have already dealt with – notably the glamour of the four-stroke victories in the TT races – and it is true that until about 1938 Brough, Norton, Cotton and Velocette swept all before them.

The British four-stroke engine was supreme until 1938. It made a lot of noise. It went very fast. The top riders wanted to have four-strokes. The two-stroke was known as a putt-putt and for a British designer to be put on two-stroke work was, from the prestige point of view, like giving him the bowler hat and his cards. However, this attitude was welcomed by British designers for the simple fact was that Continental two-stroke design was so far ahead that it could not have been overtaken even had the board-room willed it. One of the main causes was a German named Schnurle who in 1930 took out a patent for a scavenging system in a two-stroke engine which allowed the use of a flat-topped piston.

Previously two-stroke engines had used deflector pistons. The incoming mixture was pumped from the crankcase through a transfer port and so into the cylinder. It hit the steep side of the deflector piston and travelled up the adjacent cylinder wall. After combustion it slid down the shallower slope of the deflector piston and so out as exhaust gases through the exhaust port.

This, or a variation of it, was the system universally used with two-strokes. Ever since Clerk's day engineers had tried other methods – especially a system of auxiliary pumps – to get the mixture in and out. No better solution had been found though in England two-stage pistons had been used and in Austria Puch developed their effective double piston arrangement. It was left to Schnurle to introduce simplicity. He abandoned the deflector piston entirely, which was a good start, for there were endless problems of piston distortion, it was impossible to get high compression ratios, and too much of the fresh mixture was forced with the spent gases through the exhaust port. Schnurle made two transfer ports on the opposite diameter to the exhaust port, so angled that the fresh mixture came in two streams which joined forces opposite the exhaust port and them climbed to the top of the combustion chamber for ignition.

This was a revolution, but British engineers little noted it (Norton were just coming into their own) though DKW in Germany saw the value of the idea and quickly adopted Schnurle scavenging for their motor cycles and cars. It made a fortune for DKW and Auto-Union because they not only recognised the patent's value but tightened it up so that any two-stroke engine designer using a flat-domed piston was in danger of infringing the Schnurle patent, which was held by DKW–Auto-Union until 1945, when all German patents were released for world use. Almost every two-stroke engine maker adopted it, though Piaggio for many years remained faithful to the deflector piston.

There was one pre-war exception of note – Zundapp. This remarkable firm had taken out a completely new patent, that of a Berlin engineer called Schauer, whose line of attack was – briefly – a third transfer port. This by-passed the Schnurle patent and very soon Zundapp were making two-strokes (the first in 1933) with treble ports and flat-domed pistons. The modern Zundapp variation is for two transfer ports to be used as normally but the third transfer port lines up with a window

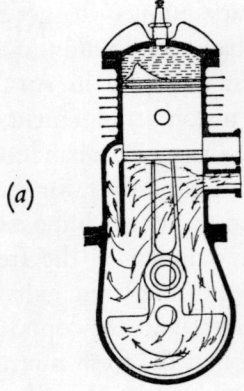

(a)

1st Charge
2nd compression completed
Charged ready to fire
2nd Charge
Induction completed

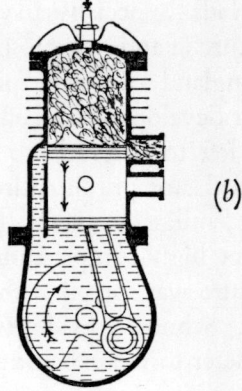

(b)

1st Charge
End of Power stroke
Exhaust commencing
2nd Charge
1st compression in crank-
case completed

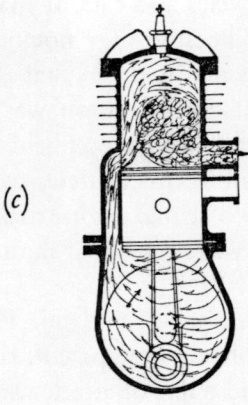

(c)

1st Charge
Exhaust nearly completed
2nd Charge
Transfer of partly compressed
gas from crankcase to cylinder

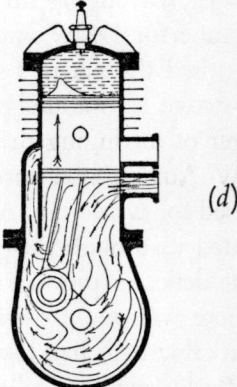

(d)

1st Charge
Ended
2nd Charge
2nd compression
3rd Charge
Induction commencing

in the piston skirt. The fresh mixture then passes from the underside of the piston, through this window and then through the third transfer port into the combustion chamber.

British design continued to lag behind. In 1967 it was the turn of the Japanese to make another startling advance. The Italian Grand Prix victory of Yamaha was based on a five-port 125cc engine. Shell-moulding techniques had allowed foundries to turn out very accurate castings so that transfer ports could be smoothed and aligned. To get such accurate castings had not before been possible. A further drawback of the Schnurle system was that the burnt mixture in the upper half of the combustion chamber did not receive the full force of the

---

2. **The two-stroke cycle of operations**. The sparking plug may, in practice, be offset and not placed centrally as here. The arrangement and number of ports will vary from one engine to another, as will the shape of the piston. Here we have shown the deflector-type as used in Vespa engines. However, the diagrams will show how the mixture moves from the carburetter to the crankcase and then through the transfer port to the combustion chamber.

(a) The piston is at the top of its stroke, ready for the spark to ignite the mixture thus compressed above the piston. Both transfer and exhaust ports are closed but the inlet port is open and a fresh charge of mixture is being drawn from the carburetter into the crankcase.

(b) There is a spark at the sparking plug. The compressed mixture burns and expands rapidly, forcing the piston downwards in its power stroke. As the piston moves downwards it blanks off the inlet port and uncovers first the exhaust port and then the transfer port.

(c) The piston is at the bottom of its stroke. The exhaust and transfer ports are both open. Fresh mixture is being forced through the transfer port into the cylinder and this helps to drive out remaining burnt gases through the exhaust port.

(d) The piston continues to move upwards, blanking off the exhaust and transfer ports and compressing the mixture above the piston. At the same time it uncovers the inlet port and fresh mixture is drawn from the carburetter into the crankcase. This continues until position (a) is reached and the cycle of operations is repeated.

stream of incoming mixture. The extra Yamaha ports overcame this difficulty in a neat and effective way. They were incorporated in the Yamaha production 125cc motor cycle in the following year – rapid progress indeed.

Having briefly noted some of the later developments of the two-stroke engine we might with advantage now consider how it all began. We must first deal with the basis, the four-stroke cycle of operations and this is shown in Fig. 2.

This is the cycle as described by de Rochas. Rather more accurately, it is one possible way of interpreting his all-embracing language. It was this cycle which was given practical application by Dr. Otto, who made it work, and it is therefore always known as the Otto Cycle. It gives one power stroke for every two revolutions of the crankshaft. As soon as people recovered from their wonder at seeing the four-stroke engine work they remarked that the piston could be made to work harder. In the Otto Cycle it took a holiday every second trip down. Sir Dugald Clerk made the piston work double-shift and though the Clerk engine has been modified and improved it is truly he who invented the two-stroke engine.

The Otto engine had two ports – or holes. Fresh mixture came in at the inlet port. Burnt gases went out through the exhaust port. These ports were controlled by valves which opened and closed in phase with the piston and were operated by a cam, gear-driven from the crankshaft. Clerk did away with the exhaust valve and all its mechanism. Even for this he deserves a place in history. In the side of the cylinder he cut holes which were covered and uncovered by the piston as it moved up and down so that at one moment the fresh mixture could enter and at another the exhaust gases could go out. Such an improvement depended on good machining and was not possible until accurate machine tools became available. It was a great improvement but the inlet valve, in one form or another, remained and some of the attempts to make an engine without an inlet valve were more complicated than any four-stroke engine. Indeed, one of the signs that a given idea has outlived its usefulness is that its applications become hung about with coarse modifications, backward-looking improvements and other drawing-office jobs-for-the-boys.

For some time after the four-stroke engine arrived there was little further progress. No single reason accounts for this, but progress often moves in jumps, with long pauses between. Otto was providing new power. His engines were stationary engines, prime movers and it was long before his idea was applied to vehicles. He was, in addition, engaged in endless patent lawsuits and, since the four-stroke was so successful, the way of the two-stroke was more difficult. Its very success diverted effort from other ideas. Perhaps a stronger reason was that even the best designers tend to get into a rut. They improve rather than find new solutions. So it was with the inlet valve. In the Otto engines there had always been an inlet valve. It had always been at the top of the cylinder and it was not easy to get away from this convention.

It was an Englishman, Day, who provided a simple and ingenious solution by abolishing the inlet valve altogether. The mixture was introduced into the cylinder through the crankcase, which was made gas-tight, the mixture being forced through a transfer port in the cylinder wall. There were no valves. In their place there were three ports – inlet, transfer and exhaust – and by spacing them on the cylinder wall they were covered and uncovered by the piston as it moved up and down. It is at first difficult to visualise even when you know how it works. To visualise it before it had been given practical shape was a remarkable feat of imagination. The cycle now was:

1. The piston moves upwards. In so doing it covers the transfer and exhaust ports and uncovers the inlet port.

2. The piston moves downwards on its power stroke. In so

doing it uncovers the exhaust and transfer ports and covers the inlet port.

These two operations are repeated for as long as the engine fires and they are all that is required to perform the work previously done by the four-stroke engine. In practice the ports overlap. The transfer port opens before the exhaust port is completely blanked off. The transfer port is the connection between the crankcase and the cylinder. The inlet port is the connection between the carburetter and the crankcase. The exhaust port leads from the cylinder to the silencer. Broadly speaking, what happens is:

While the piston moves upwards the mixture in the cylinder is compressed and fresh mixture is drawn into the crankcase. While the piston is moving downwards fresh mixture is forced from the crankcase through the transfer port into the cylinder and at the same time the burnt gases are driven through the open exhaust port.

The operation will be better understood by referring to the diagram showing the arrangement of ports and the four stages of the cycle. The mixture does not go straight from the carburetter to the cylinder as in the four-stroke engine. It is drawn into the crankcase and is then pumped out into the cylinder. If it is difficult to visualise the porting arrangement it is even more difficult to visualise the crankcase as part of a pump. Most people are familiar with the pumping action of the piston as it compresses the mixture in the cylinder but it is sometimes forgotten that the underside of the piston is acting as a pump in the reverse sense and is drawing mixture into the crankcase through the inlet port.

Not all two-stroke engines were made as simple as possible. Even with the inlet and outlet port mechanisms made surplus to requirements some engines retained a compression release valve. This was operated by a Bowden cable from the handlebars and by lifting this valve the combustion chamber had a direct outlet to the open air. Compression vanished and, though the engine might turn, it quickly stopped with a hissing noise. No scooter has such a device today though it was fitted to some motor cycles and is still fitted to some 50cc machines.

We have stressed the advantages of the two-stroke but there are some basic disadvantages which have not been completely overcome:

1. The engine runs hotter.
2. Cylinder pressures are lower.
3. It is difficult to get a full charge into the cylinder.
4. A percentage of each charge is wasted.

Early attempts to disperse the engine heat were ingenious. Water cooling was tried, but this became too complicated. The number of ports was increased. There was even an attempt to cool the piston crown. None of these methods survived and today cooling is done by a fan driven from the crankshaft and usually located on the flywheel. Some very complex solutions to the other problems were attempted, but the biggest difficulty was in getting a full charge into the cylinder. One maker fitted two opposed pistons to the single cylinder. This gave excellent scavenging and loading but resulted in a very long engine and two crankshafts. Stepped pistons were tried and so were engines where the scavenging was done by compressed air; this was getting back to the original Clerk engine where there was a separate charging chamber with its own piston.

There is the story of the racing motorist who, for a wager, undertook to start from Putney at 3.30pm and drive to Piccadilly Circus at an average speed of 60mph for the whole distance. He accomplished this by driving from Putney to Brooklands where he lapped the race track at 90mph until he had built up a sufficient margin of time to trundle back to Piccadilly Circus well within the average speed of 60mph for the whole distance. This was considered unsporting – and something of the same kind happened with two-stroke cooling. The two-stroke runs hot, since it fires at twice the rate of a four-stroke. This excess heat was considered a major disadvantage and for the motor cycle designer this was perhaps true. His engines were traditionally air-cooled, by the air passing naturally over the engine and it was left to Vespa to fit a fan to the flywheel with the vanes running close to the cover. This system is almost universally used for two-stroke engines of more than 50cc. Today it is the four-stroke which is subject to overheating problems and these seem likely to increase as motor cycles are more and more enclosed in panelling. The flywheel-mounted fan may not be an engineer's dream but it works and it is one of the details which has helped to put so many foreign-designed two-strokes on British roads.

The two-stroke cycle of operations is repeated very quickly, about 5,000 times a minute when you are doing 45mph. If the piston is a good fit to the cylinder the engine may be efficient. If not, most of the power will be wasted through gas leaks. In the first steam engines a good fit meant that you could hardly get a sixpence between piston and cylinder. Today a scooter engine cylinder will be made to a standard dimension with the following limits:

Minus   Nil
Plus   .007 ins.

while the piston to fit this cylinder will be made to limits:

Minus   .004 ins.
Plus   .004 ins.

These are close limits. If there is much more clearance you will need a new piston or cylinder. By the same reasoning the crankcase must also be gas-tight. The two-stroke is simple but it must be well done.

The biggest problem in engine design is to get the correct mixture into the combustion chamber and from it to obtain the maximum power. It is not possible to turn all the mixture into power, nor is it possible to get as much mixture as you would like into the combustion chamber. The ideal, for instance, in a 150cc engine is to push nine cubic inches or so of mixture in for each charge. In fact you cannot do this, even with a four-stroke though the latter comes near to the ideal.

Our two-stroke cylinder has the transfer and exhaurst post open at the same time so that burnt gases are going out while new mixture is coming in. The obvious happens; the two get mixed slightly. Not only do you not get a full charge in but even that which you push in is adulterated. It is not easy to say which is the more difficult – getting clean mixture in or getting burnt gases out. Pressure in the crankcase is only some three or five pounds per square inch so the speed of the mixture going into the cylinder is not high. At low engine speeds the mixture speed is correspondingly reduced and there is great loss of unburnt mixture. This loss diminishes as engine speed increases and if it could be eliminated the two-stroke engine would have a thermal efficiency equal to that of a four-stroke. Its power output would be greater, perhaps by as much as fifty percent.

The work of German designers has led to the present-day tremendous and widespread use of the two-stroke engine. It was a great achievement. The four-stroke designers had difficulties but they were mostly of mechanisms and materials – to push the fresh mixture into an empty cylinder, to burn it, and then empty the cylinder before pushing fresh mixture in. We will ignore valve overlap for the moment. Even this system is not perfect, for there is a small space in the combustion chamber which is not completely cleared, but with two-strokes there were fundamental design problems, problems of theory, and the sudden introduction of novelties like the third port or the two percent mixture show how serious these problems were.

A singular development since 1946 has been the 50cc two-stroke. Year after year this continued to be a best-seller, annual sales in France topping the million. In Germany and Austria it was a money-maker and the best brains in the industry concentrated on it. Because of its small size the utmost possible power had to be obtained and nobody should be surprised that in those countries the two-stroke engines became miracles of endurance, efficiency and lightness. Fichtel and Sachs (Germany) sold 1,000 engines a day. Of the Puch (Austria) 50cc mopeds almost a million have been sold.

Scavenging was one of the most important problems tackled because it has great influence on the power developed and on fuel consumption. Every design alteration has to be watched carefully, so that too much of the fresh mixture will not be pushed unburnt through the exhaust port; and alternatively that too much of the unburnt gases are not retained to dilute the incoming mixture. Efficiency is easily lost through both of these faults.

When the piston moves downwards on its power stroke the gases are at high pressure and when the exhaust port is uncovered the gases will tend to escape through it because the pressure outside is lower. However, when the piston is at the bottom of its stroke the pressure in cylinder and exhaust box would tend towards equality and if equilibrium were reached the cylinder would be left full of gases at atmospheric pressure. This is a very real problem, for these gases must be pushed out to make way for the new charge, and the only practical way is to raise the pressure inside the cylinder by introducing fresh mixture, at greater pressure, through the transfer port. (There are other methods, but here we are not concerned with special engines.) This is why the two ports must be open at the same time. The fresh mixture rushes in, the pressure in the cylinder rises and the burnt gases continue to be pushed out through the exhaust port. Inevitably they take with them some of the fresh mixture – and some of the engine's power.

This is a damaging criticism and is unanswerable except by saying that the system works. It is also here that tuning – which we said was not possible – can be done. A racing mechanic will not be satisfied with the porting of the standard engine. He will want the transfer port to open sooner, perhaps, and he can achieve this by grinding a trifle from the top edge. Or he may want the exhaust port open a fraction longer – so he grinds a little from the lower edge; or he gets similar effects by fitting a piston made to his own design with a different skirt profile. These are quite separate from attempts on the compression ratio – they are alterations to the designer's idea of the most suitable porting. Like most improvements these alterations will have their drawbacks. The designer will have had to cater for a wide range of users, whereas the two-stroke tuner's interest will be limited to a narrow range of speeds, etc. Perhaps he has tuned it to give tremendous power above 5,000rpm. Alas, the engine will be almost impossible to start and may stall if the engine speed drops below 2,500rpm. It will not be the ideal machine for a run to town. Low-power engines usually give reasonable acceleration combined with good fuel economy. With bigger engines the emphasis is often on a high cruising speed with good fuel consumption. Below that speed a certain roughness is tolerated. Some of these big engines four-stroke badly when ticking over at low speeds, a sign that the designer has written those speeds off and has concentrated on higher things.

The porting on your scooter will be a compromise, though the limits may be wider. It does serve to show that you cannot get a best scooter and must be satisfied with the best for your particular purpose. If you buy a big scooter and never move out of the built-up areas you will break the designer's heart, for he probably dreams of his brain-child roaring (or purring) down the motorways or eating up the miles on the roads of Scotland or the South of France. In crowded traffic your big engine is often working at half efficiency, gulping the fuel down instead of chewing it.

As we have seen, the scavenging system used universally until 1930 was known as "reverse-flow" and depended on a deflector piston, with a hump off-centre and of irregular section. The steep side of the hump faced the transfer ports and when the incoming mixture hit the side of the hump it was forced up the adjacent cylinder wall. The exhaust port was on the opposite side of the cylinder. It was a very simple system but it was widely claimed that the piston was unbalanced and led to engine seizure because of piston distortion. It is probably true that engines with deflector pistons were dirtier and less efficient; Vespa was long faithful to them right up to the time when it introduced the two percent mixture engine. Perhaps because of this the recommended period between decarbonisation was shorter with Vespas than with Lambrettas.

The more modern system was loop scavenging, which was ingenious and at first glance not likely to work. The transfer ports are placed close to the exhaust ports and on the same side of the cylinder. The incoming mixture is blown straight across to the opposite side of the cylinder. It passes up the cylinder wall and as it fills the cylinder it forces the burnt gases out of the exhaust port. This method, or a variation of it, is now in general use. It is said to give 25 percent more power and to use 15 percent less fuel. It requires great care in cylinder casting since the angle of the transfer ports is vitally important. Improvements in loop scavenging include the Yamaha five-port engine but for mass-produced engines considerable improvement – not development – depends on improvements in foundry techniques. The so-called rotary valve engine introduced by Vespa is rather an advance in lubrication and carburation than in scavenging.

With loop-scavenged engines the standard piston has a slightly domed crown with a bevel or taper towards the edge. Pistons are made of aluminium alloy. The cylinder is made of cast iron, though one or two engines were made with a steel cylinder liner. When the engine is running the cylinder expands but the piston expands much more, and if it were a tight fit when cold it would quickly seize or bind in the cylinder once the engine warmed up. Therefore the piston has a set of sealing rings held in grooves. They are made of cast iron and fit to the cylinder walls to make an almost gas-tight joint or seal. The rings are slit, with a gap of 0.25mm between the ends. When this gap widens to 2mm it is time to fit new rings.

The top of the cylinder is detachable and contains the sparking plug. The cylinder head is always made of aluminium alloy. The inside is hemispherical, though it may in semi-tuned engines be irregular – known as a squish cylinder head, very popular with Lambretta riders in track events and fitted to a few standard models. When the piston moves to the top of its stroke it does not come quite to the top of the cylinder barrel. The space above the piston crown is called the combustion chamber and its shape is the result of much research. When the mixture burns the flame should spread evenly to give maximum power and this requires a well-designed combustion chamber. If the flame left some mixture unburnt or, worse still, if a pocket of the mixture at some point remote from the flame began burning you would get great fuel waste or serious and damaging detonation.

In your scooter the cylinder head will have a cautious internal shape to give good results under most conditions. People who tune their engines often start with the cylinder head, machining a fraction (something like 0.025 ins.) from its flat face. This reduces the volume and raises the compression ratio but the expert could, without difficulty, devise a different shape for the internal surface – such as the squish head, which for certain conditions would give better results. If the cylinder head is machined there is a danger of a ridge being left or the squish shape being upset, both of which might reduce efficiency. Excessive machining may lead to the piston actually striking the cylinder head.

The best combustion consumes all the fuel but in a two-stroke this is not possible. The oil mixed with the petrol leaves some residue and though oil research continues to improve the oil or reduce the proportion needed some residue remains to accumulate on piston crown, cylinder head and plug. These deposits may also build up and block the exhaust port, seriously reducing engine efficiency. Then no spark appears at the plug or hot spots develop on the piston crown and you get pinking or pre-ignition. It is then necessary to decarbonise the engine – scrape all these deposits away.

This is a serious disadvantage of the two-stroke engine. It is what engineers call a dirty engine. The fault lies in it having to burn both oil and petrol. The obvious step is to reduce the amount of oil used. With the first scooters the standard mixture was one pint of oil to two gallons of petrol (1:16) and this proportion was used for many years. A great step forward was taken by Vespa and then by Lambretta by building scooter engines which needed only one part of oil to fifty of petrol. A few makers specified 1:24 or 1:32 but curiously enough these reduced amounts scared many scooterists who as a safety measure used much more oil than the makers suggested.

At one time the engine really could be called dirty, for decarbonising was suggested every 1,250 miles. From 1960 onwards the interval was set much higher. When the Li. range of Lambrettas appeared the owners were told in no uncertain terms that they must not be decarbonised until at least 5,000 miles had been covered, and might not be needed before 8,000 or 10,000 miles. Apart from the saving in repair bills such an advance showed that the fuel was being used more economically.

Being a simple engine the two-stroke is air-cooled, but while most motor cycle engines are cooled by the air which flows over them as the machine travels, scooter engines are force-cooled by a fan driven from the crankshaft. Because of this the engine is encased in cowlings. The cool air is sucked in at one end, circulates through the cylinder fins and so passes to the open air. Fan cooling is essential for an engine so enclosed. While this enclosure has advantages it leads to the mixture containing – literally – hot air, whereas cold air might give better results. The air within the covers soon became very warm and as it was drawn in to be mixed with the fuel it interfered with the carburation, which was based on cool air being fed in. Very soon manufacturers fitted air filters and sealed up the carburetter air inlet so that the air had to enter direct from outside the scooter. It is not an ideal solution, but it worked.

Here is another example of two birds being killed with one stone. A scooter is usually less noisy than a motor cycle of the same power. Partly this is because of the engine enclosure, but partly also due to the effectiveness of the air filter, for much of the noise of any internal combustion engine comes from the carburetter end. This part of the noise can be cut down by fitting an air filter and by enclosing the filter itself. This became common practice on scooters and did much to meet the objection that the early engines were too noisy. German and Italian instruction books commonly included a paragraph saying that the silencing had been done to comply with legal requirements; owners were earnestly requested not to modify it in any way. Unfortunately competitive events soon showed that some standard exhausts were inefficient; they seriously reduced engine power output and this gave scope to the production of amateur exhaust systems which gave more power but very much more noise. The manufacturer was then compelled to build a different, more efficient, exhaust box as standard.

The two-stroke engine has a characteristic noise. Critics dislike it, say it is the mark of a fussy engine. There is something in this and efforts to meet the criticism were carried so far that they absorbed a lot of the engine's power. The problem is how to allow the burnt but highly compressed gases to expand into the atmosphere without the ear-shattering explosions that are such a delight on the race circuit. The expansion box is fitted with baffles so that there is not a straight-through path but this means that since the exhaust port is opening and shutting rapidly the pressure fluctuations are violent and continuous. A badly designed box reduces noise but absorbs an undue amount of power. The early exhaust boxes could be taken apart or could be soaked in caustic soda solution for cleaning, which meant they could easily be modified by the owner. Later boxes were one-piece and packed with wadding which became a solid mass when wet. Infuriated owners cut them open with hack-saws or simply drilled holes to give a straight-through passage. Exhaust systems on scooters are more efficient and better secured than on most motor cars – but there is still much room for improvement.

The noise is not so objectionable in the open country but can be disturbing in city streets. That scooters are quiet-running when they come from the production line is beyond dispute. You can stand in the testing shed at Pontedera and have two Vespa engines running on test rollers only a few feet away – but you will still be able to hear normal speech. However, the two-stroke engine must be kept running at a fair speed to develop power. Below 500rpm the power output is low. Even when ticking over at traffic lights a scooter engine

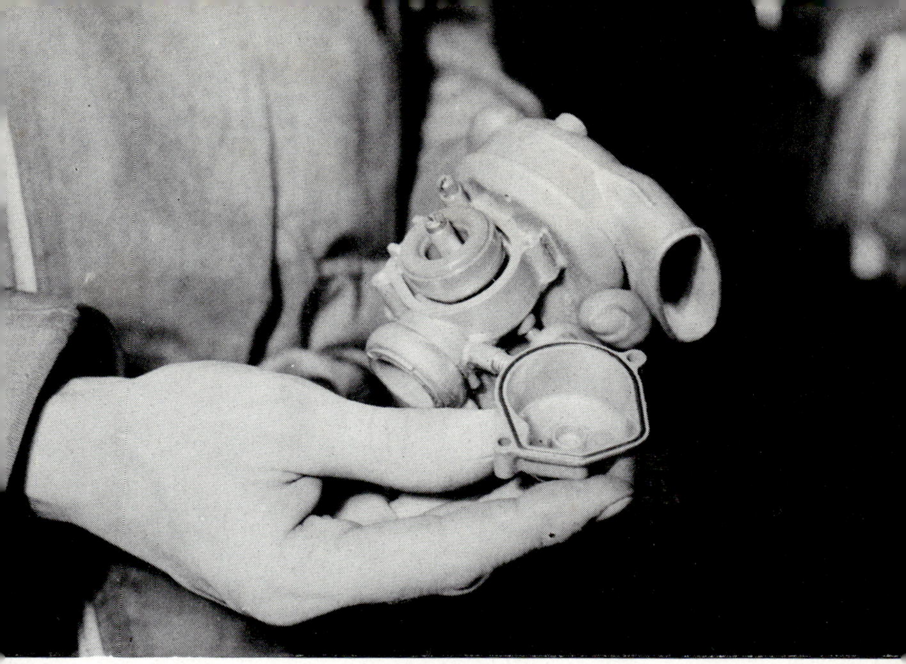

The Dell'Orto carburetter in its later version. It made extensive use of plastics. The needle jet has disappeared.

The Wal Phillips fuel injector, here fitted to a Lambretta as an alternative to the standard carburetter.

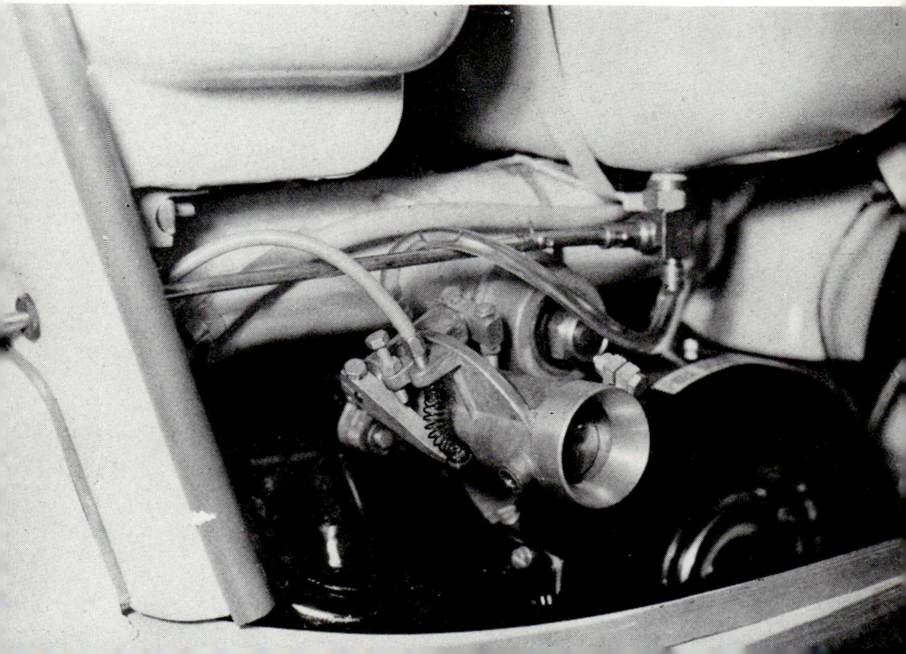

Scooter acrobatics. Rally organisers introduced this see-saw event as much to test the competitors' nerve as their riding skill.

must be kept running fairly fast and it is not possible to trickle along in top gear as you can do with a four-stroke. The power output curves of scooter engines show this very well. The power below 2,500 is hardly worth recording. Take an engine like the Sachs 200.L.AZL-R. This develops about 10bhp at 5,000rpm. At half that speed it developed half that power but below 2,500rpm there was little useful power.

If you go down the scale you would find that the Sachs 50cc engine such as was fitted to many mopeds developed 3.2bhp at about 7,000rpm but had to reach 3,000rpm before it developed a single bhp. That is why moped engines sound so noisy – they have to maintain high engine speeds. The power output of a two-stroke engine is not a straight line graph nor does the output curve tell you how the scooter will behave in action. You may find that it hangs between gears – you may get away snappily from rest but when you change from second to third the vehicles you have passed begin to overtake you once more. In the same way you may see a scooter performance curve showing the machine's road speed plotted against time. It goes up in a magnificent curve, the road speed steadily and rapidly increasing up to 40mph. When you ride such a machine you may find that the curve (if plotted) would run in a series of broken-back wobbles, and this would be a true picture of the machine's performance.

This might be due to the spacing of the gears. It might be because of the engine design. Performance curves are often obtained on the test bench, the engine taken from the assembly line, coupled to ignition and fuel circuits – or perhaps run on town gas – crankshaft speed will be read from a tachometer and the power output at various speeds taken from one form of dynamometer or another. In Germany and Italy there are standardised sets of conditions which must be observed and quoted by any manufacturer publishing engine-test reports. These are widely accepted and so you can safely compare one engine with another on the basis of these reports. You will know that test conditions will have been similar, but of course these conditions will have nothing to do with the conditions under which your engine will run when it is part of a scooter on the open road. On the test bench the engines have no silencers. The carburetter is fed with cool air. The transmission has a minimum of friction. There are no sudden changes in engine speed.

Performance curves for British scooter engines were rarely published. One maker even went so far as to maintain silence about the power output of his engine. This gives the impression that the engine was open to criticism, especially when the refusal was accompanied by the statement that Continental power curves were unreliable and misleading. This may have impressed some British customers but in fact when figures for power or fuel consumption were quoted the makers invariably quoted the conditions (DIN in Germany, CUNA in Italy) under which the results were obtained. British makers were always reluctant to quote standardised test results. They argued that what mattered was the finished machine, that bench tests were no guide, that you could get power on the bench that never reached the rear wheel, but it cannot be denied that this shyness in Britain went hand-in-hand with a very rapid development of two-stroke engines outside Britain, to overcome the serious disadvantages of the two-stroke such as noise, weight, high operating speed, internal fouling. At the same time, let it be said that British designers have shown their ability. The rotary valve two-stroke was tackled by British Anzani, though no such British engine is in production today. Similarly, the BSA/Triumph scooter engines had independently lubricated crankshaft bearings but they also are no longer in production.

The scooter engine of today is a highly developed unit and for the first time in history one part of oil to fifty parts of petrol may be used in a production two-stroke. Most of the developments have been dictated by the customer, above all by the girls who bought scooters. This is especially true of cleanliness and ease of starting. There are still theoretically many paths along which further improvements could be made. Few of them are new. One of the most attractive is some form of forced fuel injection to get a bigger charge of mixture into the cylinder. It will be remembered that the first two-stroke had a separate compression chamber with its own piston. Another line is the introduction of valves, to get better scavenging. A third is one form or another of oscillating piston or even a duplication of pistons, again to get better scavenging. None of these would be as simple as the present-day engine and it is only slowly being realised that simplicity is what the customer wants.

(b) The four-stroke engine

The four-stroke engine is rarely used in scooters though notable exceptions were the Heinkel 175cc single-cylinder Tourist and the BSA/Triumph twin-cylinder 250cc scooters. It has a somewhat complicated system of valves and the cylinder must be lubricated by oil from a pump-driven supply. To get the valves opening and shutting at the right time calls for periodic attention. This process, known as adjusting the tappets, requires some mechanical knowledge.

The engine was developed from the free-piston engine, an idea that sounds extraordinary when described today. A vertical cylinder was held in a framework and a piston fitted into it. There was no connecting rod, no crankshaft, no gearbox. Gas was introduced into the cylinder at the base and there ignited. The explosion sent the piston upwards and as it fell under its own weight it caused a heavy wheel to revolve. This power was transmitted by belting and when the piston reached the bottom of its travel a further explosion sent it up again . . .

and so on. Two Italians, Barsanti and Matteucci, put the idea into practical form, obtained (after some argument) a British patent for such a machine in 1854 and very soon afterwards had it in production. A single-cylinder machine of this type made in 1863 by Bauer of Milan gave a steady 4hp and Barsanti machines were soon installed in machine shops in Florence and, made with twin cylinders by Escher-Wyss of Zurich, were producing the equivalent of 20hp. The free-piston engine with which Otto won his Paris Exhibition gold medal in 1867 had many points of resemblance to the Barsanti machine. It was to the Paris engine that Otto and Langen fitted an articulated piston. The four-stroke engine as we know it today is a refinement and a development of that.

Otto built an inlet valve into his first four-stroke engine and there is one there in present-day models. Overhead valve (ohv) engines are considered superior and if the camshaft operating the valves is above the cylinder (ohc) the engine is even better. However, this introduces many complications. The drive must come from the crankshaft at the other end of the cylinder and there are formidable problems in the way of getting this drive to the camshaft. In both Heinkel and BSA/Triumph scooters the valves were push-rod operated – a camshaft is gear-driven from the crankshaft. The push-rods are raised and lowered by these cams and the top ends of the push-rods push upwards a series of pivoted bars (rocker arms); as the other ends of the rocker arms rest on the valve stems the valves are pushed downwards with some force. The valves return rapidly since they move inside powerful springs.

There are many refinements and the timing of valve openings is almost a science. Two things will be obvious at once. Since the valves must close quickly and since the closing depends entirely on the action of the springs these springs must be powerful. Failure of a valve spring may have serious consequences and the springs are therefore made with a very great margin of safety. This at once means that the pressure (and therefore wear) between push-rods and camshaft is considerable. Thus a further adjustment is introduced to each rocker arm.

The advantages of four-stroke engines, viewed as engines, are considerable. The first and greatest is that a heavy charge of mixture can be put into the cylinder. This will be very little contaminated by burnt gases. The scavenging process is almost complete. The inlet and exhaust ports can be adjusted separately without interference between them or can be given any required degree of overlap. This is important for tuning.

The Heinkel was a single cylinder and the BSA/Triumph twin cylinders, but both work on the same system. The piston moves downwards on its induction stroke. The inlet valve opens and since there is a clear path through the choke tube and the inlet manifold and since there is practically a vacuum inside the cylinder when the valve opens the mixture rushes in at atmospheric pressure – which is nearly 15 lbs per square inch. Compare this to the crankcase pressure forcing the mixture into the cylinder of a two-stroke, which is rarely more than 5 lbs per square inch. It is much easier to get a heavy charge of mixture into a four-stroke engine. The faster the air moves through the carburetter the more fuel it picks up.

The compression stroke is made with inlet and exhaust valves closed and they remain closed until the exhaust stroke begins. Then the exhaust valve opens and the full pressure of the piston is used to drive the burnt gases through the exhaust port. The exhaust valve closes and the cycle begins again. There is infinite scope for owners who wish to delay the opening of the exhaust valve, or advance the opening of the inlet valve. If these adjustments are too fine the engine may overheat or a valve stem may be bent. It is easy to maladjust a four-stroke engine and that may be why the two-stroke is often recommended to the owner who has no mechanical knowledge whatsoever.

The fuel of the four-stroke is petrol alone. All the moving parts of the engine must be lubricated. This is done by fitting a sump or reservoir for oil and pumping it round the engine so that cylinder and bearings are continuously supplied with fresh oil, the volume being sufficient to allow solids to settle rather than continue circulating. Although crankshaft main bearings may be ball or roller bearings it is quite normal to use split solid bearings or to use both in the same engine. Big-end bearings are often split bushes as on the BSA/Triumph scooters; these were lubricated through holes drilled in the crankpins. It will be seen that the risk of bearing failure in a four-stroke engine is remote. Engine speeds have little effect on the efficiency of lubrication.

Since there are so many moving parts which require lubrication the oil consumption (comparing engines in good condition) will be about half that of a two-stroke. The former will use one percent, while the later Vespas and Lambrettas use two percent. If we compare worn engines the two may show an equal oil consumption, for the two-stroke uses the same proportion whatever its condition. This is sometimes overlooked. With an old four-stroke engine the comparison may be even less favourable.

8 Transmission and Gears

Scooter manufacturers are still trying for a final solution of the problems of transmission. Some makers had little choice. Others have used one system after another, apparently haphazard. There are three main types.

1. The Vespa system of direct drive. As might have been foreseen, these Old Originals worked out an excellent system on their first scooters and have stuck to it throughout their range. In it the drive from the crankshaft goes direct to the gears on a layshaft which are in constant mesh with the gear pinions on the rear wheel shaft. All the gears are spur gears; no bevels, no chains, no torsion shafts.

2. Chain drive. Used on almost all motor cycles, this is the simplest to design, simplest to manufacture. When not enclosed it is dirty, subject to rapid wear in dusty, muddy or gritty conditions.

3. Belt drive. The belt is V-shaped running on grooved expanding pulleys. This has many theoretical disadvantages but was used in the Concorde (later known as the Hobby in Britain), in the Moby and Raleigh mopeds, and was adopted by BSA/Triumph when they discarded the Dandy and turned out the Tina 98cc scooter. This system has great advantages for the light scooter. Its silence, ease of operation and the elimination of the gearbox combine to make it a favourite for low-cost, low-power machines. Its success on the 74cc

DKW scooter in France was sensational. Its lack of attraction for British customers was due to social, rather than mechanical or financial conditions.

There was a fourth transmission system – by means of shafts with sets of bevel gears. It was used on early Lambretta and NSU scooters. The former dropped it because the money and skill needed for correct maintenance proved too high. The latter started with full shaft drive, but in their later models reduced the shafts to such tiny sizes that the drive became, for all practical purposes, direct through a set of spiral bevel gears. A genuine shaft drive was built into a British scooter – the Velocette Viceroy – but this was a lamentable failure and according to some was responsible for the firm's subsequent disappearance from the scene. The Viceroy was a twin-cylinder, horizontally opposed engine of unusual design. There being two cylinder heads, it was important not to mix them up when decarbonising. The primary drive to the clutch was by duplex chain, the final drive by a shaft with universal coupling. This gave a rather long propeller shaft with final spiral bevel gears.

Except with scooters having an infinitely variable belt drive all have a gearbox. This is not an exact way of putting it. The best that can be said about the average gearbox is that the customer will not pay for a better job. Most designers have a better one tucked up their sleeves, only waiting for the board of directors to give the green signal. There is no sign of the signal being given.

Few things about the scooter get worse treatment and harsher language than the gearbox. What with clashing of gears not engaged and the screaming of gears when they are engaged, many a beginner sighs for the synchromesh of father's car. Many a good engine is wrecked through the gearbox, usually because too high a gear is engaged. So common is this misuse that an accessory might well be fitted for the first 500 miles –

3. The engine and transmission layout of the NSU Prima V 175cc scooter. The engine was located centrally but at right angles to the rear wheel. Final drive by shaft was retained, but the shaft was very small. The drive went into the four-speed gearbox through spur gears, but out of it by a spiral bevel gear. The engine pivoted on a shaft parallel to the piston and just above the engine.

a supplementary clutch that would slip if you engaged top gear when you should be in an intermediate.

If an engine gave a good steady push you would not need a gearbox. Most people have seen a canal barge being towed by a single horse – or on occasions by a single man. It is the steady push that does it. If you had time enough and a different fuel (steam, for instance) you could do much the same thing with your scooter; no gearbox, no noise, practically no acceleration. If you insist on petrol you must have a gearbox. The two-stroke needs one with a low bottom gear – the Lambretta GT. 200 had a bottom gear of 4.46:1 while for the lightweight Raleigh Roma it was 7:1 and even lower on the Capri 80cc. This sounds contradictory and is certainly confusing.

Here is one gear ratio:
  11 teeth   35 teeth   Ratio 3:18

Here is a higher ratio:
  13 teeth   35 teeth   Ratio 2:7

In fact, the lower the ratio the higher the gear. If you look at your gear-change indicator on the handlebar you will find gears 1, 2, 3, and usually 4. You can call first gear bottom gear but its ratio is always higher than that of the higher gear. This is one of the absurdities which need not have happened and has no compensating advantage to offset its confusion. Perhaps that is why scooterists continue to drive their machines in too high a gear? When you engage top gear you engage the lowest ratio, not the highest. Incidentally, your gear ratios always take into account the tyres you use. If you use smaller section tyres than the makers intended you will cut down your top speed. You will get the same effect if you under-inflate them. This is known as the intervention of Providence to help the careless.

Since gearboxes are common to so many scooters it might be convenient to deal with them first. There are two variations: (*a*) Those operated from the handlebars; (*b*) Those operated by the foot lever.

Whichever system is used, the gears are totally enclosed and run in a bath of oil. There must be just so much oil and the level must be maintained. Some kind of indicator is fitted – it may be a dipstick with a groove to show the correct level. More usual on scooters is a level plug. You unscrew this, pour oil in and when it starts to overflow you have the correct amount in. Level plug and filler plug may be combined. There may even be a single plug which serves for levelling, filling and draining. This economical method is not always satisfactory.

It is unkind of you to run with too little oil in the gearbox – or with too much in. The best level is just below the centre of the spindle carrying the gears but this is not always possible as you may have a train of gears arranged vertically or gears of different diameters. If so, some gears will have too much oil, since you cannot risk any gear having too little.

Gear pinions running like this, totally enclosed and with the correct amount of oil, will run indefinitely. There is no reason why a gear train should ever need replacing, except for misuse for the gears are working in ideal conditions and the loads they carry are well within their design limits. It is useful to think of them as levers. The mechanical advantage you get from a lever depends on the relative distances from the fulcrum of load and effort. There is a saying that, given a lever long enough – and a fulcrum – you could even move the earth. This statement ceased to be correct soon after Einstein was born for it then became clear that if you pedalled to the end of this lever you would be in a region where you would be weightless and so unable to apply any pressure to the lever. Probably a gear would be more useful.

Gears usually come in trains. Two make a pair. More is a train. Technically a pair of gears consists of two wheels with mating teeth. If the power is transmitted by chain the wheel is a sprocket; if by a belt the wheel is a pulley. The smaller of two gear wheels is usually called the pinion. The gear ratio is obtained by dividing the number of teeth in the larger gear by the number of teeth in the pinion. In a train of gears the calculation must be made through all the mating gears. A gear is identified by stating the number of teeth and the gear-box for which it is intended.

Scooter engines have straight spur gears. These are sturdy, easy to manufacture and tolerably quiet. Gear dimensions are kept as small as possible to keep down the size (and therefore weight) of the engine. For many years a pressure angle of $14\frac{1}{2}$ degrees was used – and this is still used by some firms – but the British Standard was set at 20 degrees. Gears cut to this pressure angle – Villiers used it throughout, for instance – have greater strength at the root and although they have a smaller arc of contact the relative radius of curvature is greater. All these remarks apply to gears cut or hobbed, not to cast gears, with which we need not concern ourselves.

The strength of the gears in your engine can be taken for granted. These have been carefully calculated. Here an odd point crops up, which shows how difficult it is to think clearly and at the same time to make progress. When running pipelines through a mountainside the strength of the pipe was thought of as being the strength of the pipe alone. Then some bright fellow realised that if the pipe was always full of water the strength of this solid bar of water should be taken into account. . . . In working out gear strengths the designer may work either on the strength of the tooth as originally made (which is one thing) or he may assume that after two years the gear teeth will have worn down a bit – and work on this reduced figure. If he guesses wrong he may soon be looking for another job, for the thought of thousands of gearboxes giving trouble after the second year is too hideous for words. However, transmission gears which are properly designed give little trouble. A shock load can break a gear down and so can a load reversed, which is much the same thing. You can get shock loading in such things as starter gears, where the pinion is thrown forward into engagement. Eventually the teeth on the starter ring are worn down – and the pinion does not look healthy either. You get shock reversals in the back axle, especially in the old type motor car; you stall the car and the crownwheel teeth break up.

Accuracy pays in cutting gears. Accurately cut gears make less noise and last longer. However, gear cutting is a costly process, two or three teeth being cut at one time. There are machines which will cut a spur gear in thirty seconds, all the teeth being cut at the same time but the cost is fabulous and not to be thought of unless you deal in vast quantities. One of the wonders of the Innocenti works was to see such a machine at work. You see the gear blank put into the machine and half a minute later you were handed the finished gear.

The number of gears in a gearbox depends on your scooter. On the 50cc mopeds you may have only a single gear. The engine will be a high-revving, peaking at 7,000rpm. Such an engine may stall at 2,500rpm and under, but when you open the throttle it will steadily climb up its brave little power curve until it screams away at top revs doing about 34mph and it will continue doing this for days on end if you so wish. On the other hand there are 50cc engines with three gears. First and second gears will then have been put in to enable you to get up hills, for it is a drawback of the single-gear machine that on some main-road hills you will slow down to 6 mph and perhaps have to pedal – or get off and walk. Some main roads in Cornwall – and even near Dover – are awkward for such machines. The choice of gear ratios is not easy and those fitted to machines for use in Switzerland may be unsuitable for use in, say, Holland. Spectacular tests are sometimes organised to show that a machine will, for instance, get further up some famous hill than any other. It looks fine to see marked on a photograph the place where the Honda gave up, or the Kreidler, or the Benelli – and here is the Zundapp reaching the top, but this does not mean that the Zundapp is a better buy than the Honda, though the organisers of the test may wish you to think so. If those same machines were run on a race circuit it might be that the Honda would cover 15% more ground in 24 hours – it would depend, in both tests, what gear ratios were used.

Single gears are fitted to reduce costs, a simple and praise-worthy ambition. In Holland the single-gear moped was very popular but in Britain there would be many places where, to quote an old rhyme:

> You'll find, in spite of all their talking,
> You'll have to walk, and pay for walking.

Two gears? Three British machines – the Sun Geni, the BSA Dandy and the DKW Bambi – had only two gears, but these are exceptions. It is usually found that bottom gear takes you only up to about 10mph without a bit of a scream, so that it was used only to get the machine moving. There was a wide and inconvenient gap between the two gears, a gap you notice when you try to change down, and find you are doing this at 18mph.

Three gears? Scooters began with three gears on both 125cc and 150cc machines. With top speeds of about 35mph this was reasonable but as speeds increased there was a tendency to fit an extra gear. Light scooters such as the Capri 80cc had three gears from the beginning.

Four gears? The German scooters were the first to have four

gears fitted as normal. They had 175cc or 200cc engines with correspondingly high speeds and the three-speed gearbox left rather big gaps between the gears. If your top speed is 65mph and you need a bottom gear low enough to get started from rest you are left with a gap between 15 and 45mph and this is too large a gap for one gear ratio. Four gears were therefore essential but in addition to being more costly this raises a problem where the changes are controlled from the handlebars, for the linear movement may be so great that it becomes awkward for the wrist. This was the case with one or two 150cc scooters when, for the first time, they had four gears. The twistgrip movement which had been comfortable with three gears was a strain with four. No such problem occurs with foot-controlled gear changes for each change was accomplished by a push forward (or back) on a short, stiff lever. It will be remembered that the first Lambretta was given a foot-controlled gearchange, but all models since then have handlebar controls. This is probably the only case of such a switch being made. Manufacturers early decide on the method they prefer – and they stick to it. They do, however, seem to have no settled policy about the number of gears. The Vespa 90cc appeared with three gears, but the sports version had four, as had the even smaller 50cc Sprint. The Lambretta 50cc had three gears but the 75cc had four.

There is a certain element of fashion about the number of gears. Dealers report that, other things being equal, customers often purchase a four-speed machine thinking it must be better than one with only three. It is not easy to follow this line of reasoning, but Italian scooters such as the Iso Milano with a 150cc engine were made with four speeds from the beginning. Lambretta put four speeds on their Li.125, Li.150 and TV.175 machines. Moto Rumi put four on the 125cc scooters but it was not until 1959 that Vespa introduced four speeds – except for their GS sport scooters. At the other extreme the Laverda, with a 60cc engine, appeared with four-speed gears.

It is easy to see how suitable a four-speed box is for high speed machines. Top gear is then something in the nature of an overdrive, to be used only on the open, unobstructed road. As soon as the run is checked the rider must drop to third gear to pick up speed again. That is reasonable. It saves fuel, saves wear on the engine – solid advantages in the big machine. However, it is not easy to see why machines of moderate speeds are so fitted. On a 125cc scooter top gear will be a running rather than a pulling gear and for town work third gear will be much used. There is a certain fashion element in this. The tendency is here and as long as people want four-speed boxes the scooter makers will fit them. It happened with cars – Ford, who stuck to three gears for so long, eventually bowed to fashion and fitted four.

These references to a gearbox should not be misunderstood. Most scooter engines have the gears built into the crankcase (as in the Iso Milano) or into the transmission casing (as in Vespa and Lambretta) and even where the gears were mounted in a separate compartment (as in Villiers or Zundapp) there is no true gearbox as we have them on a motor car. You will read in technical descriptions that the gearbox is a built-in unit with the engine or "cast integrally with the engine crankcase". You might criticise the phrasing or the translation, but the meaning is that the gearbox is not a separate unit.

The position of the gears is governed by the final drive. If you have a chain drive you can put your gears almost where you like and you will want them as close as possible to the gear-change lever. There were many advantages of the foot control and both British and German makers used it extensively, as did the Austrian and the Japanese. Indeed, it was not only popular but was used in some scooters where it was not obviously the best method. The great advantage was that it operated through solid rods. This gives a very positive movement. Secondly, the movement necessary did not increase with the number of gears. You pressed the pedal down an inch to get second gear; the pedal returned. You pressed it down an inch to get third gear; the pedal returned – and so on. Nothing could have been simpler.

The system is derived from motor cycles. There you had only one pedal. You tapped the pedal to change up; you put your toe under it and lifted for changes down. This is still widely used on motor cycles but with scooters it was converted into the heel-and-toe or rocking pedal change. There were many beginners pardonably confused when told that the scooter had heel-and-toe change. The standard motor cycle gear change is not likely to be used on mass-produced scooters.

There were some variants of the rocking pedal. On Diana and BSA there was a single pedal which could be pushed forwards or back; the Rumi had a pivot with two levers; the Sun Wasp had two pedals side by side – cumbersome and inconvenient. Undoubtedly the best system was to have a single pedal fixed to the gear-operating spindle but this meant bringing the engine forward alongside the foot. This was done on the Rumi Formichino and the problem of enclosure there was solved by not having the engine enclosed. In the Velocette Viceroy where the engine was mounted forward the unorthodox shaft and coupling transmission shifted the gearbox back alongside the rear wheel; the gear-change pedal (similar to that on the Rumi) operated through a series of linked rods; one could not help feeling the designer would have preferred some other method. The most common fault which developed was bending and twisting of the rods, usually because the driver stamped heavily on the pedal and the pedal stuck. Occasionally it was difficult to engage the gear. The best procedure was to declutch, open the throttle slightly and try again. If you stamped hard on the pedal you might do no good and some damage. The position was similar to finding a door stuck. You pull at the handle but the door is jammed at the bottom. If you continue to pull at the handle you may pull the handle off – or actually twist the door, whereas if you closed the door and tried again it might open easily.

Another difficulty, strange in view of the system's reputation for being positive, is that neutral is often elusive. This was a genuine difficulty, though the manufacturers or dealers denied it. With a rocking-pedal you may engage first gear by pressing on the rear pedal and then second gear by pressing down the other, with neutral somewhere in between. It was quite usual to see machines halted at traffic lights with the owners testing (by means of the clutch) whether neutral was engaged or not. One or two makers fitted a separate neutral finder – in some a lever on the handlebars; in the Diana by pressing the kickstart pedal down with the engine running – but such devices underlined the fact that with foot gear changes, as with international politics, it is sometimes difficult to find neutral and stay there.

The system was popular with British scooters but, except in the Velocette and the Rumi – already described – the solution was less than very satisfactory. It is in the nature of things that transmitting motion through a series of loosely linked rods cannot be a best solution, but the alternative (total enclosure in a rigid frame) was too costly and presented formidable constructional obstacles going back as far as crank-case design. The foot gear change adopted by so many British scooters was mechanically inferior to that on motor cycles. In this respect the trend towards scooters has not improved machine design – even a great firm like Heinkel fell down here.

Almost all Italian and French scooters had a gear-change control through a Bowden cable linked to the clutch lever on the handlebars. It is not known whether this was a necessity forced on d'Ascanio when he put his Vespa engine alongside the rear wheel or whether he would have reached the same solution if given a completely unfettered choice. The question is academic. It must be emphasised that there is no difference in principle between the two methods; the selector lever and the indexing plate on the Vespa have their counterpart in the operating quadrant and sliding fork of the Villiers engine – and the main difference is that the latter is moved by a rigid lever, the former by a pair of Bowden cables.

Cable controls are not an immediately obvious solution and British designers preferred the rigid bar, so it is no accident that handlebar gear change controls were not fitted to British scooters. It is true that the Villiers engines (which carried the British scooter industry on its shoulders for so many years) was somewhat flexible and that a cable gear change would have meant great production problems in the early days, but it could have been done. That it was never done smacks more of tenacity and training than of deliberate choice.

Foot gear changes go far back in motor cycle history and is linked to the motor-cyclist's liking for a petrol tank which he can grip with his knees. It is not clear whether this is the cry of a race of thwarted foxhunters – a yearning for horseflesh instead of horse-power. Perhaps so. It certainly left the lower limbs free to waggle pedals. The foot-operated pedal gave trouble, but so also did the handlebar cable control. In principle there is a flexible sheath, fixed at both ends, within which the cable is free to slide. In practice cables gave trouble – dust, ice, lack of lubrication – and it was several years before these troubles vanished. It was not these troubles which deterred the British and German designers. If you look at the arrangement of gears on the mainshaft and layshaft of Lambretta and Iso Milano, for instance, you will notice how compact it is. This is because an entirely different gear-change system was adopted – a system with great advantages of economy and convenience. It was a truly revolutionary innovation.

On a typical British gearbox, as in the Villiers or BSA engine, you have two sets of gears on parallel shafts. The gears engage by means of dogs on their faces – an odd but descriptive way of putting it – and the drive may go through more than one pair of gears. It follows that there must be spaces between the gears along the shafts and this makes such a gearbox bigger than it need be. In modern engines the gears are almost always built into the crankcase, which economises in space, but the disadvantages of these dog-engaged gears have not been completely overcome. Due to their big masses, such gears are operated by solid rods, foot-controlled.

For the other type, handlebar operated, let us take a typical Lambretta engine, where the differences can be seen easily. The gears are mounted on the rear wheel spindle (for chain-driven machines the wheel is quite separate) and on a parallel shaft is the main gear group unit. These four gears are in mesh with the corresponding four gears on the wheel spindle and they stay in mesh all the time (constant mesh). Since all four have different ratios, chaos is averted by making sure that the rear spindle is driven by only one of the four gears at any one time. The other three idle round at their different speeds until the rider changes gear.

How is this particular gear chosen? The gears have no driving dogs on their faces, but they have something equivalent – slots on their internal diameters – and the drive is taken through these slots. This is a refinement of the way in which clutch plates are driven, but greater accuracy is required with the gears and the slots are carefully machined in solid bosses. We now require something to fit into these slots and so transmit the drive to the rear wheel. This something is a sleeve with six arms each ending in a stub which just fits the slots. No machining is needed here; on Lambrettas they are sintered, a moulding process used for small parts. The extraordinary thing is that the stubs are less than a quarter of an inch square. True, there are six of them – at least on the later models – but that is not a very big driving section. It is ample, though, and carries the load.

There is some confusion about the naming of parts. Mainshaft, layshaft, secondary shaft, countershaft and other terms are not always used to describe the same thing. What Lambretta calls a layshaft is a mainshaft to Villiers and a secondary shaft to Iso Milano; though because of the difference between the two systems the parts are not strictly comparable, but please remember the variations in nomenclature when drives are discussed.

However, you can follow the drive which comes from the clutch to the mainshaft with its four fixed gears all meshed with the four change gears on the rear spindle. Three of these four will be free-wheeling, only the fourth being engaged by the six-armed sleeve. When you want to change gear the Bowden cable control works a lever which pushes (or pulls) the sleeve so that the arms engage with a different gear wheel.

The gears run in oil, so all the surfaces are well-lubricated and the sliding action is easy, especially when the engine is running, but if you have followed the description you will see why, if you stall the engine in gear, you may find it difficult to get into neutral. The sudden shock will have made the gear slot grip the sleeve stub tightly. If you try to pull the engine into neutral by the handlebar control you may stretch the cable – or break it – actually the cable rarely breaks but it may pull out of the end nipple. The best thing is to give the stub a bit of play by rocking the scooter backwards. It will usually free itself and allow you to operate the handlebar control easily. The same sort of jamming may occur with dog-operated gears and the same solution applies.

Both gear systems are popular. The internal-driven gears are compact and light though British designers do not like them, thought them suitable only for small engines. This was not unreasonable since the Italian scooters for many years kept to 175cc or less but when the Vespa GS and the Lambretta GT 200 sports engines were developed they had internal-driven gears and proved satisfactory. As these machines could be tuned to give 80mph it was a fair test, but it was argued that if your firm made engines up to 500cc it was reasonable to have one uniform system of gear-changing in them all so the obvious choice was dog-driven gears with a foot control. You could use these for small and big engines. For the former your gearbox could turn out to be oversize and you might sigh for the compactness of the internal-driven gears but you could use many parts unchanged from one engine size to another and so cut costs.

An unusual case was the NSU firm, which started with its Prima D engines using cable-controlled gear changes and then turned over to dog-driven gears with foot control for the III.KL and Prima V.

One advantage of the cable gear change is that the gears are selected positively and so is neutral. You may get an old scooter with sloppy changes but when in good condition the handlebar change is clean and the selection of neutral both easy and certain. In this regard it is superior to the average foot change. The positive action is a great help to the beginner, who knows the gear has engaged because he can feel or hear the catch going home. This little device may be a spring-loaded roller as on the Vespa, a spring-loaded ball engaging a serrated spindle as on the Lambretta, or some other equally effective device. On the early Heinkels there was not this positive engagement. On the early Vespas and Puchs there was a rod-and-ball joint linkage instead of a cable.

There are two major disadvantages:

Difficulty in lubricating. On some early scooters there were continual complaints that cables broke or – more usually –

pulled the nipple off. In some cases this was due to the cable and sheath being trapped in an acute bend, but more usually the cable had jammed in its sheath because dirt and grit had accumulated there, or perhaps water had leaked in and rusted the cable. Some early Lambrettas were very liable to this trouble and many were the calls for ways of pushing oil down the cable. For a time lubricating nipples were fitted to the sheath and the grease gun used regularly, for to lubricate from the handlebars was not easy and in any case meant partial dismantling. After a time the cable makers improved their products, some makers using plastic-lined cable sheaths with a very smooth action. Gradually cable complaints dwindled, but for many years a set of cables was considered a necessary spare for any lengthy trip and rally riders fitted duplicate cables in situ.

Length of travel. This has become a problem with the introduction of the fourth gear. The handlebar control requires one position for each gear plus one for neutral. When a gear is selected it is retained by a ball or roller which engages in a notched bar or quadrant. These notches must be sufficiently deep to retain the gear even when there is considerable vibration, which means a certain minimum width so that for a scooter with a four-speed engine the travel of the handlebar control, in inches, is considerable and on one or two machines the length of travel, combined with the angle of the clutch lever, made gear changing tedious and uncomfortable. This problem was solved in time but when buying a secondhand scooter it is advisable to check that the gear-change control lever is comfortable to use.

These are the two main disadvantages, though neither is noticeable on modern scooters. Minor troubles are usually connected with wear – the cables may stretch so that the gears do not engage properly or they jump out easily. This was serious with some earlier scooters but became of little importance when the retaining device was made so positive that a little slack in the cable does not mean the gear jumping out of engagement. Again, the cable sheath may become frayed or burred; or grit and water may lodge inside the sheath, sometimes freezing and making it impossible to move the cable. When this has happened some strong owners have actually pulled the cable from the end nipples. When Bernard Thompson did his run to Milan he had duplicate cables fitted ready to be hooked into the levers should one break, and many owners still dislike cable controls, but today they are reliable and there is no sign of any maker abandoning them once he has started fitting them to his scooters. On the Bond, indeed, one rod linkage was changed to cable control – on the footbrake, an unusual arrangement.

A singular advantage of the internal-driven gear system became plain when sporting events became popular; alternative gear ratios were readily available and the complete set of gears could be fitted quickly. The Italian Malaguti appeared at the Milan Show in 1962 with three alternative gear ratios as standard. It was a powerful scooter capable of an easy 80mph and the alternative sets of gears were standard accessories. This machine did not go into production and it was left to Lambretta to market the first scooter with alternative ratios. This gave Lambretta owners a choice of five different ratios. Riders could then weigh up the track they were to ride on – its curves, straights, gradients and so on – and select the gear ratios best suited to it. Broadly speaking they could choose between top speed and acceleration. Though five sets were available the choice of gears was not quite as wide as it sounds, for the complete train had to be fitted. It was not possible to alter top gear alone, for instance, but it did mean that 150cc gears could be used on a 175cc engine and in some events this would give sufficient edge to win, perhaps on a track with many sharp bends.

Transmission systems

Direct drive. To change the up-and-down motion of the piston into rotation of the rear wheel a crankshaft is used. In the two-stroke engine this is necessarily unbalanced and places a strain on the main bearings – a problem not completely solved in some of the earlier Lambrettas. The crankshaft in the Vespa was at right angles to the long axis of the scooter and the drive to the rear wheel was direct through a cush drive. All the gears were straight spur gears. All the shafts were parallel. This was a simple and effective system. It was totally enclosed. Parallel shafts mean easy machining of parts and quick assembly. The gears were lubricated by the simplest method; if the oil level in the gearbox was maintained the gears picked up sufficient – nothing could be simpler.

Direct drive was also used in the NSU scooters but in the Prima III and V models the engine was placed across the machine so that the crankshaft ran parallel to the long axis. There was a separate gearbox behind the clutch and the drive emerged from the gearbox as a stubby shaft with a bevel pinion. This was a most unusual arrangement and meant that if a kickstart was fitted the pedal moved outwards from the side of the scooter – not very convenient.

In both these drives the engine was set close to the rear wheel and a good deal of machinery – and weight – was offset. Classical teaching sets weight on the central axis where possible and both Vespa and NSU were criticised for their weight distribution. One answer was that the weight was placed much lower than on some machines, but the best answer was in the Vespa sales figures.

Lambretta adopted direct drive only gradually and started with their engine mounted centrally. This led them to make much play in their sales talk with the static unbalance of certain other scooters and undoubtedly created difficulties when the Lambretta engines, so to speak, moved sideways. Even then, the engine was a separate unit and the clutch was driven by a duplex chain. This gave some accessibility but made for a bulky crankcase.

The NSU and Vespa drive systems were very compact and when well designed made things easy for the owner – in some early Vespas it was almost impossible to do a complete decoke without removing the complete engine from the frame. Undoubtedly direct drive has its limitations, especially on engine size. NSU appear to have been happy with it up to 150cc but when they wanted more room for the engine, as in their 175cc Prima V they preferred not to have such a large mass offset. Vespa were happy with it to 150cc and many people thought this was the limit, but Vespa went first to 160cc and then to the big 180cc and as far as engine layout is concerned this was simply the smaller engine enlarged. It cannot be said that bigger engines will not be built using direct drive – firms are willing to convert the Vespa SS.180 to 200cc, or the Lambretta GT.200 to 225cc – but the makers seem to have called a halt at this size with a single cylinder and the prototype 250cc scooter which Lambretta made was a twin-cylinder. Above 200cc there is a problem with the clutch. It was possible to tune the bigger Lambrettas to give so much power even at 200cc that special clutch parts were needed. British designers are not attracted to direct drive.

Chain drive. This is very popular in Britain and in Germany. It is exceptionally flexible and where the final drive is by a totally enclosed chain running in a cast housing it is highly efficient. When replacements are needed they are usually chains or sprockets.

This is a curious position, because the chain is not a perfect transmission medium. A chain drive has a tight side and a slack side. The slack is essential and should be on the underside. The driving sprocket should have an odd number of teeth and will wear rapidly if it has fewer than eleven. All chains wear, and ideally the sprocket centres should be adjusted from time to time because a slack-running chain will quickly wear out. Chains must be continuously lubricated. If a chain is replaced the sprockets should also be replaced.

These are all disadvantages either for the designer or the owner – and there are many other snags. However, chain drives have come to stay for all their drawbacks. Two reasons are: roller chains are of surpassing excellence and reliability and a chain drive can be designed even by the lazy and incompetent.

A very simple form was that used in most British scooters fitted with Villiers engines. The gearbox had a shaft carrying an external sprocket. There was a larger sprocket on the rear wheel spindle. A chain was run over the two and joined up by the usual type of spare link. On some scooters lubrication of the chain was left to take care of itself, the owner being recommended to keep the chain lubricated. Frequent chain tensioning was necessary. Since the rear wheel was invariably carried in a fork the fork ends were flattened and slotted and adjusters similar to those on pedal cycles were fitted. Adjustment was carried out in the same way, too. The securing nuts were slackened off, the adjuster screwed up or slackened and then the securing nuts were (we hope) securely tightened.

Sometimes a chain drive is fitted with more or less complete chain guards and there may be a drip-feed lubrication pipe. However, on none of these machines is chain lubrication as efficient as it might be, so chain wear is heavy, for the road dirt, water and grit mixes with the oil and grease to form a grinding paste which works havoc on both chain and sprockets.

An improvement – or rather a radically different attack on the same problem – was the totally enclosed chain running in a cast case. The case may be part of the crankcase but is more usually a frame member carrying the rear wheel. One of the earliest examples of this was the Motobecane Moby. A British example was the BSA/Triumph. Beginning with the Li. and TV models Lambretta used it for the primary drive to the clutch. It satisfies most of the requirements of a transmission system.

Its main drawback is that it involves the manufacturer in a great deal of capital outlay. Engine and transmission casing must be designed together. This at once means manufacture – and therefore sales – in big quantities. It almost demands that the scooter and engine be made in the same works. Other important advantages follow: great thought is given to making the assembly easy to service, joints are between machined faces, grit cannot get at the chain – and so on. It becomes an engineering job.

However, few things come without strings attached and the fundamental objection to a chain drive remains. Unless the driver sprocket centre coincides with the centre of the arm about which the rear wheel pivots, the chain centres will vary and the chain will run alternately slack and tight as the rear wheel moves up and down. This leads to chain wear outside the normal range. It follows that the chain centres should be adjusted periodically and this is hardly possible if both centres are fixed in a single casting. BSA and Lambretta got over this by fitting a slipper. One or two makers let things go by default, perhaps thinking the chain will never wear, for they fitted no adjuster. Where the drive is in two parts, as it was with the Diana, the rear sprocket and chain are in the swinging arm. Adjustment of the chain centres was by means of an eccentric and the whole swinging arm moved – a more agreeable system than having a separate adjuster on each side.

Belt drive. The only kind of belt drive with which we are concerned is the no gearbox type where the gear ratio is infinitely variable by using a pair of expanding pulleys. This was used on the Motobecane and Raleigh mopeds, in the Concorde 98cc and in the BSA/Triumph Tina and T.10

automatics. There is a certain amount of slip in all belt drives, which is why they are useless for timing drives but for final drives this can be accepted. The system is simple. The pulley halves are held against powerful springs and the effective diameter is set by the position of the belt. It is best visualised if you think of the machine running along a flat road at an even speed. The effective diameters of the two pulleys will remain constant. This means that the gear ratio will be the ratio of the two diameters. When you come to an upward slope the load on the driver pulley will increase. This will increase the sideways push of the belt on the movable pulley face, which will slide out a trifle, though still held by the springs. When it has moved out sufficiently to reduce the effective diameter of the driver pulley it will settle down at that until the next change in load. While this has been happening the load on the larger pulley will have diminished; its movable face will have crept in a little and increased the effective diameter to a corresponding degree. Thus the gear ratio will have changed slightly without any gearbox being necessary.

These changes are only slight but they are constantly being made. In theory, therefore, the Concorde was always runnng in the most efficient gear ratio; instead of having no gears it had an infinite number, each coming into use when the appropriate load was being applied. It is essential to remember that these changes in pulley diameter are being made all the time, the pulley faces moving in and out continually. The natural objection to this kind of drive is that the belts wear quickly, but this seems to be only theoretical. In practice the drive is reliable and has a long life.

A more valid criticism is that snappy acceleration cannot be obtained with this system. For the rider who wishes to have a sporty mount the standard gearbox has the greater appeal.

There are also limits to the size of engine. It was limited to scooter engines of less than 100cc (although quite large motor cars use it, none made in Britain) and because the shafts on which the pulleys moved needed constant lubrication there were design problems. Further, although we have dealt with this as a transmission system it was not carried to its logical conclusion. The final drive to the rear wheel was by roller chain. The V-belt was here a substitute for a gearbox and no attempt was made to carry the driven sliding pulley back to the rear wheel though there is no basic reason why this should not be done.

There are other types of drive but they were little used. The fully automatic drive through an oil-driven torque converter was used in production scooters in Japan but was never seriously considered in Britain because of the high cost and power losses. Prototypes were, however, made by Ducati (Italy) and NSU (Germany).

The shaft drive was once popular but was dropped successively by Lambretta (who used duplex roller chains for primary drive) and NSU (direct bevel drive on the III.KL and Prima V) though the latter continued to use it in the Prima D. A form of shaft drive was fitted to the Velocette Viceroy. Here the shaft ran between flywheel and clutch, with Metalastik couplings at either end. The final drive was similar to the NSU Prima direct bevel drive. This was a remarkable innovation and since the engine was a vertically opposed twin-cylinder two-stroke, made it one of the two really interesting scooters to be produced by British firms. The other was the beautifully styled DKR Capella where, for the first time, a British scooter was obviously the work of an artist.

The clutch. This is a form of shock absorber, though it is rarely considered in that way. If your engine had no clutch you would get it started in a very energetic manner; by pushing it along the flat with the decompressor valve open (if you had one) and first gear engaged, simultaneously leaping abroad, closing the valve and switching the ignition on.

By using the clutch you can run the engine at any speed without regard to the speed of the rear wheel. This is not exaggerated – it is literally true. You could set the engine at 5,000rpm and yet have the scooter trickling along at 8mph in top gear by slipping the clutch. Your journey would be short and would be accompanied by clouds of blue smoke from the burning clutch, but you could do it.

You can get an equally dramatic picture of a clutch from the moving platforms at a fun fair. These revolve at different speeds and with a bit of luck you may be thrown from a fast one to a slow one. As you land you will feel a certain amount of heat being generated between you and the new platform. This continues until you and the platform are moving at the same pace. This is exactly what happens in the clutch.

There are usually three or four steel plates with inserts of some friction material gripped between other steel plates (the two kinds being alternated) and the clutch bell (internal) and the clutch bell (housing). When the six plates are held together by the clutch springs the whole unit revolves.

There are many variations. Single-plate dry clutches were once popular and were fitted to the NSU Prima as late as 1965 but were followed by the type technically known as "multi-plate running in oil". When you see these words you should picture a clutch housing, three of four plates with friction pads sandwiched between the same number of slightly dished plates – also of steel – and a clutch centre. The terms may vary. Lambretta called the clutch centre a bell; Villiers called it a sliding sleeve, since they make it that way; Puch called it a clutch hub. You may think it would be as well to have some standardisation but clutch design did vary – Villiers and Iso Milano had very individual styles.

The way of working, though, was much the same. It is not readily understood because the whole working is hidden and for many years the standard textbook description of a clutch was of a single-plate dry clutch. There was no difficulty about understanding this. You could see it working. The newer clutches were hidden and when you took them apart you needed special tools, otherwise the needle roller bearings fell into the crankcase or the springs flew out all over the place. People tended to leave the clutch alone and mutter something about it all being done by friction.

The clutch is driven from the crankshaft. The latter carries a sprocket of, say, twenty teeth and a roller chain from it drives the clutch sprocket of, say, forty-three teeth. The clutch housing is fitted to this sprocket and looks like a very solid round tin lid with slots cut in the rim. The clutch plates with friction strips have projections on their outside diameter which fit these slots.

The other set of clutch plates are of smaller size and have smooth rims. They have their centres removed and the inner diameter is slotted to fit the clutch hub, internal bell or whatever you call it. There are other discs, flanges, plates, etc., according to machine, but in addition there is a set of springs and an operating lever so that you can compress or release the assembly which is mounted about a common centre.

You thus have two units which can revolve independently. The clutch sprocket is chain driven from the crankshaft. The friction plates are slotted inside the housing and are carried round with it. That is one unit. You also have the dished steel plates sandwiched between the friction plates and carried on the slotted clutch hub. That is the second unit and until all these plates are pressed together the housing and the friction plates can revolve alone.

The clutch hub is machined very accurately. It has a splined centre and fits on the gearbox mainshaft. When your machine is at rest but with engine running the whole clutch unit will be revolving and so will the mainshaft. The parts that are turning will be crankshaft, clutch housing, all the plates,

Track events were organised at most of the British racing circuits. Here is a Rumi fighting for the lead with a Lambretta at Cadwell Park.

A feature of the popular Isle of Man Scooter Rally was the introduction of sidecar racing for scooter outfits over a course marked by straw bales in Nobles Park.

The British-made Velocette Viceroy scooter. Made by the famous motor cycle firm of the same name it was heavy and extremely powerful.

the clutch hub and the mainshaft with all the gears carried on the latter. However, none of the gears will be engaged, so no power will be transmitted to the rear wheel.

This is the normal thing. The clutch plates are normally all pressed together. When you start the engine you turn them all and you also spin the mainshaft with them. If you now declutch by pressing the clutch lever the pairs of plates will separate. The mainshaft with its gears, the clutch centre, and the dished plates will cease to revolve. The only parts revolving will be:

> Crankshaft
> Clutch housing
> Friction clutch plates

You will now see why some people declutch when they use an electric starter. This was long known as a useful way of reducing the load when starting a car for it means the starter has to turn over less weight of material. If the engine is very cold, if you have left the machine out one frosty night, the oil in which the clutch plates rest may not be as easy-flowing as it ought to be, especially if you have the wrong oil in. You will then materially reduce the load if you declutch. Owners of scooters with electric starters will benefit more from this advice than those who have huge funds of energy from which to draw additional kicks.

You are often warned, by mechanics or by writers of instruction books, not to declutch for longer than is necessary. You are particularly warned by them not to declutch while waiting at traffic lights or behind other traffic. The warning is sound advice, but it is often disregarded because the advice is given without any reasonable explanation. The correct reason is rarely given, either because the instructor does not know or the manufacturer hates to admit that any of his

G

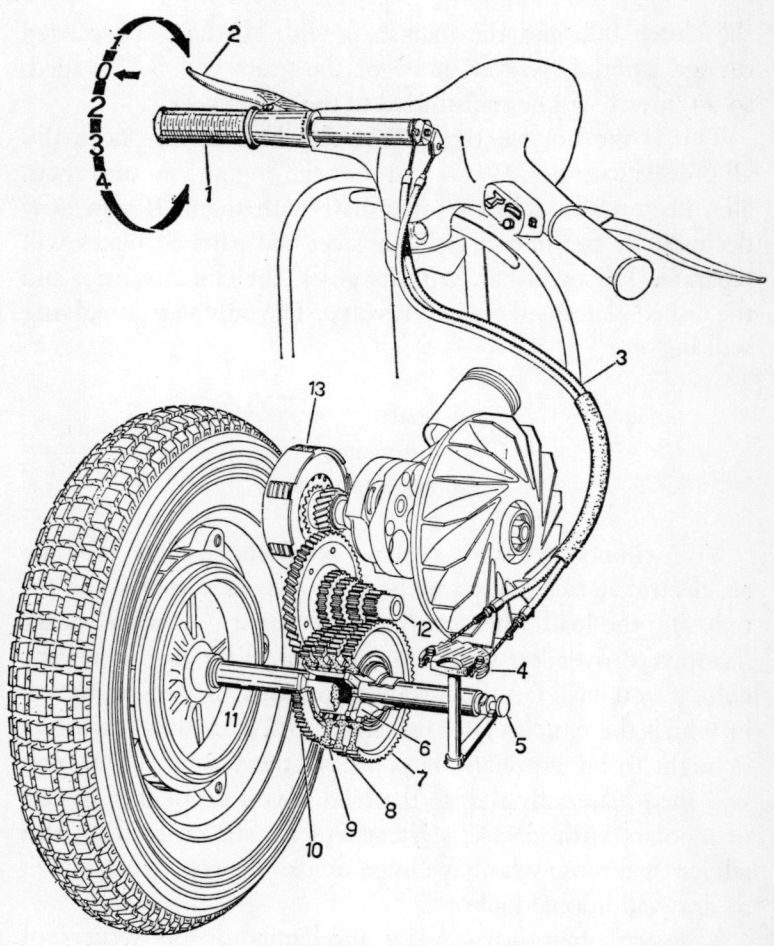

4. General arrangement of clutch, gears and gearchange controls on the Vespa. Parts are numbered as follows:

1 Gearchange twistgrip **2** Clutch control lever **3** Gearchange cables **4** Gear shifter **5** Selector stem **6** Selector spider **7, 8, 9** and **10** Gear pinions **11** Mainshaft **12** Spring gear **13** Clutch components is less than perfect. The average multi-plate clutch is far from perfect, though it gives almost no trouble in use.

The correct explanation is simple and there is no reason to hide it. When the plates are pressed together the clutch and mainshaft constitute a nice solid unit, revolving on bearings and generally behaving itself. The moment the clutch plates separate the clutch housing continues to revolve at a fair speed but it is then an unbalanced unit with three or four loosely fixed friction plates, etc., revolving with it. This is not the kind of service for which any ball bearing was designed and the danger is that the unbalanced load will destroy the bearing. You are warned that although the cost of a new bearing is not great you will have to remove the clutch unit complete – and on some scooters remove a good deal more – to get at the bearing. Even the kindest service stations will present a hefty bill for doing this.

We have not described any particular clutch in detail as there are so many different types. The force necessary to overcome the spring pressure holding the plates together is transmitted through a Bowden cable connected to the handlebar clutch lever. There is almost nothing to go wrong with it except that, if badly adjusted, the plates will either not separate completely – or they will not hold together. About the only things that can go wrong are:

1. The plates do not separate completely; you get noisy gear changes, since the mainshaft is always being driven, even when you declutch.

2. The plates do not hold together; then when you accelerate suddenly, or put an extra hill-load, on the plates will slide against each other continuously. You will notice a loss of power at the rear wheel, and ominous smelly smoke from the burning-out clutch.

Provided you keep the adjustment correct – see your instruction book – neither of these will happen and the clutch will last for years. If you have bought a secondhand scooter you should check the clutch, not only to see that it works properly, but to find out whether the previous owner has modified it for sports events. He may have fitted more powerful springs, having found that with the extra power from the engine the standard springs allow the clutch to slip. In some engines it is possible to fit an extra clutch plate. When servicing the clutch – or having others do this job – you should know beforehand what changes have been made.

9 Suspension Systems

The scooter framework is a rigid structure. Certain components are attached to it but have freedom to move relative to the frame, the movement varying according to load, speed and road surface. At an early stage the designer has to settle what proportion will be carried on the framework and what proportion will be allowed this relative movement. For instance, the front wheel must be carried on the suspension system and you might add most of the front fork, as was done in the TWN Tessy; or you might carry most of the front fork on the frame, as in the James and Velocette – and in most others.

Moving further back, he has to decide about the engine. Should it be anchored rigidly to the frame? BSA did that. Should it be anchored to the rear wheel? Vespa did that.

There are many variations within these two broad systems and as there are so many variations perhaps none of them is the ideal, but all work reasonably well. For the front wheel the variations are:

Leading link. Here the pivot is behind the wheel centre. This solution is usual with mopeds and light scooters. It was used in the BSA Dandy (70cc) and the Sun Geni (98cc) but is not usual on big machines. However, it was used in the Rumi Formichino, which was a speedy, sporting machine.

Trailing link. The best-known examples are the Vespa and Lambretta. Here the pivot point is forward of the wheel centre.

These two systems are uncomplicated and they are satis-

197

factory for medium speeds and loads. They are not used for heavy machines, and British manufacturers have never been keen on either since the telescopic fork was adopted, though on a well-known motor cycle – the BSA Ariel two-stroke – an ingenious trailing link front fork was used. NSU originally used a leading link system on their Prima D but abandoned it. In their TV.175 Lambretta kept to their trailing link but added an external helical spring in much the same way that Gerard Daric did when he raced a 125cc Lambretta at Montlhery. This may be taken as a sign that the original front suspension needed assistance at high speeds. Road shocks are absorbed by coil springs but if the springs are made from small diameter wire (soft suspension) there is a comparatively large movement up and down of the frame relative to the wheel. This dipping of the frame above the front wheel was a prominent feature of the first scooters and caused much amusement among motor cyclists accustomed to very firm and stiff front suspension.

A third system has the front wheel centre at the corner of a triangle. The steering-head is continued in a curve to a point level with the front hub. From this point a pivoted arm goes to the wheel centre and the triangle is completed by a third arm carrying a hydraulic damper between the steering-head and the wheel centre. In practice the wheel centre is rarely used, the junction being just behind it. The two extremes were the James, where the point was moved far back, and the Jawa Manet, where the point coincided (or very nearly) with the wheel centre. The DKR, the Diana, the Puch, etc., came somewhere between these two extremes. This continues to be a popular system, giving medium-hard springing. It was used on some fast scooters such as the DKR Manx. It requires little maintenance. Neither Vespa not Lambretta have used it.

The fourth system is by telescopic forks. With one peculiar exception this was used only on the bigger machines, machines used for high speeds, usually by firms with a strong motorcycle tradition. The straight line of the steering-head is continued to the hub centre and along this line a pair of telescopic tubes fit closely one inside the other, with powerful springs inside. The tubes are partly filled with oil to damp the spring vibrations. Telescopics are fitted in pairs, as forks.

This system has been taken direct from high-speed motor cycling but with the important modification that the telescopic tubes are not carried so close to the handlebars. The twin telescopics going straight-lined to the handlebars are always seen on the more powerful machines. Where this system was adapted to scooters the twin tubes were shorter and combined into a single steering column just above the front wheel.

We mentioned a single exception to the rule that twin telescopics were confined to the bigger machines. It was strange to find it on the 74cc Concorde. Perhaps the explanation was that this was made by the DKW concern originally. We should also mention the Puch scooters, where twin telescopics were used through the whole range, right down to the 50cc models.

In these various suspension systems we have ignored the possibility of using a fork instead of an arm. The Vespa has a trailing-link arm. The Lambretta has a trailing-link fork. Except for the telescopics, the other systems may be used either way. Nobody has yet built a scooter with a single telescopic damper on an arm and it is unlikely that such a system will be introduced.

Bearing in mind the influence of front-wheel suspension on road holding and cornering at speed it is remarkable that there should be so many different systems. It was even more surprising to note that one or two makers (such as NSU and Zundapp) should have begun on one system and then switched to another for machines of the same capacity and, roughly speaking, of the same speed.

If the variations in front-wheel suspension are many, what can we say about the rear suspension? We can set out the main types diagramatically:

1. The engine, transmission and rear wheel form a single unit, pivoting about a point above the engine. This is normal with shaft drives but can also be used in chain drives having a solid chaincase.

2. The engine is bolted into the chassis. The rear wheel is mounted on a solid arm which pivots about a point coinciding with the centre of the driver sprocket. Hence the chain centres remain constant.

3. As in 2, but the pivot point is distant from the centre of the driver sprocket and so the chain centres vary with load and acceleration.

Rather confusingly the rear suspension is sometimes described as swinging arm or pivoting arm (or fork) regardless of what swings or pivots. Indeed, swinging-arm suspension has become a general term which has lost some of its original meaning.

With Lambretta, Vespa, NSU, Iso Milano – and most of the original scooter makers – the engine and rear wheel were built as a unit and moved together. With British scooters the rear wheel alone was sprung without the engine, whether by an arm or in a fork. One or two powerful telescopic dampers are anchored firmly to arm and frame. This is a difference in principle. It is easy to say that the first type was suitable only for small machines, and this was often said, but it was used with great success in the bigger scooters up to the BSA 250cc twin.

The overwhelming advantage of the first system – with engine and rear wheel built as one unit – is that it limits the size of engine used. This may not seem to be much of an advantage, and a designer working for a firm with a wide range of big engines waiting for employment would consider it a great nuisance, so the decision by BSA to use it in their 250 twin scooter was most unusual.

A second advantage is that such scooters have a very pleasing appearance. The engine is tucked away. There is a lot of space. The panelling is streamlined.

A third advantage is that the designer of such a machine has a challenging assignment. He must often resort to original thought.

Is there much in this argument? Does the scooter owner get anything out of it? Does design really matter? Well, two solid benefits have already been obtained:

1. A clean machine.
2. Easy wheel changing.

Had the Vespa and Lambretta started out with rear forks it is doubtful that these advantages would have been obtained on any scooters. Not every scooter has an easily detachable rear wheel, but BSA and Bond pioneered it in their scooters and others may follow, whether with motor cycles or scooters. It would be an advance.

An early attempt at torsion bar suspension was made by Lambretta and NSU. This was very interesting but was soon dropped. Instead of springs a bar of high tensile steel was used. One end was firmly gripped in the frame. The other end was fixed into the unit carrying the whole load of engine, transmission and rear wheel. Swing motion was absorbed by the torsion bar and a very satisfactory suspension system was obtained. Unfortunately, special tools and knowledge were required for its proper maintenance. Also, the original design was not adequate and it was supplemented in later models by a conventional sealed damper. It seems unlikely that this experiment will be repeated, especially on any of the larger scooters.

A very unusual variation was adopted on the Moby. In its front suspension Neiman rubber bands were used instead of conventional coil springs and, though many critics scoffed, the system worked splendidly. In the rear suspension rubber was used again. There was a single unit consisting of two Evigdon rubber blocks, one somewhat softer than the other. This system was used by Moby for many years, but its example has not been followed by others.

Even more unusual was the Peugeot rear suspension. Here a system of tie rods led from the rear wheel underneath the machine to the front of the footboard. A set of Neiman rubbers was anchored under the footboard with a turnbuckle to the chaincase which also carried the rear wheel. The unit pivoted on a steel shaft through the chaincase mounted in cams. An unfortunate feature of this system was that the suspension had to be slackened off when the chain was being tensioned – and it then had to be reset. Again, this worked well but the example was not followed by other manufacturers here or abroad. It must also be said that the Peugeot suspension unit picked up a colossal amount of dirt and mud from the road, and this required regular cleaning out – not a pleasant job.

The most popular, reliable and effective system depends on helical coil springs. There is an important relation between the thickness of the wire used and the inside diameter of these springs, and as this proportion falls within fairly close limits the rear springs of all scooters tend to look much alike. Where there is a chain drive it is important to limit the vertical movement in the interests of long life for the chain and sprockets. The springs may therefore be tapered top and bottom, may have sections with different numbers of coils per inch, may be assisted by an internal cylinder and plunger. The object is to give a different rate of deflection as the load increases.

With such a unit the springing will be relatively soft under normal loading and at normal speed. Above that point the proportional vertical movement of the rear wheel will be reduced. The springing will become harder, otherwise there would be too great a movement up and down by the frame relative to the rear wheel.

These open-coil springs require no servicing. The ends are usually fitted with a bush, of synthetic rubber or similar. On some scooters, however, the rear suspension consists of a sealed unit which not only does not require servicing by the owner, but definitely must not be tackled by him. If servicing is required the complete unit should be removed and handed in to the service station, which will provide a fresh one, not necessarily new, but on a service exchange basis.

10 The Carburetter

Carburetters and ball-taps alike do a lot of good work unseen. They are among the most reliable of gadgets. Nevertheless, if anything goes wrong with a scooter, the owner first of all tackles the plug. If that does no good, he blames the carburetter.

Although the engine runs on fuel the power ultimately depends on the amount of air which can be pushed into the combustion chamber per minute. The proportion of air to fuel with which the average engine will be satisfied varies between nine and twenty to one. For petroil engines between thirteen and fifteen to one is best. The considerable weight (and the ratio refers to weights, not volumes) of air must be passed through the engine and burned efficiently, and it is on the efficiency of this burning that the engine's power largely depends.

Does this seem strange? However much air there is in the cylinder it is clear that adding enough fuel is simple; you could do that by fitting a larger jet. But it is useless to add more fuel unless there is sufficient oxygen present for its combustion. In the early days the golden rules of engine design were:

1. High piston speed.
2. Clear passages.
3. Low mixture temperature.

On the first point designers were in some difficulty, for although they got increased power with the higher piston speeds they got greater mechanical efficiency with the lower piston speeds. Also, manufacturing cost increased with the higher speeds and so designers had to compromise – a process which continues today.

The mixture of fuel and air is a thorough mixture, evenly graded, where every particle of fuel has its attendant fifteen particles of air. This 15:1 is the correct proportion but it does not give the greatest efficiency because some of the oxygen may not be burned in the combustion chamber. In practice a mixture with 10 or 15 percent more fuel (say 13:1) will give best results.

If you weaken the mixture, power will fall rapidly. With a 20:1 mixture – which is very weak indeed – you will get popping back through the carburetter. The flame-spread with these weak mixtures is so slow that combustion will continue the whole power stroke. This is not a good idea. The flame-spread should, in good practice, be over when the piston is four-fifths of its way down. The last fifth of its travel is taken up by clearing the exhaust gases through the port which is now opening and the flame-spread should have finished before this starts. If the gases are still burning when the inlet port is uncovered the incoming mixture will be ignited. If this happens on a four-stroke you will get a magnificent display of flame and smoke from the carburetter, which can be dangerous. On a two-stroke this is highly unlikely (though just possible) and what is more likely to happen is the familiar popping back in the carburetter – the pressure inside the crankcase will have been increased and will be relieved by a puffing explosion in the carburetter. A weak mixture like this may be caused by fitting an incorrect size of jet, by a partially blocked jet or by an air leak. With weak mixtures, therefore, a greater ignition advance will be necessary than for the correct or slightly rich mixture because of this slow rate of flame spread.

The basis of modern carburetters is the venturi tube. This was not always so. In the first internal combustion engines

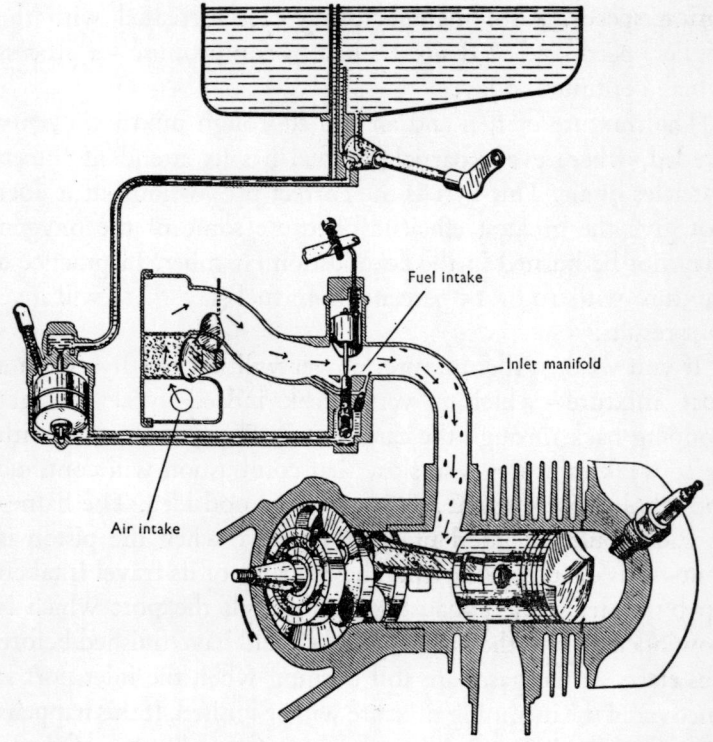

Fuel intake

Inlet manifold

Air intake

5. In the earlier Vespas the carburetter was arranged as shown, and there was a fairly lengthy inlet manifold.

there was no venturi tube. You had what was really a pot of petrol. You fed air down a tube and across the surface to pick up petrol and this pretty rough mixture was fed into the engine. You made things easier by heating the petrol – which then evaporated more quickly – but the amount of petrol picked up by the air stream could not be controlled accurately. For instance, you would get too rich a mixture when the engine was warmed up and running at top speed, but starting would be a bit tricky. However, it worked in a way, though it was

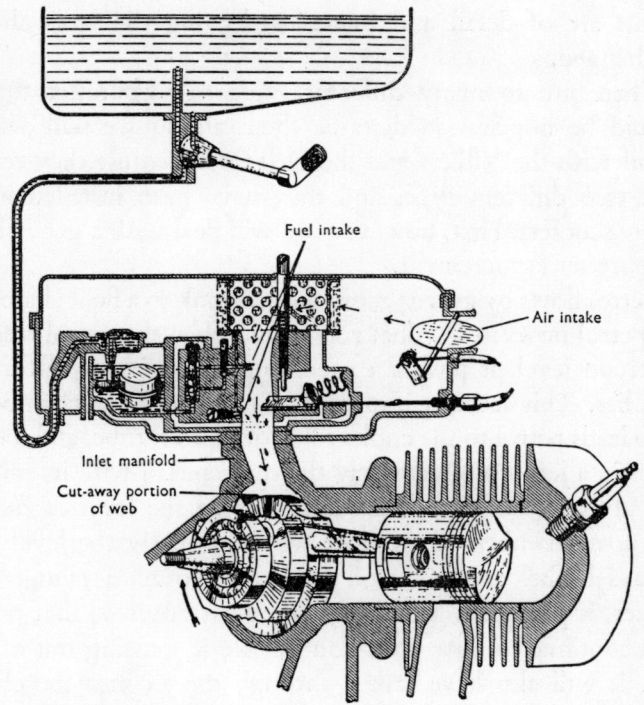

Fuel intake

Air intake

Inlet manifold

Cut-away portion
of web

6. In the later 125cc and 150 cc Vespas the carburetter was placed on the crankcase above one of the crank webs, a portion of which was ground away to admit the mixture, thus acting as a rotary valve. Only 2% of oil was needed in the mixture. The inlet manifold length was reduced. On the big 180cc Vespa the length was reduced even further.

soon abandoned in favour of the float chamber, jet and venturi tube which is the basis of scooter carburation. The basis has not been changed by the introduction of the 2% petroil engine, the rotary valve of Vespa nor by the various automatic mixing devices of various makers, both Italian and Japanese – although these are important advances they are advanced in mechanical details only. Again, the so-called needle-less carburetter is more compact and in some ways more adaptable but the improvements are of detail and materials, leaving the basis almost unchanged.

There are so many different types of carburetter that it would be hopeless to describe them all, so we will deal in detail with the Villiers and the Dell'Orto because they represent two different types and they have been installed in so many scooters. First, however, we will deal with a generalised carburetter arrangement.

Petrol flows by gravity from the fuel tank to a float chamber. As petrol flows in the float rises until, when the petrol reaches a certain level, it pushes a needle up and so cuts off further supplies. This level is important. From the float chamber a tube leads petrol to the choke tube, or venturi tube, and terminates in a jet (more accurately the centrepiece) with its surface just above a horizontal line drawn from the level of fuel in the float chamber. If the float works properly the level will always be below the tip of the jet, but often a plunger, or tickler, is provided. This pushes the float down so that petrol will continue to flow until you can see it spurting out of the top. It will also have leaked through the jet into the choke tube. This is known as flooding the carburetter and is a practice so hated by the manufacturers that some of them have removed the tickler. With such carburetters you cannot do any flooding. What is more awkward, you cannot tell whether fuel is reaching the float chamber. On some Dell'Orto models this is made of transparent plastic, a practice which might well be more widely adopted.

Left to itself with this arrangement the fuel would never flow. The jet, however, is placed in the air inlet at a point where this narrows and so constitutes a venturi. Another word for it is a choke tube. When air is passed down such a tube the air velocity at the narrow part increases and the pressure decreases. Since the fuel in the float chamber is at atmospheric pressure the petrol is forced out of the jet and into the air stream. The result is a thorough mixture of fuel droplets and air, ready to go through the inlet manifold into the crank-case and from there to the cylinder.

The venturi effect is best known in its application to the standard scent spray but it is also used on a big scale – for instance in some of the experimental wind-driven generators built in Scotland. In the old type of windmills and in the familiar wind-driven water pumps the air blows on vanes or sails tilted at an angle. The new type have hollow arms. One end is open to the air. The other end terminates within a vertical hollow structure containing the rotor which drives the generator. As the wind rushes across the open ends of the arms a terrific blast of air is drawn up the vertical tube and so drives the rotor.

The mixture you need for starting from cold is one thing; the mixture for high-speed running is a second; the mixture for ticking over at traffic lights may be different again. Various ingenuities are built into the carburetter to take care of these, but they are secondary – the engine would run without them. It would not run without the jet and the choke tube, the float and chamber or the fuel supply – these are the fundamentals.

Carburetters were originally made with the choke tube horizontal. The air travelled along a horizontal path through the carburetter. In some engines this was an awkward arrange-ment because the carburetter is a bulky article and to accommodate it the inlet manifold had to be bent through a right angle or perhaps had to be longer than the designer thought it should be for best results. As we shall see later, a short straight inlet manifold gives greater economy and snappier acceleration. This type is known as a horizontal carburetter. Examples are the Villiers S.19 as used on the DKR Dove and the Dell'Orto T.A.18.D used on the Vespa 150cc scooters in 1955.

There are manufacturers who prefer to arrange for a vertical airflow. This also means a vertical mixture flow. The float chamber is then parallel to the choke tube. The jet projects horizontally. The arguments are highly technical and since Vespa went over to vertical (down-draught) carburetters with their Sportique, but Lambretta stuck to their horizontals even with the sporty Vega 75cc, there is probably something to be said on both sides. Down-draught carburetters permit of very short inlet manifolds, they take advantage of the inertia of the mixture, they are very compactly made. It is perhaps significant that many of the later Dell'Orto carburetters were down-draught and with the Vespa it was possible to tuck the unit away very neatly which gave better silencing – since so much noise comes from the air intake – and a better chance of feeding cool air. On the other hand, the down-draughts used by Lambretta had advantages when the scooters were being tuned for competition work. The standard carburetter was usually discarded but there arose a great demand for the famous Amal monobloc introduced in 1965. The 30mm model became almost standard on the race circuits; so great became its reputation that the Amal monobloc was fitted to some engines for which it was highly unsuitable.

Carburetters are also made with the choke tube tilted at an angle, or even with it inverted, so that the airflow (and the mixture-flow) travels upwards. This is usually because of some awkwardness in engine design. Mention should also be made of the fuel injector. Originally used in competition motor cars this was later adapted to motor cycles and scooters, particularly for sprint work, where many records were obtained by its use. The best-known model was designed by Wal Phillips. This has been used in touring scooters, but is best suited to competition work. The adjustment calls for some skill and any one setting has a rather narrow range of engine revs and weather conditions within which it gives best results. Initially the Phillips fuel injector was available only for

Lambrettas but in 1968 a type suitable for the big Vespas was introduced and became popular. The multiple controls of the standard carburetter are missing and so adjustment is at once simpler and less flexible.

Having got the fuel and air mixed the problem is to get the right amount and the right proportion. This is done by two or more jets but there is usually a control fitted to each jet, so the number of adjustments you can make is considerable. As the jets are not labelled and as the settings are easily disturbed there is a possibility of confusion. This is made worse by the unfortunate use of the words "needle jet" to refer to something which is not, properly speaking, a jet at all. It might help if we took the jets in order.

The main jet is a genuine nozzle. It is made of brass, with a very fine hole drilled through its centre. The diameter varies from one engine to another and is identified by a reference number. For a 125cc engine a Dell'Orto jet might be No. 105 while on a Villiers S.19 it might be a No. 90 – this indicating the number of cubic centimetres of fuel such a jet would pass under standard conditions. The main jet measures the maximum amount of fuel which will be supplied to your engine. The size of the main jet does not interest the average scooterist. It is fixed by the manufacturers, who have chosen the right one. You may feel like experimenting with a different size main jet. Please do not. You may be advised to fit another. Unless the advice comes to you from the makers, or is confirmed by them, take no notice. The main jet should not be altered.

Rather confusingly, the main jet is threaded at one end and has a slot machined in the opposite face, straight across the hole. However, fit a screwdriver in the slot and screw the jet home into what Villiers call the centrepiece (Dell'Orto call it the atomiser). Then fit the washer, if provided, and finally screw home the bottom nut. You now have the fuel flowing from the feed pipe into the float chamber, through the main jet and into the atomiser. This controls the maximum amount of fuel you can spray into the choke tube. You can interrupt the flow, or reduce it, but you cannot increase it without fitting a larger main jet.

We now proceed to manufacture the so-called needle jet. The amount of air passing through the choke tube is controlled by the throttle slide which may completely block the choke tube – or leave it completely open. This is operated by the throttle cable from the handlebar and to it is attached the throttle needle. This has a number of grooves at one end so that it can be held in a clip. The needle is ground to a taper and fits down the centrepiece or atomiser. It will move up and down as you open the throttle and it may blank off a portion of the atomiser or leave it completely free. From the top end of this the fuel is sprayed into the choke tube and is carried along by the airstream into the crankcase. The amount of air which passes at any given engine speed can be varied by opening or closing the throttle but the amount of fuel sprayed out can be varied by moving the taper needle up or down in its clip. If you fit it in a higher groove you restrict the opening and so get less fuel into the same amount of air. In this way the taper needle is really a tap, not a jet.

The third jet is the pilot jet, alternatively called the slow-running jet or idling jet. This is entirely separate and its position varies from one make to another. It has an accurately drilled hole through it, identified by a reference number. It has the same kind of slot for the screwdriver. It has its own regulating device. It has its own fuel supply. It is a complete system. It comes into operation when the engine is idling or with the throttle closed.

If you have a tuned or souped-up engine or one which has been converted for competition work – or one of the British scooters – your Villiers or Amal carburetter will have a clearly written and most interesting set of instructions about the way in which these two jet systems can be varied to give richer or leaner mixtures. If you have a scooter with a Dell'Orto carburetter you may be able to get their equally informative handbook which, however, is not readily available in English.

All carburetter adjustments are made in an attempt to get the correct proportion of fuel and air into the engine. The adjustments are:

To the main jets: You can fit a bigger or smaller size. Please don't.

To the needle jet: You can raise the taper needle, giving more fuel, i.e. a richer mixture for normal running.

You can lower the taper needle, giving less fuel, i.e. a weaker mixture.

To the idler jet: By means of the adjuster screw you can admit more air, giving a weaker mixture, or you can admit less air and get a richer mixture.

On some models (but not all) you can control the amount of fuel passing through the idler jet.

To the throttle: On some models you can adjust tickover speed by means of an angled screw. This halts the throttle slide at a higher point as you turn the screw clockwise. On some machines a similar adjustment is made on the throttle-cable fixing.

There are other adjustments: you can fit a different taper needle, or a different throttle slide. You can even fit a different size choke tube . . . but these are unusual. We have mentioned the engine conversions, with a bigger cylinder capacity through fitting a bigger barrel and probably fitting a bigger carburetter, say the Amal 30mm size. Now in experienced hands this gives excellent results and you have a bigger engine all round with a bigger performance. Remember that you must preserve the balance – fuel and air taken in, the mixture efficiently burnt and the exhaust getting the waste away. Some scooterists simply bore out the barrel to take the next size bigger piston; and even bore out the choke tube. This is not really good practice. The barrel porting is calculated for a given size and is upset if you bore it out 25cc bigger; the choke tube is only one unit in the carburetter and the balance is upset if you merely increase its diameter. Choke diameters, like jet sizes, should be understood before they are altered.

All the adjustments listed above are to vary the amount or the strength of the mixture. On these depend power output, engine running temperature and efficiency – which means economy. The people who made your carburetter know a lot about the subject and it is unlikely that you will be able to make any general improvement. They have tried to give you the best overall settings. Overall is the key word there. The engine requires a different mixture for almost every speed, every load, every change in temperature and humidity in the same way that you need an infinite number of gears for every change in speed and load. This has been done with the infinitely-variable V-belt drive, so perhaps some day a carburetter may be built on the same principle.

They have not done it yet, but remember that the carburetter designers are clever people and you will rarely be able to improve on their work. Unfortunately, these adjusting screws are a great temptation. People love to fiddle with them and they also like to delude themselves that they have made some improvement. No great harm follows, but probably no improvement either.

There are people who know that you love fiddling with carburetter adjustments. They know you want to get more miles per gallon and they are prepared to sell you a gadget that can do it – cash in advance, of course. These fuel econo-misers can be numbered in their scores and the best that can be said about most of them is that they will not harm your engine. The usual claim is that the gadget will overcome some particular deficiency in the carburetter mixture control. During the Suez crisis when petrol was rationed dozens of different devices were introduced and they made fortunes for some people. Some of the devices were well-intentioned but some were plain deceptions, in that the gadget imposed alike on inventor and customer. Some of the gadgets were so expensive that it would have been an economy to discard them.

Fuel economy depends very, very largely on your style of driving and on having the correct carburetter settings. You will always get more miles per gallon if you change speed more gradually. This is a real saving. You can try a smaller jet – main jet, that is – and this may possibly be a real saving. You can run on a weaker mixture but this may in the long run not be a saving at all.

In truth, the average fuel economiser is based on a misunderstanding about carburation principles. The commonest delusion is that your engine gets the same dense mixture at high and at low speeds. Therefore, says the gadgeteer, weaken the mixture at high speeds and you must save fuel. There is little substance in this for it assumes that the mixture charge varies in volume, whereas it actually varies in weight. At high speeds on level roads, with no appreciable change in loading, what you want is not a weaker mixture but a higher gear. That really would save fuel. However, that extra gear would be so high that if you were slowed by traffic in the slightest degree you would have to change to a lower gear – the high gear would give you almost no pulling power.

That really takes care of the carburetter's first duty, which is to measure the amount of fuel fed to the engine. Your main jet sets you the maximum; the taper needle decides what proportion of the maximum gets through at fairly low running speeds.

The second duty is to atomise the fuel. In the very early internal combustion engines the petrol was vaporised. Today we concentrate on atomising, to get a uniform mixture. The fuel does evaporate, of course, mostly in the induction pipe. In doing so it takes heat from the air and from the surrounding metal and in early motor cycles this sometimes gave trouble. The inlet manifold was fairly long and was not heated, so that in certain conditions of temperature and humidity thick frost would form on this pipe even when the engine was running, a disturbing sight until you got used to it. As the engine warmed up heat would spread to the manifold and the frost would disappear, but you can easily imagine an engine in which the manifold would stay cold. The frost would accumulate and might even block the air inlet in time. This phenomenon caused a lot of trouble in aeroplane engines, especially in moisture-laden air at fairly low temperatures.

In modern scooter carburetters – whether with or without the needle jet – evaporation can be ignored. It is the atomising which is important and this is done by the centrepiece. The fuel emerges from this in a fine spray into the choke tube and there it is thoroughly mixed with the air passing through. In theory the mixture should be of uniform density, every cubic inch having the same number of particles of fuel. In practice the mixture consistes of a central core of vapour surrounded by layers of air and fuel particles in suspension. Each successive layer, as you move out from the centre, is richer in fuel – and so moves more slowly. The layer lining the induction manifold is, at full throttle openings, richest of all; it is practically a layer of liquid and moves slowest of all.

Reference has been made to the airflow through the choke tube and the way in which this behaves in the venturi. This airflow is only possible if there is a difference in pressure between two connected systems – in the two-stroke engine the systems are the atmosphere and the crankcase. Not much pressure can be built up in the latter. The volume of mixture burnt at each power stroke does not vary (since the piston displacement does not vary) but its weight can vary – it could contain more fuel and more air if the speed of the airflow could be increased and if this increased volume of mixture could be compressed into the space available in the cylinder – which is the engine capacity, 125cc, 175cc or whatever the rating is.

This is a tempting line of thought and many inventors have followed it. They have tried various dodges for compressing the mixture in the crankcase so that a greater weight could be packed into the cylinder. These compressors have a long history, and started with a separate piston and cylinder between the carburetter and the crankcase but the complications outweighed the advantages. A promising line of thought which has not been followed strenuously aims at reducing the crankcase volume after the mixture has been admitted to it – it is surprising that this has not attracted more attention for it is merely a mechanical problem, not particularly difficult. Instead more attention has been given to reducing the crankcase volume; naturally the less the volume the greater the compression. The reduction is popular with competition riders and is known as padding the crankcase – usually by filling the balance holes in the crank webs with cork or some equally light material, though some riders reduce the volume by filling the underside of the piston, a solution which has raised many problems of overheating. A further system is the use of an actual compressor or supercharger but as these were forbidden in motor cycle racing their use has never become popular. These are really fans for blowing the mixture into the cylinder at higher than normal speed. Particularly with two-stroke engines the mixture enters the cylinder at a relatively low speed and it is this which, more than anything, limits the power which can be developed. It may be deduced from the multiplicity of these devices that there is some inherent defect in the carburetter, in the whole idea of using such an instrument. This is probably so, that even the best carburetter is a poor instrument. Since 1960 there has been a steady trend towards fuel injection of one kind or another on the part of motor car makers. It is a significant trend. For the two-stroke owner the sluggish airflow is a handicap inseparable from the carburetter.

Do not imagine the airflow as continuous or even. When the engine is turning over at 5,000rpm the inlet port is being opened – and shut – 5,000 times every minute, and the airflow starts and stops that number of times. You can picture the result. The mixture acquires a vibration, the period depending on the engine speed and its own mass. It is this vibration which accounts for much of the noise in a badly designed engine, for a great deal of engine roar comes from the carburetter. If you wish to silence an engine, therefore, you must attend to the induction as well as to the exhaust – though on one famous engine almost as much noise came from a vibrating crankshaft. To get some idea of the problems, work out the speed at which the air is rushing through the air inlet.

You will also get some idea of the uncertainties which surround carburation. You have the piston's pump action causing rapid vibrations – and therefore fluctuations of pressure – in the mixture. You have the mixture which did not even start off with uniform density – there being more fuel in it the nearer you get to the side of the choke tube. Add to these the fact that under pressure some of the fuel is precipitated; there are some confusing variables to be taken into account. No wonder the average scooterist swallows the fuel economiser's arguments.

The amount of air picked up will vary according to the speed of the airflow through the choke tube. The faster the air travels the more fuel will be picked up. However, the proportion of fuel will not vary. If it is one-thirteenth at 20mph it will be one-thirteenth at 50mph; the exact proportion will depend on the manufacturer who chooses a jet of that particular size. Opening the throttle does not vary the strength of the mixture – this is basic to the venturi effect. Where the choke tube is narrowed the speed of the air increases, causing a reduced pressure just there. The pressure reduction depends on the air speed and since the fuel is pushed out of the centrepiece under uniform pressure (pressure of the atmosphere) the amount of fuel pushed out into the choke tube varies inversely with the pressure drop. It is no use opening the throttle quickly in the hope of catching the venturi asleep. However, if a taper needle is fitted you have in that device what is really an infinitely variable jet, so though the venturi effect is not disturbed the mixture strength does vary most of the time. The absence of a taper needle in some carburetters is another sign that makers do not want scooterists to be able to make adjustments.

If you do open your throttle suddenly you may also get a weaker mixture. Many riders have suddenly opened the throttle and found, to their dismay, that the engine has almost stalled. Certainly it has faltered – and then picked up. The cause is interesting. A certain amount of mixture is always waiting to enter the crankcase. This has passed the jet and its density is already settled. When you open the throttle suddenly you increase the pressure on the fresh mixture and this increased pressure will be communicated to the waiting mixture so that some of its fuel will actually be precipitated, much as you squeeze water from a sponge. Having lost some of its fuel that portion of mixture will be weaker and the engine, instead of picking up immediately, will falter. Some engines are more lively, respond more quickly, than others. Some have this lag in pick-up in a pronounced way. It is often explained that this is due to the engine getting (for a moment) too rich a mixture, but the opposite is the case. An overlong inlet manifold is a major cause of this trouble.

The throttle is very accurate and highly developed, far

removed from the metal disc revolving on a spindle that was fitted at one time. It is now almost totally enclosed, machined to close tolerances, sliding in an equally well-made chamber. Its shape is not of importance to the average scooterist since the throttle slide fitted as standard is the best all-round solution to the problem. Each slide has a reference number and a slide with a different number will give different results – a point to check if you have to fit a replace slide. The lower edge is shaped. Villiers reference numbers indicate the amount of cutaway in sixteenths of an inch. Amal give an arbitrary number – 2, 3, 4 and so on.

As this slide is raised more air can pass through the choke tube and therefore more fuel can be fed to the engine. It is not quite true to say that the proportion of fuel to air does not change as the throttle is opened. The rates of flow of fuel and air do not vary exactly at all speeds and there is a tendency for the engine to get a richer mixture at high speeds. In this case there is usually an additional compensator air jet fitted to admit extra air to the mixture, but this need not concern the scooterist, on whose engine this effect is neglible.

A point which will at once occur to the reader is that since the choke tube is circular in section the amount of air admitted will not vary exactly with throttle openings. A quarter-inch rise in the slide will give a bigger change at half-throttle than at nearly wide-open throttle.

Another point is that although we talk of throttle openings the throttle slide is not the only control – on those fitted with a needle jet – except for the range between three-quarters to fully-open. Up to three-quarters open the main control is the taper needle, governing the fuel flow.

When the engine is running on its pilot jet you have, on some models, only one adjustment – a screw which admits more or less air and thus acts as a kind of second throttle slide. On other carburetters there are two adjustments – you can regulate the flow of fuel and you can also regulate the amount of air. During this period the main jet is out of action and your machine will be ticking over waiting for you to move off. You can waste a lot of fuel if the engine is running too quickly on the pilot jet. As you will have gathered, the pilot jet on the Dell'Orto is given great importance and their instructions for adjustment are lengthy and very clear.

The amount of fuel admitted through the pilot jet should first be adjusted; if the screw has to admit full flow through the jet to get a reasonable tickover speed, a bigger pilot jet should be fitted. Then the air screw should be adjusted to give the correct mixture; a racing engine means too rich a mixture. These two adjustments should be balanced one against the other. On the Dell'Orto needle-less models the possible adjustment was reduced and there have been murmurs that this gives an inflexibility and also a less economical use of fuel.

Your own carburetter may not have both these control screws – or you may have both plus a third – but the principle is the same. Although the tendency is to cut down the number of possible adjustments, Amal in particular adhere to the older system and it is significant that in competition work, where accurate carburation is vital, most riders in the top brackets find the standard carburetter inadequate, and try the Amal – or a true fuel injector.

For the second range of openings, from one-eighth to one-quarter, the control is by means of the bevel or cutaway on the lower edge of the throttle slide. You are not likely to fit a different slide, except by accident. The cutaway has been carefully chosen for your machine. With the Series II Lambrettas, using needle-less Dell'Orto, the same carburetter was fitted to different capacities, and it was possible to fit the wrong slide. With all two-strokes, you are dealing with quite low air-speeds and by altering the cutaway slightly you will be able to make a significant change in the mixture.

For the third range of openings, from one-quarter to three-quarters, the amount of fuel in the mixture will be governed by the taper needle, where this is fitted. By raising or lowering this in the holder you can get a weaker or richer mixture. It is important to note that this taper needle upsets the normal working of the venturi effect, insofar as more or less fuel can be mixed with the same amount of air. If you are not satisfied with the range of adjustments in the taper needle you can fit a needle with a different taper, but this is a drastic change and you are advised against it. These remarks do not apply to carburetters like the Dell'Orto SHI and SHB.

For the fourth range of openings, from three-quarters to full throttle, the venturi effect takes over. The amount of fuel mixed with the air is controlled entirely by the main jet diameter. The only adjustment you can make here is to fit a different size main jet.

There are many other variations in carburetters. For use when starting there is the choke, which cuts off the air supply and so gives an exceedingly rich mixture. This is normally operated from a separate control. You are very properly warned that the choke must be disengaged when the engine has warmed up. In practice this means that you should not run with the choke out. On some machines the choke control is linked with the throttle twistgrip. As soon as you open the throttle the choke is disengaged. On one unfortunate machine quite the opposite happened; you pulled out the choke control to start and pushed it back when the engine was running nicely but as the engine was running the vibration caused the choke lever to move to the closed position, leaving you to wonder why the engine misfired and the plug fouled, to say nothing of the ghastly fuel consumption. On the Puch the air inlet was through the louvred door at the side, which contained the air filter and a rubber sleeve which fitted against a flange on the carburetter. Here the choke control was a knob which

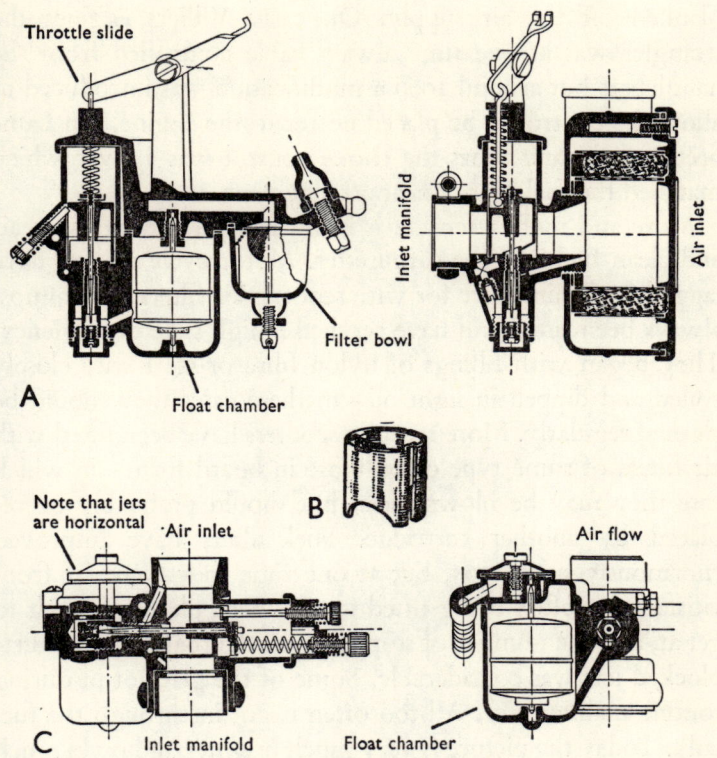

Throttle slide

Inlet manifold

Air inlet

Filter bowl

A

Float chamber

Note that jets are horizontal

Air inlet

B

Air flow

C

Inlet manifold

Float chamber

7. A shows a typical and widely used horizontal carburetter – the Dell'Orto type used in Lambrettas. It is unusual in that there is a transparent filter bowl held by a spring clip, which made cleaning simple. In horizontal carburetters the choke tube (and hence the airflow) is horizontal. In the right-hand sketch above the air filter is in place.

B is a view of a throttle slide showing, on its lower edge, the cutaway. This cutaway controls the amount of mixture passing through to the engine when the throttle is closed.

C shows two views of a Dell'Orto down-draught carburetter. Here the choke tube, and hence the airflow, is vertical. The jet is placed horizontal. The float chamber is vertical. This down-draught (or vertical) carburetter takes advantage of the mixture's inertia and gives a very compact arrangement, with a short inlet manifold.

blanked off the air supply. On early Villiers engines the strangler was at one time always cable controlled from the handlebars but around 1960 a modification was introduced to allow the control to be placed nearer to the engine. On Lambrettas for many years the choke control was a lever which matched the fuel tap – a neat arrangement.

More and more attention is being paid to getting clean air and clean fuel into the carburetter. Motor cycle makers have lagged far behind here for with scooters air filters have almost always been fitted and have reached a high state of efficiency. They began with fillings of nylon fibre or steel wire closely coiled and dipped in light oil – in these cases they should be cleaned regularly. More recently scooters have been fitted with air filters of some type of cellulose in board form – in which case they may be blown clean but should preferably be replaced by another cartridge. Fuel filters have improved enormously since 1965, but at one time they were far from satisfactory, often being fitted in awkward places, difficult to get at, and the number of stoppages on the road through dirt-blocked jets was considerable. Some of the grit got in during routine maintenance. All too often it got in through the fuel tank. Today the picture is very much brighter and owes much to the introduction of the neat filters of nylon, one in the carburetter itself, one in the fuel line. These are so easy to get at and to clean that blocked jets are rare.

If the fuel is dirty and the filter damaged, dirt may easily give trouble. The jet holes are fine and easily blocked. When this happens the jet must be cleared without delay. The stock advice is not to clean jets with a needle since this might damage the jet and enlarge the hole. How this leg-pull started is shrouded in history – certainly before scooters were invented. It is unlikely that you would get a needle very far into the average jet so there is no danger of you making the hole oversize. However, you would probably do no good with it either and the traditional bristle – or a good blowing through – would do the job. Where no taper needle is fitted the effectiveness of the spray may be impaired by scratching the tip of the centrepiece, which usually has a carefully designed chamfer. Dell'Orto make a special point of mentioning this – they say you should periodically examine the centrepiece (which they call the atomiser) into which the needle fits, in case it should have been damaged. They also recommend that in case of doubt it should be taken to a service station which, say Dell'-Orto, will have means of checking the rate of flow and the efficiency of the atomiser as such. The service stations where this facility exists must be widely spaced in Britain.

If the upper face of the centrepiece is below the level of the fuel in the float chamber, fuel will leak through into the inlet manifold and from there it will drip into the crankcase or out through the air filter, depending on the way the carburetter has been fitted. In either case there would be waste of fuel and you may get badly fouled plugs which will hamper starting. You will get this leakage if you set the carburetter at an angle. Usually it should be fitted vertical, say the instruction books, and this is the advice given verbally as well. This used to be a great problem, especially as there was no index mark by which you could check the vertical setting – and also the fact that vertical on an unloaded scooter might be a considerable angle on one with pillionist and luggage. It was all the more confusing because you could not even get a good look at the carburetter. Fortunately, current models rarely raise this problem because you can fit the carburetter in only the correct position.

It will be seen that there have been vast changes in design, usually as the result of complaints from scooterists. Lambretta seems to have had continuous problems with the air intake; when it was located under the seat scooterists would stuff gloves, scarves and the rest across the inlet, blanking it off

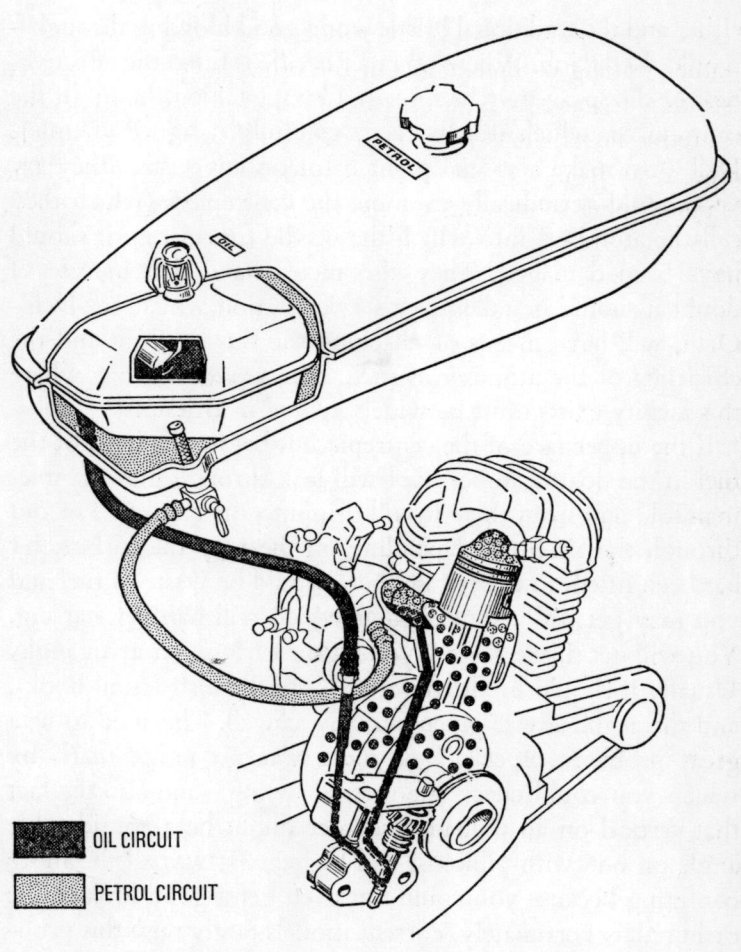

OIL CIRCUIT

PETROL CIRCUIT

8. The two-stroke engine may be fed with oil and petrol from separate tanks with a crankshaft-driven pump delivering oil direct to the inlet port as here in the Lambretta Lubematic system. The proportion of oil can be varied from 2% to 2·7% which allows for closed throttle downhill riding or stiff uphill climbs.

completely, all unawares. The rubber sleeve also gave trouble, either leaking or blocking. On the other hand Vespa moved steadily towards a highly rational solution – fitting the carburetter in its own compartment directly above the engine and away from dirt. In both cases the body is of plastic. The shut-off plug which cuts off the fuel supply when the correct level has been reached is of neoprene. The float swivels, instead of bouncing up and down.

Whatever carburetter is fitted to your scooter, it is a marvellous device, very accurate, and before you begin altering jets or slides, think several times. The ones already fitted have been chosen to give good all-round results and it is unlikely that you will make any improvement which will cover the full range of speeds. The engine is a balanced unit and the parts of the carburetter have been given as much thought as the ports, the shape of the piston or the ignition timing. If somebody suggests that you alter any of these, think twice. There are people who can tackle the job but they are usually professionals or competition riders. For instance, it is possible to get more power from your machine by raising the compression ratio. This is relatively simple – just skim the face of the cylinder head. You may then find that the piston crown overheats and soon has a neat hole in it; or you may get so much power that your main bearings crack and disintegrate.

People who tune engines usually tune them for a special purpose and to follow them blindly is wrong. What they consider to be an improvement may have a different aspect in you own engine. Perhaps they want snappy acceleration between 15 and 25mph, so they alter the carburation to suit. In so doing they may make starting difficult and idling impossible below very high engine revs. Or you might set the carburetter to give you great economy on long solo runs at 35mph but to get this result you might have to put up with poor acceleration and bumpy running in city traffic. Generally speaking these people who claim to have improved their carburation have done so only for a certain range of speeds or loads and they may have done so at the expense of other sectors of the range. The best service you can do to your carburetter is to keep it scrupulously clean. Fit a filter in the fuel line if there is not already one. Many scooter fuel tanks have no protecting lip round the filler hole. The garage attendant may, with the best will in the world, run a cloth over the top of the tank after filling and in so doing sweep dirt and grit into the tank. Get the filter in the fuel line as near the tank as possible and you will indeed be unlucky if you ever afterwards have a blocked jet.

11 Ignition and Lighting

At one time there was a sharp distinction between scooters which had good lights and those which had poor lights. This brought them into disrepute. Early models were not fitted with a battery at all and so they had no parking lights and though this did not trouble the Italians or the French it did not go down well in Britain. The engines were fitted with a flywheel magneto and when the engine stopped the current stopped. Also the current output varied with the engine speed and since the current was not at a constant voltage the headlamp brilliance fluctuated according to this speed. The headlamp bulb shone most brightly when the engine was racing in neutral but if you rode along in top gear at 25mph your headlamp on these early Italian scooters was often inadequate and many riders, when they wished to see where they were going changed to a lower gear; the increased engine revs for the same road speed meant a brighter light.

Even when a battery was fitted it was small, had little staying power and was often dead flat. After all, there is a size below which a battery – while possible – is not satisfactory. It can fairly be said that although the ignition system was first class the current supply to headlamps was little regarded and parking lights either did not exist or were served inadequately. Parking with such a scooter was a question of hoping the police had kind hearts and could imagine light where light was not.

There was, of course, no provision for the fitting of stop lights or winking indicators.

Around 1955 there began a sudden and dramatic improvement in scooter lighting systems, particularly with the Italian scooters, for it was with them that improvement was most necessary. German and Austrian scooters were usually made by firms having a long tradition in motor cycle manufacture and were fitted right from the start with good and sometimes excellent lights. In addition some other accessories such as winking indicators, stop lights, headlamp flashers were obligatory fittings and called for an electrical output almost double that on most Italian scooters. In Britain the big battery, the ample current supply was obtained along a different route – the major reason was that the manufacture of a road vehicle without effective parking lights was unthinkable. Rear-light units, coils and batteries were therefore on a bigger and more robust scale from the start and one of the early British scooters – the BSA Dandy – though having only a 70cc engine, had brilliant lights front and rear. The Dayton and Piatti, though with no motor cycle tradition behind them, were fitted with components made by firms brought up on the high standard of motor cycle equipment, and these two British scooters again had good lighting systems.

The improvements in lighting owed much to the growth of the British market for Italian scooters. There were other factors: engines became bigger and also faster; parking lights became essential fittings; those interested in road safety had an easy target in the poorly-lit scooters; the fittings of a tiny battery led to serious ignition troubles – and many other factors could be mentioned, but as motor car lights improved and the roads became brilliant with speeding vehicles at night the scooter simply had to fall in line and shine with the rest. Today scooters have good lights and, as a corollary, separate HT coils located on the frame. The earliest flywheel magneto systems had the HT and lighting coils mounted on the stator plate – not a satisfactory arrangement, especially where HT coils were wound on LT coils. Not only was the lighting improved, but the mechanics of the lights. The early scooters had the headlamp fixed rigidly to the frame but after 1955 there was a general movement in favour of streamlining the handlebars, and in the process the headlamp moved from frame to handlebars, pivoting with them and giving a much better spread of light. With the streamlining came experiments in the headlamp shape, from circular to hexagonal and a determined effort was made to fit a speedometer that could be read by night, usually built into the headlamp nacelle. However, one original handicap still remained on the majority of scooters – that if the engine cuts out, as it does when a plug whiskers, the headlamp fails completely. This can be dangerous at night. The only way round this is to have the headlamps fed from a battery, which in practice means converting the circuit to 12 volts. Vespa and Lambretta were reluctant to do this and it was left to scooterists themselves to work out a simple 12-volt conversion. Where this was done the scooters could truly claim to be equal to the growing demands of travel by night.

Electric current is needed for:
Ignition at the spark plug
Headlamp (twin-filament bulb)
Parking light (front)
Parking light (rear)
Stop light
Horn
Ignition warning light
Speedometer light
Fuel-level warning light
Winking indicators
Fog or spot light

The manner in which these are supplied with current will vary from one machine to another. In some countries, for instance, the scooterist must not use his headlamp beam in built-up areas. He will thus drive for long periods on his parking lights and if these are battery-fed provision must be made for the additional battery-charging necessary. Driving on parking lights alone has obvious dangers and an increasingly popular fitting is a blinker switch whereby the headlamp can be switched on for a moment as a warning when approaching crossroads at night. The blinker switch became popular first in Germany and became a standard motor car fitting, intended for use in town traffic where the use of the hooter was forbidden. For night travel it thus came into competition with the demand that dipped headlights should always be used. Linked with headlights was the hooter, that lamentably inadequate fitting to early scooters. The hooter was fed direct from the flywheel magneto and the resultant sound was often a miserable croak, unimpressive and almost inaudible in busy traffic. High-frequency horns which got their DC current from the battery were fitted to many scooters and were invariably fitted with the conversion to 12 volts. They obviously cannot be used where no battery is provided.

The generation of current for lighting and for ignition is done simultaneously and a single circuit is used but it will be simpler if we treat them separately. First, consider a scooter with no lighting whatever. Electric current would then be required for two things only:

1. To make a spark at the plug.
2. To sound the hooter.

To jump the spark plug gap and to make a spark in so doing you would need a high-tension (HT) current. A voltage of around 7,000 volts (7kV) will give you this current.

You can generate this voltage from the engine, but the simplest way would be to fit a battery, feed its low-tension voltage to a high-tension coil and connect the spark plug between the output side and earth. You would need a rapidly opening switch and if you timed the opening and shutting correctly you would get a spark at the plug which would fire the mixture in the combustion chamber. Your 6-volt battery, used with the HT coil, would give you more than 7,000 volts at the spark plug. This is coil ignition at its simplest and coil ignition is used on a very great majority of motor cars with internal combustion engines, though it may be accompanied by magneto ignition as a safety measure. Coil ignition is very efficient, its main requirement being a battery in good condition and with a fair charge.

The HT coil consists of two separate coils of insulated wire wound in layer fashion round a central iron core. Roughly speaking the relation between the LT voltage you put in and the HT voltage you get out depends on the relative number of windings on the two coils. This HT voltage is said to have been induced in the bigger coil and the phenomenon will be familiar to those who have experience with inductance coils. These, fed from a flashlamp battery, can be persuaded to give you a surprising but not dangerous shock. These well-named shocking coils do not require a mechanical make-and-break switch. The principle is also used in the domestic battery-operated doorbell.

It cannot be applied to the scooter engine, which requires one spark for every revolution of the crankshaft, so even in our hypothetical scooter which requires no lighting current we should have to fit a mechanically operated make-and-break switch. The simplest would be one which was cam-operated from the crankshaft and this, known as the contact breaker, is now standard with both magneto and coil ignition. The contact breaker is a special kind of switch, opening and closing once with every revolution of the crankshaft on two-stroke engines.

It is a simple system. Indeed, it is too simple. For one thing, the contact breaker gap is smaller than the gap at the spark plug. Since electricity will always take the easier, shorter path you would find the spark occurring not at the spark plug but at the contact breaker points, which would soon be burnt away. To avoid this catastrophe a condenser, which has two sets of connected plates sandwiched and insulated from each other (and serves as a kind of storage tank), must be fitted between the contact breaker points and the HT coil.

Another and more serious objection to this simple system is that the battery would soon be flat since the current was being used and not replaced. You could remove the battery and have it charged from the mains. If you did this you could afford to use a big battery, one giving a long life per charge. This kind of arrangement is not practical for two reasons: first, that if you use your scooter on public roads you must have a lighting system and this must be in working order; and second, that your battery would rapidly fail even if you kept it fully charged. Batteries intended for use on scooters must be kept charged from the scooter and not from the mains. To use a battery until it is flat and then to re-charge it from the mains damages the battery and makes the guarantee on the battery invalid. This point is not realised by all owners, for some deliberately fit a battery too large for their engine's charging capacity and charge it from the mains, not realising the harm they are doing to the battery.

You might go to the other extreme. You might decide to generate your current as you went along and dispense with batteries altogether, as was done in the earliest Vespas and Lambrettas by the very ingenious flywheel magneto. The first examples were of the utmost simplicity and they had to fulfil only the smallest demands for current. A flywheel with four magnets equally spaced round its periphery was fixed to the crankshaft and revolved with it. Two coils of wire were fitted to a fixed plate. One coil was for lighting current and the other

was for ignition current. These were spaced inside the hollow
of the flywheel but remained stationary. As the crankshft
turned the flywheel magnets revolved about these coils of wire
and so generated a current in them, the current in one coil
being used for headlamp and tail lamp, the current in the other
coil being used for ignition at the spark plug. With such a
system you can generate a certain amount of current and so
long as your engine is running you do not require a battery.
If you find the supply inadequate you can generate more current
by fitting bigger magnets and also bigger coils. We will say
here very briefly that the original flywheel magneto systems
were developed in just this manner. To take the Lambretta
scooters – in their Slimstyle range the magneto was given six
magnets as against the original four. The stator plate was
given five coils; the first two supplied current to the direct
lighting circuit; the third coil supplied current for the ignition
through the contact breaker points and a condenser; the fourth
and fifth coils supplied current through the rectifier for re-
charging the battery. Current from the battery fed the horn
and so at last the scooter has a DC horn with a piercing note.
This was still a 6-volt system but it had an 11 ah battery of
considerable capacity and it could with little difficulty be
converted to the 12-volt system with headlights fed from the
two batteries.

The disadvantages of the earliest systems rapidly became
intolerable. With coil ignition you will get a good spark as long
as your battery is in good order. True, the HT current produced depends also on the speed with which the contact breaker
points open but this is a minor matter and the current does not
depend on the speed at which you turn the engine over; an
average push at the kickstart pedal is enough.

With magneto ignition the HT voltage depends directly on
the flywheel speed. This follows because with this system you
are turning physical energy into electric current; the more

energy exerted the more current is produced. You need a current of at least 7,000 volts to get a spark (and one designer spoke, in an unguarded moment, of his engine preferring 10,000 volts though this is on the high side) and to produce this 7,000 volts you need a crankshaft speed of around 200rpm. As the HT voltage – and the ease of starting – depended on the speed at which the engine was being turned over the system of magneto ignition has been abandoned on most motor cars except where it is fitted as a spare. It is still used on most scooters, though some of the bigger machines did standardise on coil ignition.

We have said that the earliest scooters had the coils mounted inside the hollow of the flywheel, mounted rigidly on a stator plate. The size of these coils was limited by the space available and when it became necessary to fit extra coils in order to generate current for lights and (later on) to charge a battery, the HT coil became a separate unit and was mounted outside the magneto on the frame. On these earlier machines where parking lights were not fitted the electrical output could not easily be increased and this was a serious disadvantage when parking lights became almost obligatory. It was true that a battery could be fitted and the lights fed from that, but the battery could not be continuously charged from the flywheel magneto without an extra lighting coil.

Year by year the demand for current increased. Good parking lights came first; then a stop light operated by the footbrake pedal; then a spot lamp or fog lamp; finally, an electric starter. On today's scooters most of these items are fitted – though the electric starter was never fitted to Vespas and was quickly abandoned by Lambrettas – but flywheel magneto ignition is still very popular and it may therefore be asked what are the grave disadvantages which have been responsible for scooter makers not adopting coil ignition.

The first and most serious objection is that of cost. A good battery is essential and this must be kept well charged. Also, a special scooter battery has had to be produced and in the early days this was not available. By the time the new scooter batteries appeared the flywheel magneto system had been firmly established and it seems likely that it will continue to be the most popular system.

Those technically interested might like to know that the standard flywheel magneto system can be changed over to coil ignition without any great difficulty and at the same time the output of the generator can be almost doubled. Some electrical knowledge would be helpful and, to make the conversion cost reasonable, the spare parts must be available at second-hand prices. However, the system has been adopted by many scooterists with great success.

It consists of replacing the 6-volt battery by a 12-volt battery (the major expense) and fitting a second lighting coil in place of the ignition coil already fitted. The stator plate contains the usual ignition and lighting coils. Remove the former and fit an extra lighting coil – a standard spare – and wire it in series with the first. Remove the standard rectifier-cum-fuse-box and fit a 12-volt 6-amp bridge rectifier. This will give you an output of about 54 watts when you are doing 30mph in top gear. The wiring will differ from one machine to another. An ammeter, an old motor car-type ignition switch and a 12-volt car-type HT coil are also required. The two latter may be found in any car scrapyard. Finally, for safety, a regulator should be fitted. It could be omitted but as most later type scooters had a regulator this is no problem – if one was not fitted, it should be added as otherwise battery mainten-ance might be necessary. The regulator merely increases the charge as the battery needs it. With this converted circuit the battery may run flat but the engine could still be started on the kickstarter if the battery is disconnected, though it should be re-connected as soon as possible.

Such a conversion is particularly suitable for scooterists who require a much greater electrical output – or a bigger battery – than standard. The lights are fed direct from the battery so their brightness is constant and does not depend on engine speed.

As is clear from this, the problem is to obtain sufficient current. With flywheel magneto ignition there are two separate circuits and the current for both is produced mechanically. The first circuit consists of the units as described above for the scooter without a battery; there are the magnets fixed in the flywheel, the coil on the stator plate feeding the external HT coil, and the contact breaker mechanism protected by the condenser, with the current from the HT coil going to the spark plug.

A second and quite separate system operates at the same time. This consists of a lighting coil (or coils) fixed to the same stator plate. As the flywheel magnets revolve round these coils current is produced which is fed to the battery through a rectifier and separately direct to the headlamp.

The battery side is quickly dealt with. The current produced by the revolving magnets and the coil is alternating current – that is, it fluctuates rapidly between positive and negative. A rectifier irons out these fluctuations in one of two ways; a half-wave rectifier takes only the positive half of the current and feeds it to the battery while a full-wave rectifier takes the whole of the current and feeds it to the battery. Most scooters are fitted with half-wave rectifiers and thus the charging rate is relatively low, although if an electric starter is fitted the full-wave rectifier is normal. Again, the current is generated by mechanical effort. The greater the effort the greater the amount of current. If you put in bigger magnets and coils, or more of them, you will produce more current than you would with standard equipment. For competition work the top riders realised that this mechanical effort was exerted at the expense of engine power. This is not idle fancy – it actually takes some power from the engine to get the magnets past the coils – so some riders stripped their engines, cut out the lighting circuit and in theory obtained more engine power, even if it was only a slight advantage. This is why the rules specify that scooter engines must have a complete lighting circuit and why competitors tried to get round that one by carrying a battery-fed set of lights, discarding the battery when the lights were not needed.

This current is produced continuously and if you do much daylight running the battery will soon be fully charged and further charging will damage it. A regulator is therefore fitted, and, usually by means of a spring, by-passes the current when the battery charge is high. Because this is mechanically operated it is possible for the regulator to malfunction. The spring may stick in the "off" position so that the battery gets no fresh charge and is soon flat. For this reason many scooterists, especially those with the bigger engine or those having converted to coil ignition or a 12-volt system, wish to fit an ammeter so that they can check whether the battery is being charged and at what rate. With the 12-volt conversions, for instance, there are alternative circuits for a 5-amp or a 9-amp charge. With the latter two big batteries are essential.

The ammeter is a standard fitting for the majority of motor cycles and was fitted to some German scooters – and British – as standard. By means of it you can check the state of the wiring circuit – a badly made or loose connection will mean a heavy loss of current and the ammeter will show this – the needle may move over to the discharge side when the engine is switched off. The ammeter will also show whether the charging rate is satisfactory, due regard being paid to the regulator, for when this cuts only a trickle charge will be coming through. When the battery voltage drops below a certain level the regulator cuts itself out and the full charge goes to the battery until the voltage rises to a given level, at which point the regulator operates to by-pass the current. With a 12-volt battery the upper figure may be 15 volts. The regulator is in fact something like a thermostat such as you have on an immersion heater or refrigerator.

The mechanical type of regulator continued to be used long after its manifold inadequacies had been plain. All too often the spring stuck in one position or another and wrecked the battery. With the bigger outputs a more refined device was devoloped – by electronic engineers who wanted a more reliable method of current control. One such device in the Zener diode which, linked to a heat sink, has proved reliable. The diode diverts surplus current to the heat sink, the latter being merely a piece of metal (usually aluminium) which is heated by the surplus current, the heat dissipating in the outside air, since the heat sink is bolted to the scooter frame. This combination of diode and heat sink proved instantly popular and efficient. Indeed, the whole level of electrical accessories and equipment has steadily been raised. The battery fitted as standard has a bigger capacity; in the 1950 Lambrettas most had no battery, including the fairly advanced Li.125; the Series III, included a 6-volt 8 ah battery – quite a powerful type and in time the 4-pole magneto was replaced by a 6-pole; for the popular 12-volt conversion the batteries were 6-volt 11 ah and the flywheel magneto had an output of about 56 watts, comparable to that of a good motor cycle. Each time a single unit in the electrical system has been improved all the others took a step forward. One obstinate problem was the controlling switch. This, fitted to the handlebars, started as a poor affair which gave endless trouble. It leaked in wet weather. It became unreliable when condensed moisture settled on exposed surfaces. The internal copper strip lost its spring and so failed to function, blowing light bulbs fore and aft. The switch was constantly improved, but when at last it was made a sealed unit another snag developed – inaccessibility. To get inside the switch was almost impossible, so when a fault showed itself, or when the owner wanted to alter the wiring, a new and expensive switch had to be fitted. The lamps themselves improved tremendously, not only in size but in efficiency. There is little doubt that the greatest improvement in Italian scooters has been on the electrical side.

There are still many scooters where the headlamp relies directly on the flywheel magneto for current coming direct from the lighting coils. This is known as the direct lighting system. In such scooters a battery may be fitted also, but it may be so small that it barely supplies enough current for the parking lights, certainly not for any extended period. The current for the headlamp (and for the battery) is created by the magnets in the flywheel revolving round the lighting coils on the stator plate and this current varies with the engine speed. The faster the engine runs the more current will be reproduced. In short, more power is generated up to a maximum which depends on the size of the magnets and the number of turns of wire in the coils. Let us assume that this maximum is 30 watts.

A peculiarity of the direct-lighting system is that the current must be used as fast as it is produced. It cannot be stored – except when fed to a battery. Every scrap of power must be used the moment it is made and if you produce 30 watts you must feed it to lights, etc., which together use that amount. You could thus, for instance, have a 25-watt headlamp bulb, a 3-watt rear light plus perhaps a speedometer light and the total is about 30 watts. We have said that many German scooters had big electrical circuits, but the Diana with flywheel magneto ignition had a Noris /ULZVS/25/30L with a total output of exactly this amount and Lambrettas, for instance, fitted a bigger rear light bulb.

As long as the balance is maintained all the lights will work well. However, should the headlamp bulb fail, all the current would pass to the tail light and speedometer bulbs and one of these might fuse immediately. It might even happen that if you had a 3-watt tail-light bulb its failure would cause the headlamp bulb to blow. This is one good reason for fitting small-wattage tail-lamp bulbs. On some scooters, should the headlamp bulb fail the engine would cut out, for the ignition circuit is continuous through the bulb filament. With some scooters the stop light is so wired that if it blows the engine stops whenever you apply the rear brake. True, you can then re-start the engine without difficulty but the ignition will cut out every time you press the rear brake pedal. The cure is to fit a new stop-light bulb.

It is important to check the wattage of any bulbs you fit and to see that the total wattage of the bulbs in a direct-lighting circuit is not substantially below the maximum output of the flywheel magneto generator. The headlamp may be fitted with three bulbs – normal beam, dipped beam and parking light. More usually there are two, a parking light and a twin-filament headlamp bulb. If you add a spotlight as an alternative to the headlamp you should get one of the same wattage – usually 25 watts. This can be operated by a simple on-off switch and may be useful in fog, for some scooter headlamps throw a good deal of their light backwards in fog, – you can fit a headlamp cowl to reduce this nuisance. If you fit bulbs with a total wattage of more than that generated the light given from all bulbs will be correspondingly reduced. On the other hand, if the output falls, as it is liable to do after some years (in which case have the flywheel remagnetised, a simple job for any service station) you may be getting only 27 watts instead of 30 watts. You would notice that the head-lamp gave an appreciably dimmer light, more yellow than white, and you could improve this by fitting a bulb with a lower wattage, but the better course is to have the flywheel magneto checked over. It would not matter how the current was distributed as long as it was all used as produced. The blowing of scooter lamp bulbs is a nuisance which continues. At one time the trouble arose in the main switch; in changing from main beam to dipped a copper strip should keep the circuit balances, but when it failed to maintain contact the entire current would be loaded on the tail-lamp bulb which promptly fused. New bulbs would similarly fuse until the fault in the switch was corrected.

Since the current generated depends on engine speed there are great variations in the light given from such a system. This is most noticeable in bottom gear, when engine speed can be increased very rapidly. There is a real danger of fusing the bulbs if connections work loose, putting one bulb out of action. There is a lesser, but still present, risk of fusing all bulbs through excessive engine speed and this is liable to happen with engines souped up for competition work.

A final note about the direct lighting circuit. The hooter is usually on alternating current. It is a curiosity that this direct lighting circuit should produce alternating current and that direct current (DC) should be supplied from the battery. Where an AC hooter is fitted it usually has a low croaking note and causes the headlamp to dim when the two are operated simultaneously. Recently there has been a tendency to fit DC hooters and to operate them from a sizeable battery. Obviously an AC hooter makes no noise when the engine is not running.

If intermittent lights, such as stop lights, winking indicators, etc., are fitted, they should get their current from a battery. The current consumed by these is so great that they would seriously affect the light from the headlamp and if a headlamp bulb of lower wattage were fitted in compensation the bulb might fuse at high speed and the best result obtained would be poor. A stop light taking 15 watts would be a considerable drain on a small battery, so it is not clear why scooterists, halted at lights, keep the rear brake pedal and the stop light glowing for a couple of minutes on end – it is a great drainer of batteries and if the winking indicator light is flashing at the same time the battery will soon be flat. It is essential to balance wattage used against wattage produced and this should be a major consideration when fitting further electrical accessories. As a general rule winking indicators should not be fitted to scooters unless there is a good battery – at least 8 ah.

The second kind of current produced is HT current for the ignition. It is made in the same way as the lighting current and while it is not necessary – nor very helpful – to go into details of magnetic poles and lines of force the reader should be quite at home with the following fact: If a magnet revolves about a suitable coil of wire an alternating current will be produced.

For the HT current the magnets are in the rim of the fly-wheel and the ignition coil is mounted on the stator plate. The current produced in the ignition coil is low tension (LT) current and it is fed from the ignition coil to the familiar HT coil mounted outside the flywheel on the frame. The use of one word with two meanings is not helpful but is now normal. The HT coil consists of a laminated iron core with a continuous very fine insulated wire making thousands of turns round it. Another thicker wire, insulated from the first, makes several turns round the inside of it. The current produced by the flywheel magneto is led through this thicker wire coil and creates a magnetic field in the core which, when interrupted, induces a high-tension current (and a voltage of anything up to 30,000 volts) in the outer coil. This HT current goes, via the HT lead, to the spark plug.

The interruption is caused by the contact breaker, a very simple device, a kind of switch opened and closed by a cam mounted on the crankshaft. The switch opens once for every revolution of the crankshaft in a two-stroke, and thus once for every time the piston moves up the cylinder. Every time the contact breaker points open the ignition current jumps the spark plug gap and in so doing makes a spark. When this happens the mixture inside the combustion chamber burns rapidly and the pressure thus created inside the cylinder head drives the piston downwards and so moves the scooter on the road. Since the burning of the mixture is not instantaneous the spark is timed to occur just before the piston reaches the top of its stroke. In this way maximum pressure is developed as the piston begins to move downwards.

The timing of the spark is vitally important. It may be specified in something like the following terms:

Ignition timing; 0·16 to 0·18 ins before TDC with contact breaker gap of 0·012 to 0·016 ins.

It will thus be seen that accuracy of spark timing is essential – the limits are fairly close. If the ignition occurs too soon it may be that considerable pressure will be developed before the piston reaches the top of its stroke. Two things are then possible – the piston may continue to move upwards but will absorb some of the engine's power wastefully in so doing, or the piston may actually be driven violently in the wrong direction, as happens when you kickstart an engine with the ignition too far advanced. The kickstart pedal will then kick back, sometimes with painful effect. If ignition occurs too late (timing too retarded) the full flame-spread may not occur until the piston is moving downwards and some of the force of explosion will then be lost. In both cases the engine will be running at less than full efficiency and there may be serious overheating. The ignition timing and the contact breaker gap are both adjustable and the instruction book gives very detailed information about this. Rather curiously, having said that the settings must be made within fine limits, we must add that with the

Lambretta circuits the contact breaker gap cannot be given accurately for any particular engine. The setting is fixed when the scooter is delivered but subsequent adjustment is a matter of testing to see which gives best results. This is in contrast to spark plug gaps which are specified to one-thousandth of an inch.

Is ignition timing affected by engine speed? After all, the piston is moving much more rapidly in an engine doing 5,000rpm than in one doing 2,000rpm. In the same way the reader may wonder – having been told that with the ignition too advanced the piston may be kicked back when starting – what happens when the engine finally fires, since it obviously cannot continue to run backwards?

The latter point is met by saying that it would require great skill to make a two-stroke engine run backwards. The possibility remains theoretical though if a magazine publishes a letter from a reader whose engine has run backwards there are sure to be others claiming to have had the same thing happen with their machine, though none of these readers seems able to reproduce this astonishing phenomenon when others are present. On the question of relating engine speed and ignition timing, it is rather surprising to find that there is some variation in the attitude of manufacturers. The automatic advance-and-retard mechanism fitted to motor car engines as standard has no counterpart in scooter engines where there is one setting for all engine speeds, although Lambretta had a centrifugal device fitted to some models which operated at fairly low speeds.

There are many differences between machines in ignition circuits and layouts. For instance, the negative earth system (whereby the battery negative terminal is connected to the earth terminal) is adopted by some but not by all. Again, on some scooters it is so simple to adjust the ignition timing that the owner is almost invited to do it, whereas on the Villiers engines the contact breaker base plate was locked by a solder-filled screw. Again, with a coil ignition system as that on the BSA scooters a special switch was fitted to give a magneto-ignition circuit in case you had to start the engine when the battery was flat. BSA – along with Lambrettas – used the energy-transfer system, with the ignition coil primary connected in parallel with the contact breaker points, in place of the more usual connection in series. Some engines had a warning-light which lit up when the ignition was switched on and the engine was not running. This was very necessary with coil ignition where, if the ignition is accidentally left switched on overnight, the battery may be flat the next morning. Another gadget was fitted to a few German machines – a warning-light to show when fuel was getting low. This replaced the more usual reserve fuel supply and did away with the need for a three-way fuel tap. Generally speaking the electrical load became heavier year by year, causing designers to specify more substantial circuits and components. Batteries improved and had greater capacity. Switches were better designed and more robust. The lighting itself improved out of all recognition.

Electric starters. Very few scooters have electric starters but something should be said about them because they represent one feature which is ripe for future experiment and development if still further improvements in scooters are under consideration. Good lighting, good brakes and easy starting are the three lines along which improvements would make the scooter more generally popular. Easy starting is still not obtained with all scooters. Some are better than others but with magneto ignition all depends on getting sufficient crankshaft speed by means of the kickstarter to get a spark at the plug, assuming connections, timing and carburation are correct. The voltage required for a spark across a plug gap of about 0·018 ins is of the order of 7,000 volts and on a machine in good condition this should be obtained with a crankshaft speed of about 200rpm. This is easily obtained on the average scooter but kickstart modifications continue. Lambretta have made many variations. Between the two versions of the TV. 175, the pedal itself moved. In the Series II models it was fitted to the rear wheel spindle, driving direct on the first gear wheel This is the position it had always occupied with the Vespa.

Electric starters were fitted to some scooters – NSU, Maico, Diana – as standard equipment, with or without auxiliary kickstart pedals. Plainly with these scooters the electric starter was considered the normal thing to use. With the exception of the Maico, an electric starter involved the use of 12-volt lighting. The 6-volt batteries were used and immediately the standard of lighting improved, parking lights became a reality and additional electrical equipment could be fitted without having to balance wattage developed against wattage used, since the batteries had ample reserves. It should be emphasised that 12-volt circuits are not twice as powerful as 6-volt circuits. For many years American cars fitted 6-volt lighting circuits as standard and though they have changed to 12-volts some Volkswagens, for instance, kept to 6-volts. The great advantage of the 12-volt system to scooterists was that the two batteries gave him not so much bigger lights as a bigger reserve. Compare a typical scooter.

Kickstart model: One 6-volt 7-amp/hr battery.
Electric starter model: Two 6-volt 13-amp/hr batteries.

This is the biggest and most obvious advantage of the electric starter scooter. It is true that for a girl the electric starter requires less strength, is kinder to light shoes – but a kickstart model in good condition will start with a very light pressure on the pedal and research continues to reduce the pressure still further. The bigger battery reserve, however, is an advantage to every scooterist. The headlamp can be fed from the battery and will function even with the engine switched off. The headlamp itself may be more powerful; a kickstart model will have a 25-watt bulb while the other may have 35-watt bulbs. Also, a DC horn will be fitted, which gives a more pleasing and useful sound. Stop lights and winkers and a host of other gadgets may be fitted without overloading the batteries – and some will be fitted as standard. These are solid advantages when linked with the more robust wiring and switches usually employed on electric starter scooters. There are broadly three types of electric starters.

Dynamo. Two well-known makes were the Noris, as fitted to the Diana, and the Siba, as fitted to Villiers engines in the Bond, DKR and other British scooters. In these the crankshaft was turned mechanically when starting.

We have seen that by making the flywheel revolve we can create electric currents. We can reverse the process. We can arrange sets of coils round the crankshaft and by passing a current through one set we can make the crankshaft revolve, thus starting the engine. There is no mechanical connection, no gearing, no V-belt. The Siba Dynastart as fitted to Villiers engines will be briefly described, though the Noris is very similar in construction. The armature is fixed to the crankshaft, much as the flywheel was fixed, and revolves with it. The stator, which does not move, consists of twelve separate coils, one set of six for starting and the set of shunt windings for the ignition, lighting and battery charging. There is an external HT coil, a condenser, etc. When the starter button is pressed current from the batteries passes through the set of starter coils and the Dynastart, acting as a series motor, transforms the current into the mechanical energy required to start the armature (and therefore the crankshaft) rotating. The engine now fires and at a predetermined speed the starter coils cut out and the shunt windings begin charging the battery, feeding the ignition, etc. These dynamo starters have great capacity – 90 or 100 watts is quite normal. Voltage regulators, cut-outs and contact breaker units are fitted and the complete dynamo starter is a fairly heavy piece of equipment.

Gear driven. This is the best-known type of electric starter, being fitted to very many motor cars in one form or another. It consists of an armature would round a commutator with sets of closely wound coils. When a current is passed through the coils the armature is made to turn and by means of a shaft extension coupled to a roller clutch the motion is transmitted through a small pinion which mates with a starter ring on the flywheel and, since the flywheel is mounted on the crankshaft, turns the latter and starts the engine. The starter motor is a separate unit driven from the battery and the battery is kept charged through a standard type of flywheel generator, magnets being mounted in the flywheel and revolving round a set of stationary coils. In the later-type LD Lambrettas the drive from the starter motor was taken through the clutch and not direct to the flywheel. In such starters the driving pinion is pre-engaged; that is, when the starter switch is pressed, the first part of the movement moves the pinion into engage-ment. Further pressure on the switch closes the electrical contacts. This has the advantage of quietness and makes this type of starter as silent as the dynamo type. Gear-driven starters when fitted to motor cars are noisy because the driving pinion is not pre-engaged. When the starter button is pressed the pinion rotates and, when a set speed is reached, it is flung forward to engage with the starter ring.

Pendulum type. This very unusual type of electric starter is made by Bosch and was best known as fitted to the Maico scooters. It was a combined starter and generator and, instead of rotating the crankshaft, oscillated it – swung it to and fro. The mixture was drawn in and fired by an ignition circuit quite separate from the conventional contact breaker unit. When the mixture ignited the pressure was quite sufficient to turn the engine over normally. The standard contact breaker system then took over and the engine continued to fire on this standard ignition system. As the starter had not to turn the engine over at maximum compression less power was required from the starter and the Maico pendulum starter was fitted with 6-volt equipment and a single 6-volt 11 ah battery. Under normal running conditions the crankshaft oscillated two or three times per second and there was a separate spark for each oscillation. This was an ingenious starter motor and naturally it was much smaller than the other 12-volt types. The standard Maico headlamps had 35-watt bulbs, as might have been expected from these high-speed scooters.

Having thus described the three best-known types it may be as well to say something about their disadvantages.

All three were made by first-class firms. Even after these starters had been in service for many years – and there are German scooters such as the Bella running about after twenty years of service and still with the electric starter working perfectly – the fitting of electric starters to scooters made little headway. They were standard equipment on most German scooters. In Britain, the Villiers engine fitted with the Siba Dynastart was a standard unit so British scooters fitted with Villiers engines could offer an electric-starter model as an alternative without much design work being called for. In France, electric starters never had much appeal and in Italy only a few scooters ever had them. Lambretta offered the LD.125 and LD.150 scooters with electric starters but the three models which followed – the Li.125, the Li.150 and the TV.175 – were offered with kickstart only. As for Vespa, an electric starter was worked out on the drawing board, and prototypes were made, but no electric starter Vespa was offered as a production model, Piaggio feeling that the demand did not exist.

The number of firms which offered electric starters did increase at one time, but the number of scooters so fitted steadily declined. Many scooterists, having tried an electric starter model, went back to the kickstart. It is not possible to give a single reason for this but probably the usual reason was that the battery went flat and there was difficulty in getting the engine started at all. Additionally, since the current required for starting is over 30 amps on a 12-volt circuit the wiring must be substantial and the batteries to supply a sudden demand of this order must be substantial also – something like 6-volt 13-ah, costly items today. To keep such batteries fully charged, a fair proportion of running must be done during daylight hours, without using the headlamps and during the winter months, where the scooter is used for going to and from work, this is simply not possible. Once the battery has gone flat it is usually taken out for charging, which puts the scooter out of commission for a length of time which may be inconvenient. Ironically, the load on the batteries from lighting demands is greatest during winter when the load is increased by the strain of cold weather starting. It is fair to say that the electric starters fitted to German and British scooters gave excellent service and proved superior to others. The reason was probably that they were made against a strong motor cycle background, with a tradition of service under severe conditions. The Czechs fitted an excellent electric starter to their small scooters. The Japanese produced electric starters for even smaller engines. It is thus curious that the Italians, faced with this challenge, should have produced no equally satisfactory solution.

It is pleasant to record that one important – if limited – advance was made by Britain's Lucas – the capacitor ignition system. First shown in 1966 it was adopted by many trials riders who wished to discard the batteries. It can be fitted to scooters equipped with a 12-volt conversion, though it is slightly complicated where the energy-transfer system is used – and unfortunately most scooter engines with 6-volt ignition systems are energy-transfer. However, it can be done. Basically it incorporates the standard 12-volt battery coil ignition components (with the Zener diode mounted on an adequate heat sink) and a spring-mounted high-capacity electrolytic capacitor. Engines with 6-volt systems must be converted to 12-volt; those with energy-transfer systems will additionally require a battery charging alternator stator, wiring harness and light and ignition switches.

The capacitor itself stores the energy pulses from the alternator and supplies the ignition coil with sufficient energy to give adequate plug sparking for starting and running. Timing is less critical than with the energy-transfer system. Horn and lights can be used without the battery in circuit even at fairly low engine revs. This discarding of the batteries is a great help for trials riders. The batteries can be re-fitted afterwards for ordinary road use.

12 Lubrication

All lubrication is a compromise, but the lubrication of a two-stroke engine is perhaps more of a compromise than most. Sufficient oil must be used to preserve the bearings and cylinder bore, yet the quantity must be kept to a minimum so that the engine shall develop reasonable power. The parts most affected are the little-end bearing, the big-end bearing, the cylinder and the two bearings on which the crankshaft is carried. On one or two scooters such as the Maico the crankshaft bearings had their own pure-oil lubrication system (and on one or two Lambrettas there was actually a grease nipple for main bearing lubrication) but on almost all two-stroke engines these parts are lubricated by the petroil mixture drawn in through the carburetter.

Petroil is a mixture of petrol and oil, so it is a diluted lubricant. In the first scooters there was a tendency to use too much oil because using too little oil would cause expensive damage. One part in sixteen was usual, whereas today increasing numbers of scooter engines run happily on one part in fifty. It was hardly surprising that when these 1:50 engines first appeared scooterists and dealers alike viewed them with apprehension and were inclined to use twice as much oil as the maker recommended.

The mixture is drawn in through the inlet manifold to the crankcase. Here it is compressed as the piston moves downwards and since the big-end bearings and the crankshaft bearings are inside the crankcase some of the petroil mist gives the necessary film of lubricant. The remaining mixture is forced up through the transfer ports into the combustion chamber as the piston continues its stroke and is there ignited.

The cylinder bore, as the piston moves up and down, is lubricated for only a small proportion of the time and for the rest is open to fierce attack by friction and by the burnt gases. Here we can deal in very brief form with the three problems facing engine designers and their partial solution:

1. Oil and petrol do not willingly mix. The initial efforts to overcome this were concentrated on marketing oils which mixed more readily but the oil was made ready-mixing at the expense of its lubricating properties. Subsequently efforts moved towards spraying undiluted oil into the mixture of petrol and air. This was promising, but destroys some of the two-stroke engine's simplicity.

2. Crankshaft bearings were inadequately lubricated when they merely rotated in a petroil/air mist and failures were too frequent. Later design has the petroil mixture directed in more intense way on the bearings themselves.

3. Where petroil mixture is used the quantity of lubricant reaching the bearings depends directly on throttle openings and engine revs. When descending long hills with closed throttle the engine often receives too little oil. This problem has proved insoluble except that in engines with separate tanks for petrol and oil, the oil can be metered; though this is done at the expense of engine simplicity.

The early scooter designers were excusably cautious in settling on a 1:16 ratio of oil to petrol. They accepted the loss of power which resulted from this rather oily mixture rather than risk pistons seizing or bearings breaking up.

There was a further factor which introduced an element of confusion. It was realised that the oils then obtainable did not readily mix with the petrol in the way that heat spreads

through a cold substance and the thicker the oil the greater its
reluctance to mix thoroughly, though even light oils might
still leave pockets of neat petrol in the mixture in spite of
vigorous shaking. There was also a fear that even when mixed
the oil would separate out and this notion was given support
by repeated statements that the crankshaft bearings were
lubricated in a two-stroke engine by neat oil being squeezed
out under crankcase compression and deposited as discrete
drops of oil. The newcomer to scootering found these curious
claims made even in reputable journals and was naturally
nervous. It was quite usual to see scooterists shaking their
scooters to and fro to mix the contents of the fuel tank after
refilling – and also before starting off in the morning, a practice
which did no harm to the engine and helped to get the
scooterist's blood flowing more freely, whatever it did to the
fuel. So fixed was the idea that the oil separated out that
frequent warnings were printed – and continue to be printed –
that the scooterist should shut off the fuel tap when he was
two or three hundred yards from home so that the fuel in the
carburetter should not become neat oil overnight and foul the
plug whan the engine was next started. This was absurd if
only because on some scooters turning off the fuel was complicated; one required that you remove the ignition key, with
it unlock a side panel and rummage about inside to find the
fuel tap. Few scooterists even tried to turn off the fuel this far
from home, but the advice continues to appear in print.

From 1955 onwards the oil companies made strenuous efforts
to develop a reliable system to delivering petroil ready mixed
in a single pump. This was a great advance on the original
method of asking for half a pint of oil and a gallon of petrol,
putting the oil in first and swishing the petrol round to mix.
On many scooters this system, though messy, would serve
very well but on most the fuel tank was not large enough. A
typical early Vespa had a fuel tank holding one and a half

gallons. If you ran out of fuel and turned to reserve supply you might find when you reached a garage that the tank would not hold an additional gallon of petrol plus the half-pint of oil. In theory it should have done. In practice some petrol slopped over and was wasted, leaving your engine with more oil than it needed, since of course this was put in first.

Another difficulty was the engine which required a 1:24 mixture – only a third of a pint of oil to the gallon. Few garages had such a measure. Still another problem was getting the extra amount of oil into the mixture while the engine was being run in. On the Continent scooterists often carried fuel, ready mixed for use, in a tin strapped to the legshield. Abroad also the petroil pump – delivering whatever proportion of oil you requested – was by 1948 a normal piece of filling station equipment. Very few foreign scooterists mixed their own fuel.

These foreign petroil pumps were so reliable, so popular, so long-established that some explanation is required for the slow, erratic and sometimes ludicrous efforts to furnish British garages with some device which would supply two-stroke mixtures of varying proportions. World-famous oil companies, able to tame deserts and pierce the sea bed, proved incapable of equipping garages – which the oil companies had in most cases financed themselves – with the kind of pump equal to that which even one-man filling stations in France had used for many years. Some of the British efforts were little more than tin cans on ridiculously small wheels. From these devices the mixture was pumped by hand. Commonly the oil used was of the wrong type. Commonly neat petrol was delivered, with disastrous results for the scooterist and to avoid this the mixture was given a distinctive colour if oil had in fact been added to the petrol. There were also some companies, like Filtrate and Castrol, which marketed oil but not petrol and so neither owned nor controlled a chain of filling stations. Scooterists wanting such oils often found it difficult to obtain, for even if not actually hidden they were not displayed prominently. Eventually all these – and many other mixture problems – were solved. An effective mixture pump did appear. An alternative oil pump was provided. This could be set to give the required amount of oil for a gallon of petrol, whatever ratio was needed. The number of seized engines dropped, but it must be admitted that British scooterists had to face some problems peculiar to this country.

The situation was further complicated by some scooter manufacturers calling for SAE.30 oil and others for SAE.50 while one famous manufacturer announced that the guarantee would be invalid if ready-mixed fuel was used, in this case because of a then justified doubt about the way petroilers behaved. Greatest complication of all arose when new types of lubricants became popular. Molybdenum disulphide was one such. It rapidly became the best-known additive to lubricating oils but scooterists who used it suffered from slipping clutches since the clutch ran in the gearbox oil. Some of these problems took a long time to solve.

However the mixture is delivered, it has a double duty; of being burned to provide power and of acting as a lubricant film on bearings and cylinder. The second is complicated by the fact that the mixture does not burn away completely – it leaves a deposit of carbon behind while the process of combustion also produces a certain amount of moisture and acids.

Water is always produced when petrol is burned in air. The amount is roughly equal to the amount by weight of petrol. Normally this is vented through the exhaust port as vapour but some will remain in the engine unless the engine temperature is fairly high. The acids produced are also volatile, and these will vanish with the exhaust gases if the engine reaches a fairly high temperature, but any left in the engine will accumulate and in time will set up corrosion. It is part of the designer's job to see that the engine quickly reaches a temperature at which this acid-laden moisture will be eliminated, but the owner can interfere with these plans if the scooter is consistently run at too low a temperature. That is why there are occasional complaints of bearing failure – from running the scooter for very short periods and not allowing the engine to reach a reasonable operating temperature.

This type of failure is different from piston seizure, or bearing failure through overload (usually during running-in). It is sometimes forgotten that cooling is a part of lubrication. Where oil is used as a lubricant, as in gears, the amount of oil is calculated to produce a certain amount of cooling, by conducting the heat away from the moving parts, much as is done in the brakes, and passing it eventually to the open air. In complicated parts the lubricant is pump-fed from a distant sump and this sump is frequently cooled by external finning or even mechanically. When the two-stroke engine is being used for its first 500 miles many of the surfaces moving against each other are comparatively irregular and part of the running-in process is aimed at getting these high spots down. Thus, although there may be a film of petroil between piston and cylinder which would be sufficient as a lubricant if contact was made over the whole surface and pressure evenly distributed, it might be near the safety line at one of these high spots, and a slight overload would be enough to cause a local breakdown of the oil film. This frequently happens, causing tiny fragments of the metal to be broken off, and there are no expensive consequences. If the film breaks down where there is excessive heat which is not dissipated there is every likelihood of the parts seizing solid. This piston seizure happens fairly often without ill-effects, particularly during the running-in period. It can be a danger signal, but when the engine has cooled down it can be run as before. Only in rare cases does the seizure cause so much damage that a fresh cylinder or piston is required.

The little-end bearing at the upper end of the connecting rod was at one time a bronze bush. The design of such bearings was often based on empirical formulae and it was not unknown for a manufacturer to produce a scooter and, after a time, decide that from such and such a date a bigger diameter bush, would be fitted. This led to confusion when a scooterist, having one of the later batch and wishing to replace the bush, was supplied with one made for earlier machines. Such a bearing, working with petroil mist as its only lubricant, was working under great difficulties, and in time was replaced by needle rollers. This is similar to a roller bearing but is cageless and the rollers have a high load capacity. They are particularly suitable for service at low speeds. There is, generally speaking, no difficulty about getting good service from a bearing at the medium and high speeds. High-speed bearing failures are usually due to running at excessively high speeds for long periods so that it is impossible to dissipate the heat thus generated. Such a failure takes a considerable time, whereas failure at low speeds may be sudden. The needle roller bearing has been adopted by most scooter makers. As a small-end bearing it does not revolve, so the load is always carried by the same few rollers.

Vespa fitted such a bearing when they introduced their two percent mixture model and at the 1960 Paris Show the two percent Lambrettas had a similar small-end.

The small-end bearings, like the big-end bearings, are protected from the burning gases and are lubricated by the mixture introduced into the crankcase. Merely waving them round in the mixture would not be sufficient to lubricate them, as adequate penetration would not be secured. It is these and the main crankshaft bearings which are most likely to break down under corrosion following running at too low an engine temperature. However, as was said when dealing with the carburetter, if the mixture is subjected to pressure after petrol spray and air are mixed, some of the petroil will be squeezed out, as water is squeezed from a sponge. This happens in the crankcase also. When the piston descends the crankcase pressure is increased to between three and five pounds per square inch, some of the petroil is squeezed out as globules and it is these which help to lubricate the bearings. However, this is not the complete story, nor is the process very satisfactory and Vespa, for instance, altered the inlet manifold so that the incoming mixture was directed immediately on the big-end and main bearings.

It will be seen that in the two-stroke engine the amount of lubricant applied to the bearings increases with speed but does not increase with load. With the reduction in the amount of oil used in the petroil has gone intensive research into special two-stroke oils because the standard motor cycle oils are not the best for two-strokes. The aim has been to find an oil which mixes more readily but is also cleaner, but it has seemed impossible to eliminate one disadvantage without introducing another. Detergent additives gave a cleaner engine but reduced lubricating properties. When the mixture burns it leaves carbon deposits which accumulate on the piston crown and cylinder head and may build up to obstruct the exhaust port and upset the delicate balance of carburation and exhaust. Most of the oil companies now market special two-stroke oils, and there are also substances offered either as substitutes for the oils themselves or as additives giving specific advantages. Some claim to reduce plug fouling, or to cut down the risk of whiskering. Some of these additives were frowned on by the scooter makers but two or three were greatly favoured by competition riders whose engines were highly stressed.

Lubrication of the remainder of the scooter includes ball and roller bearings on such parts as wheels, transmission shafts, etc; working faces such as gears; oscillating or reciprocating parts such as suspension units and cables. These three purposes are quite separate and different lubricants are required.

There is no single lubricant which can be considered as best for all purposes. Ball and roller bearings have their own special oils and greases. They also have their optimum quantities – very many ball bearings fail through being given too much grease. You will get occasional bearing failures from faulty manufacture, but the life quoted by the maker is between 3,000 and 4,000 hours. This is usually qualified by saying that this life assumes a given speed in rpm, and a constant and steady load. At a 4,000 hours life you would expect your scooter's bearings to last about six years if you used it for two hours a day.

This may not seem much, but put it another way. Suppose you averaged 20mph, then your 4,000 hours would give you 80,000 miles, which is more than the average life of a scooter. Such a bearing would slightly outlast the scooter, which is probably satisfactory to the designer. In theory all the parts of a scooter should collapse at the same moment.

However, the bearing life quoted assumes good maintenance. There is no allowance for dirt being present or grease being absent. When the bearings are fitted in the first place they are given the right amount of grease. Usually they are then fitted with oil seals of synthetic rubber on either side so that the grease will be retained there. Too much grease may do damage. The temperature of the bearing will rise unduly. The grease will be churned and the grease may actually disintegrate, with rapid failure of the bearing.

If a bearing is taken out for any purpose it will be normal to wash it out. Paraffin should not be used. Petrol – or petroil – is excellent. Few owners observe this rule and in most service stations you will see bearings being flushed with paraffin – a quite wrong method. After cleaning, leave to dry, then partly fill with suitable grease. When roller bearings are fitted to rotating shafts the oil seal is very important especially on the crankshaft, where failure of the oil seal means neat oil escaping into the crankcase from the gearbox. Standard oil seals are made of steel with a retainer of synthetic material (based on butadene acrylonitrile copolymer) and, while not expensive, are not readily accessible and so replacement has a high labour content and is expensive unless you do the work yourself. If the shaft is damaged or distorted it may not be possible to get the seal working satisfactorily. A good shaft surface is essential.

Working faces such as gears are lubricated by running with a portion of their depth in oil, which is thus carried to all the working surfaces. This is known as the splash system and is used throughout all two-stroke engines. The depth of oil is usually less than half the diameter of the gear, as there is a danger of churning here if the oil level is too high. It is for this reason that gearcases have a level indicator, usually a level plug and too much oil should not be put in. On some early Lambrettas there were many cases of owners putting too much oil in the transmission cases. Churning and surging developed and oil was driven through to the brake shoes. A pressure-release hole was drilled to overcome this. A similar trouble was met in the early BSA scooters. This building-up of pressure where parts revolve in oil is a constant problem not always understood by the owner – and sometimes not by the designer. The splash system of oiling is used throughout the whole scooter range and works satisfactorily. The type of oil is usually specified and this should be used.

For other oscillating and reciprocating parts your handbook will usually specify the periods at which named oils or greases should be applied and some of the leading oil companies publish charts showing the details. Suspension units may be sealed and require no attention. Hydraulic forks and arms may require topping-up from time to time. The quantity and type will be specified as a rule in some words as 40cc SAE.50, but more usually a level hole is fitted and it is only necessary to feed oil in until it begins to flow from this. For oiling control cables, grease nipples are sometimes fitted. Other parts needing lubrication will be detailed in your instruction book.

Where a chain is fitted special attention should be given to it, unless it is running in a totally enclosed casing as in the BSA scooters or like the primary chain in the Lambrettas. If not totally enclosed the chain will be exposed to dust and unless well maintained will be subject to rapid wear. It should receive attention at intervals of not more than 500 miles.

The sparking plug is a simple, robust unit. Its two best-known characteristics are that it makes sparks and it gets fouled up, causing the engine to misfire or refuse to start. As we have seen, a current is passed from the flywheel magneto to the primary coil and induces an HT current in the secondary coil. This HT current jumps the gap at the sparking plug and makes a spark in so doing. There is occasional talk of thin and fat sparks, but a current which will jump the gap (usually about 0·020 ins) will produce all the spark you need. If it will not jump such a gap it will produce no spark at all.

The spark ignites the mixture of oil, petrol and air in the combustion chamber and that, very simply, is all the plug does. It must obviously consist of two parts insulated from each other – since it carries an electric current. As there is continual sparking it is natural that the points between which the spark occurs should tend to burn away. From its position in the combustion chamber it follows also that a greater or lesser amount of carbon will be deposited on the plug points, since the petrol is not 100 percent burnt away.

All these happen – and more. If a scooter engine ceases – or refuses – to fire, the owner is advised to check the fuel supply and then the plug; it is unfortunate that plugs should so often be connected with trouble. Few scooterists have not had a fouled or a whiskered plug, or one so wetted by mixture that the insulation was bridged and the engine would not fire.

These are troubles common to most scooters. It is only fair to say that no scooter is more liable to plug trouble than any other. No make of plug is thoroughly bad, though some are said to be better than others.

Plugs are classified by thread diameters – 14mm for scooters; by the reach (or length of thread) which is usually half or three-quarters of an inch; and by the heat range. The first two require little explanation.

The heat range of a plug is an index of the extent to which heat is required in the insulator. This is a very important factor and the use of a plug of the wrong heat range is almost always unsatisfactory. Intense heat is developed when the mixture is ignited. This heat must be carried away from the plug tip. It travels along the insulator and the longer the insulator tip the slower will be the heat dissipation. The plug with the long tip will be called a hot plug and will have a high heat value. When the insulator tip is short the heat will quickly be dissipated and such a plug is said to be a cold plug.

The system sounds – and is – extremely simple to understand. Unfortunately, each manufacturer appears to have his own system of classification. The Bosch heat range scale is generally used in Europe but British manufacturers do not normally use it – at least not in public. Each one prefers to build his own scale and to publish charts listing his own plugs along with the equivalent plugs of other makers. In such a table all the following plugs are of roughly the same heat value:—

3 HLN
N 3
43 XL
AG 3
W.240 T2
FE.100

The Sparking Plug

These six plugs are made by different makers and references quoted are the only clue to the heat range. However, while one maker's scale runs to 100 another finishes short of that and one maker had two different systems running at the same time. Again some, but not all, makers describe their plugs as harder or softer, the softer plugs having a lower heat value. In practice the plug should remain at a temperature between 450°C and 850°C to give best results. Below this figure the plug tip is too cold for the products of combustion to be burned away as quickly as they are deposited. When the deposits are so great that the plug points are bridged a spark cannot be produced and the engine stops firing. If the plug is correct this low temperature will rarely be reached, for the normal engine speeds will be sufficient to keep the plug temperature within the useful range. If, on the other hand, the plug tip temperature exceeds the top figure the heat will not be dissipated quickly enough, the plug tip will become hotter and hotter until a point is reached when the mixture will be ignited before the spark occurs and there is then a possibility of the engine suffering damage. Even when it does not, pre-ignition of this kind will very quickly destroy the plug.

This is a greatly simplified explanation of a complex problem about which different views are held. For instance, when starting a cold engine the normal temperature – that is the running temperature – will not be reached for a little time and yet plugs will often give excellent service in such conditions. Occasional high-speed driving is almost essential to good plug performance. A scooter which is constantly run at low speeds and low engine temperatures is likely to give continual plug trouble. As the running temperature rises the plug is better able to burn away the deposits from combustion – in other words, to keep itself clean.

As the engine temperature varies so greatly the plug has to

deal with rapidly changing conditions. Some riders seem to get better service from their plugs than do others so undoubtedly the driving style is important, as is general engine condition. It cannot be said too often that the two-stroke engine dislikes light loads and low speeds. The latter means low piston speeds and this means slow flame spread, leading to excessive deposits on piston crown, cylinder head, exhaust port and plug. Therefore, keep the engine revving briskly. Choose the lowest comfortable gear, not the highest, and the plug will give better service.

Sparking plugs are made by mass-production methods. There is almost no manual labour except to feed parts into conveyors and then box the finished article. The essential parts are the two electrodes, an insulator and a metal shell to be screwed into the cylinder head. The shell may be a sealed unit, in which case the plug is said to be non-detachable; or the shell may consist of two threaded parts so that the plug may be dismantled for cleaning. The tendency has been increasingly to make the non-detachable plug the standard, though some makers continue to produce both types. Where the plug could be taken to pieces it was simple for the owner to clean the various parts thoroughly, though the manufacturer felt that the insulation and the sealing of the parts suffered in the process. Non-detachable plugs should be cleaned in a machine specially made for that purpose and driven by compressed air. The plug is screwed into a holder and by passing a lever a very fine sand-spray under high pressure cleans all the exposed parts. This sandblasting is very effective and there is usually incorporated in such a machine a complete plug-testing device to check gas leaks or electrical leaks. For instance, if a plug being tested gives a satisfactory spark at low pressures but sparks at the external gap when the pressure is increased it is almost certain that the central electrode has broken. Not all these machines are of uniform design and a certain amount of skill is required to interpret the results of such tests. There is no really efficient alternative method for cleaning non-detachable plugs. The advice sometimes given to soak the plug end in petroil and set it alight will result in even worse fouling. The sandblasting method is sometimes criticised on the grounds that some sand will be left in the plug and will later damage the cylinder walls. This should not happen since as a matter of routine the plug is blown clean of all sand.

Unfortunately these machines are not always available when your plug requires cleaning and even if available, are not always working. As filling stations tended to become merely filling stations the additional services once gladly provided free of charge – of which plug cleaning was one – dwindled and as motorists rarely needed their plugs cleaned in the modern cars, the scooterist has found that plug cleaning machines are more and more often out of action. Combined with the tendency to make plugs requiring such machines this has been unfortunate. Cleaning by hand is not adequate. The trouble is often that the plug has oiled up while trying to start the machine. The petroil will have formed a film over the plug tip and will have connected the two electrodes. In emergency a little petrol may be poured on the tip and set alight. It is emphasised that to use petroil will only increase the fouling. The cavity is so small that it cannot easily be cleaned out by hand. If the fouling consists of dry deposits they may usually be scraped or brushed off by hand.

Whether detachable or not, plugs are much alike in construction. The central electrode is a stout wire held in an insulator and sealed into it. This unit is then fitted to a metal shell with an external thread at the lower end. For scooters the thread is 14mm and either half (short reach) or three-quarters (long reach) of an inch in depth. Many other sizes are made, of course. It is important to get the correct reach and although the half-inch reach is so popular, the long reach plug was specified for some German scooters and for some Lambrettas beginning with the Li. range. The lower end of the thread should be level with the inside surface of the cylinder head when the plug is screwed home. If it projects further it may be severely over-heated and cause pre-ignition or pinking; and when the exposed threads have become carboned up the plug may be difficult to remove. If you use a short reach plug when a long reach is specified the plug points will be in a kind of recess in the cylinder head. The internal threads in the head will then carbon up and this may make it difficult afterwards to get a long reach plug in. It will be seen that the cylinder head is machined to a depth suitable for a plug of a certain reach and before you use a different plug you should give the matter some thought.

The length and shape of the insulator is most important for it is this which decides into what heat range the plug goes. A short, stubby insulator nose indicates a cold-running plug. A longer insulator nose indicates a hot-running plug. You fit a cold plug in a hot-running engine – that is, an engine with a high compression ratio, normally running at high speeds. As the compression ratio increases the pressure inside the cylinder head increases and so does the flame temperature. You get these conditions in the higher performance scooters and that is why you will almost always need a cooler-running plug if you increase the compression ratio of your engine or tune it for sports use. Again, if you are entering for a 24-hour event, with your engine running for the whole of that time, you may find a cooler-running plug is required.

The central electrode in the plug is made from round wire and varies in composition from an anonymous substance to the widely advertised silver and platinum. A great deal of research has been done on this electrode, especially to find suitable metals. The earth electrode is welded to the plug shell and bent over until the correct gap has been reached. Some plugs have an overhead gap – the earth wire makes the gap with the end of the electrode – whereas previously the gap had been made with the side. Adjustment of the gap should never be made with the central electrode since this is sealed into the insulator and there is some danger of this seal being broken if the electrode is hammered in the adjustment process. On some plugs there are three earth electrodes.

The central electrode was at one time made of a conventional nickel alloy and this was quite satisfactory, erosion being normal. With modern fuels, especially where petrol or oils contain sulphur, the attack on the nickel alloy is sometimes severe and the electrode is quickly pitted to such an extent that a correct gap cannot be maintained. New materials and special plugs were developed with so-called platinum points soldered into the stout copper core which was in turn sealed into the insulator. This type was first made for high compression engines. Of perhaps more interest to the average scooterist there were also developed so-called silver-pointed plugs which had a cool-running electrode and this helped to prevent metallic deposits melting and forming a bridge – or whisker – across the points. These plugs had three earth electrodes and one central electrode.

As the number of scooters on the roads increased special plugs for their engines were designed. There also appeared a great deal of useful information about choosing, maintaining and servicing plugs. A gap gauge was made, containing wires of different thicknesses so that the correct gap could be kept. This was as useful an accessory as the tyre gauge. Coloured charts were also published showing exactly what plug points should look like and showing, in their natural colours, plugs which had suffered various forms of ill-use. One such chart had twelve coloured photographs covering almost every state of plug – oiled, sooted, overheated, pitted, etc. – one was likely to encounter as well as some one hopes never to encounter in one's own scooter. These charts were technically interesting but they are also an invaluable guide to plug choice and plug use. You can take the plug out of your engine and check it with the photographs and so find out accurately what – if anything – is wrong with your plug. In many cases such a chart is a valuable guide also to the engine and mixture condition as these are quickly reflected in the state of the plug points. For example:

1. If you get persistently oiled plugs when starting, some fuel may be leaking into the crankcase.

2. Sooted plugs, that is with a thick black deposit, usually show that you are running on too rich a mixture. This may be because you are holding the choke out too long or that the carburetter needs adjusting.

3. Light grey plug points usually mean the mixture is too weak; or that there is a leak in the air inlet; or that the ignition is too far advanced; or that a cooler plug should be used. In any case this is a sign of overheating and should be corrected.

4. The condition of the plug should be checked regularly. The points should be clean but may have a light to dark brown appearance with perhaps a light flaky deposit on the outer rim and the earth electrode.

It is curious that when talking about plugs the troubles and difficulties should crop up so regularly and so automatically. This is hard on the plug manufacturer, who has gone to so much trouble to produce the plug and to give advice on choice and use. The scooterist does not worry if the only trouble is that the plug is too sooty or too light in colour after use. Indeed, if the plug is taken out and found to have light-coloured, bleached points the owner may replace it at once, satisfied to have such a nice clean engine. The colour may suggest something is wrong but if the engine sounds well he does not worry about the colour. Unfortunately a much less curious trouble often results in an immediate stoppage of the engine because the plug points have been bridged. This means a dead short across the points and there can be no spark until the gap is restored once more. The bridging is of two kinds:

By carbon deposits. The end of the plug has a very black appearance. There are considerable deposits of a black substance, the products of imperfect combustion. When the mixture has been ignited some of the oil has not been burnt and this black powder has been deposited. Some of it goes on the piston crown, some on the cylinder head, some on the plug points. The usual cause is that the mixture is too rich, but you may get the same result from running at continual small throttle openings, or running in too high a gear. Normally, when this happens it does not long continue. You open the throttle for a burst of speed. The engine fires more happily and its running temperature rises. Piston speed increases. Flame speed increases and usually the majority of these deposits are burnt away before they do much harm. If you continue slow running, or with too rich a mixture, the deposits will accumulate and it is a matter of chance which of two consequences follow:

(a) The plug continues to fire but the deposits become so hot that the mixture ignites under pressure before the spark occurs; or after the spark occurs a local increase in pressure causes the mixture to ignite at a point distant from the flame. These are two forms of knocking and the engine will be damaged if there is much of it.

(b) The plug may cease to fire because the deposits have built up on the points and shorted them.

By a metallic whisker. This is a baffling and incompletely understood trouble. Your engine may suddenly begin to misfire. Within a few seconds it ceases to fire. You stop, check the fuel supply and then, naturally, suspect the plug. When you remove the plug you find the points are clean – in fact, light grey – but that across them is a fine metallic whisker. The points have been bridged completely and the HT current has been passing to earth just as though you had pressed the cut-out switch on the handlebars. This little metallic-looking whisker is easily removed. You can do it with a screwdriver blade or a penknife or a brush; you might even be able to blow it off. Replace the plug and the engine will run as sweetly as before.

This is plug whiskering. You may run for weeks and never encounter it, and then you may have it occur three times within an hour. Some scooterists have never met it. Others consider it a major bugbear. The causes and cures are as various as they are unconvincing for few scooterists agree on the cure and it is difficult to relate the explanations given by some firms with the explanations given by others. No engine manufacturer seems to have an opinion on the subject except that it certainly has nothing to do with his engine.

A commonly offered explanation is that plug whiskers originate in the additives included in two-stroke oils. As these additives are often organo-metallic compounds, it is said that the metal separates out and attaches to the plug points, eventually building up until the plug gap is bridged. This process is dependent on the electrical field about the plug points, being assisted by the occurrence of a spark there.

This explanation may well be correct; however, whiskering is a long-established trouble with two-stroke engines and occurred long before the special two-stroke oils were marketed. It occurs spasmodically. It seems impossible to reproduce plug whiskering under controlled conditions. Certainly no convincing paper has been put out giving results from a series of tests during which plugs were whiskered at will in the way one can get an engine to pre-ignite or detonate. There was a time when heavily leaded petrols were used in aeroplane engines – plug whiskering there could become dangerous. It could also be shown that the whiskering was directly linked to the composition of the fuel. No attempt to describe such a link with modern fuels appears to have been made successfully. A peculiarity of plug whiskering is that it invariably occurs with a clean plug. With carbon build-up there is a heavy black deposit on the points but whiskered plugs have a clean, almost immaculate appearance.

Another explanation, from a manufacturer of oil additives, ascribes plug whiskering to some peculiarity in engine construction and adds that oil additives are not the primary cause, the composition of the fuel being of greater importance.

This explanation may also be correct but it is difficult to accept that one make of engine is peculiarly liable to plug whiskering. No facts to support such a conclusion have ever been published nor has any engine manufacturer claimed that his engine was superior from this point of view. Scooter clubs have arranged many discussions, public and private, about the virtues and failures of their machines. Speed and flexibility, suspension and acceleration – these and a dozen other qualities have been claimed and discussed as being better or worse with some makes than with others. No such discussion has ever established even a suspicion that plug whiskering has been happening more frequently with any particular make.

Whiskers are distributed in such a haphazard manner that probably no simple explanation will be complete. Unfortunately, as can be seen from these two (out of many) explanations, the responsibility is variously ascribed to oil, to petrol, to oil additives, to engine construction. The makers of plugs, oil additives and petrol all make claims that their products give superior resistance to whiskering, but little objective research seems to have been done and made public. Since whiskers are distributed in such random fashion it is not easy to collect the evidence on which research must be based and in spite of the many claims it is not possible to say that whiskering of plugs is less – or more – common today than, say, five years ago.

One plug manufacturer said that where the scooter is driven for long periods at full throttle, there may be persistent plug whiskering. Against this, consider a few occasions on which a scooter has been driven at continuous high speed under observed conditions:

Rowell and Gallagher drove a Maico for twenty-four hours round the Isle of Man TT circuit, covering 1,062 miles.
Baldet and Christian drove a DKR Manx fairly hard, covering 500 miles in 500 minutes.
Thompson drove an Iso Milano – and Rowell drove a Lambretta – nonstop to Milan.
The Malta Scooter Club ran a Lambretta non-stop for ten days and nights.

On none of these runs was there a single whisker.

The next major problem is pinking or detonation. It might be thought ungenerous to include this in the section on sparking plugs but it is here because it happens when the plug sparks and on one notable occasion it appeared as though the choice of plug had something to do with persistent engine pinking.

There is a second noise, something like pinking, which is caused by pre-ignition and this may occur because the plug is the wrong type and runs too hot.

Both these result in the same kind of noise, a metallic tinkling from the cylinder when extra load is put on the scooter or when you accelerate. The noise increases as the load increases and often further throttle opening merely causes more pinking without perceptible increase in the engine's power.

The mechanism of pinking is not completely understood, but it can roughly be described as the result of uneven flame spread through the mixture. According to Ricardo the nucleus of combustion is a thin, thread-like flame at the sparking plug point. The flame moves outwards and the rate of combustion depends very largely on the temperature and density of that portion of the mixture which is just in front of the flame front.

If the speed of propagation is too high the steady flame spread will become a knock. The burning will become detonation, through the self-ignition of the remaining mixture. This will begin a wave which will be reflected back and forth within the cylinder to produce the familiar pinking sound. This auto-ignition was once considered a simple matter of compression-ignition, but later research suggests that it is bound up with the concentration of peroxides.

This simple detonation can occur through:

Too high a compression ratio. Scooter engines usually have a compression ratio of between six and eight and at this they give satisfactory results with standard fuels. If poor petrol is used there may be persistent pinking. Similarly, if you raise your engine's compression ratio you may get a pinking with standard fuels. The effect is the same – too high a compression ratio for the fuel being used.

Ignition too far advanced. If the spark occurs too soon it will start the flame-spread and then the pressure on the mixture will noticeably increase. The effect will be much as though you had suddenly increased the compression ratio – some of the mixture will detonate instead of burning.

Local hot spots in the combustion chamber. If carbon is deposited here it will usually start as an even layer. This layer will tend to retain heat so that the working temperature will rise. If this continues the plug points may become so hot that they will ignite the mixture before the spark occurs, the effect being much as though you had advanced the ignition too much. On the other hand, the layer may not be even. At some point along the piston crown the layer may become a projection, a small bit of carbon sticking up. This will tend to become incandescent. When this happens the spark may occur at the right time and the flame-spread may begin, but the pressure built up in front of the flame-front may be enough to cause the mixture near the irregular bit of carbon to ignite before it should. You will then get an effect similar to compression-ignition and the familiar knock will follow. In all these instances it should be remembered that as the pressure increases heat is generated and it is this which causes the compression-ignition effect.

Pinking which rapidly becomes worse usually means a dirty engine, which is cured by decarbonising it. The engine will then give good service once more. One of the Lambretta models gave some trouble through pinking and many were the remedies suggested – some by the British importers – for dealing with it. These ranged from bigger jets to a different ignition timing. Some owners claimed that the trouble was cured by using a short-reach plug in place of the long-reach plug normally recommended. However, the compression ratio of these Li. models was 7:1 whereas the LD models had a 6·5:1 ratio and since a short-reach plug slightly lowered the compression ratio it is possible that this was the explanation. It should be added that these scooters suffered not at all even though there was pinking. Some owners could live with the pinking and the engine power was not lacking.

Sparking plugs are connected to the HT coil by a stout lead and at the plug terminal the lead has a waterproof cover containing a suppressor so that the sparking plug will not interfere with television sets. This cover sometimes clips on to a plug terminal but sometimes the terminal must be removed and the cover is merely pushed on – an unsatisfactory arrangement, especially as you may have thrown the plug terminal away and the HT lead will not stay put without the terminal. Competition riders frequently complain of HT leads coming adrift. Many attempts have been made to give the HT lead a firm fixing – spring clips, drilled brass tabs and so on, but where a suppressor is built in the problem remains to be solved.

Another frequent source of trouble is due to the perishing of the HT lead casing or other terminal cover. Cracks may develop and water will enter them, shorting the HT current to earth and stopping the engine. This happened with one of the early type Vespas, where the onset of rain almost always meant the HT lead shorting to earth. The trouble was cured by developing a new type of HT lead and cover. In case of ignition trouble the HT lead should always be checked for this kind of shorting.

Sparking plugs are extremely efficient and require no maintenance except to clean them and occasionally to check the gap. How often to change the plug? That will depend on the way the engine is run, but a fair average is between 6,000 and 10,000 miles.

A small hint about actually fitting the plug; it is sometimes thought that to get a gas-tight seal between plug and cylinder head the plug must be screwed down hard. This is not necessary, and may be harmful. The seal is made by the copper washer. At one time these washers worked loose and might be lost, so the owner was perhaps justified in screwing down the plug hard. Later sparking plugs had the washer gripped to the plug and it is difficult to remove it. It is going too far to say the plug should merely be screwed home finger tight, but very little more pressure than this is needed to get a gas-tight seal. If excessive force is used the thread in the cylinder head may be stripped.

In standard machines the choice of plug is rarely critical but, in competition work, expensive damage may result from using the wrong plug. High compression ratios mean great heat and the use of a plug which is too hot for the engine may lead to damaging pre-ignition. In some cases the damage can occur very quickly. In one scooter race a rider had only just got going when – a bare two hundred yards from the start – there came ominous puffs of white smoke from the exhaust showed that a piston had been holed. On stripping the engine the piston crown showed a very neat circular hole which had taken only a few seconds to make – all through using the wrong type of plug.

You should always carry a spare plug and this should be clean, set to the proper gap and safely wrapped in thin polythene film – a polythene bag is ideal.

One of the best known facts about scooters is that they have small wheels. Both Vespa and Lambretta started with eight-inch diameter wheels whereas the average motor cycle wheels were eighteen inches or more. One obvious reason for the small size was cost; another was the normal low speed; a third was the different riding position.

As years passed scooter tyre sizes varied considerably; from the Vespa's eight inches to the fourteen inches of the Maicoletta 250. The most popular size became ten inches and this size was used when BSA launched their BSA and Triumph scooters. Along with the reduction in diameter went a small increase in section; 8 × 4·00 became normal, as did the pressed steel wheel, though there were exceptions. The Guizzo, the Capri, the Concorde and the Jawa Manet all, from time to time, used spoked wheels. However, it can be said that the vast majority of scooters were fitted with pressed steel wheels.

This was rather surprising for it applied to firms making scooters alone and to firms who made very powerful motor cycles. The pressed steel wheel, made in two parts, is another hallmark of scooters. The BSA Dandy and the Concorde were two exceptions where spoked wheels were used consistently for although the first Capri scooters had spoked wheels the makers quickly turned over to pressings.

The advantages were tremendous. Where they were combined with a single-sided wheel mounting they were overwhelming. D'Ascanio, talking about his first thoughts on designing the Vespa, said that he had often seen motor cyclists repairing a puncture and he had been so impressed by the difficulty of this operation, especially where the rear tyre was concerned, that he determined there should be no such difficulty with his Vespa scooter. Pressed steel wheels had come to the automobile industry and, though there had been some teething troubles, the idea was sound. In scooters it was almost universally adopted.

Simplicity marks the construction of typical split wheels. There is virtually a rim whose main duty is to carry the tyre. It is bolted to the more substantial pressing which carries a rigid centre face with four or more equally spaced holes. Through these pass the bolts which anchor the wheel firmly to the brake drum and so to the wheel hub which fits on the splined rear axle.

In another form of construction the two parts of the wheel are similar and merely hold the tyre. On some, but not all, these are identical for front and rear wheel, the hubs being separate and machined on the inner diameters as brake drums. This is in line with the tendency to standardise as many parts as possible.

On the BSA and Triumph scooters the wheels were made solid, being fixed by three nuts. Although the wheels were interchangeable care had to be taken not to fit them the wrong way round or the alignment would have been affected. In the event this proved to be an awkward arrangement which a little thought would have avoided. To make parts so that they can easily be fitted wrongly is a design error. With solid wheels of the BSA type the pressings were made separately and spot welded.

Where front and rear wheels are interchangeable only one spare wheel need be carried, so it is rarely necessary to repair a puncture by the roadside. The spare is fitted and the repair waits until a more favourable time occurs. This is an advantage when punctures are discovered in the dark or the rain, as usually seems to happen. Removing a wheel and fitting the spare is not a long job. However, on one or two scooters the necessity for removing the wheel was overlooked in the design and if you think of buying such a machine, become familiar with the drill before the necessity arises. Also, on some scooters with final chain drive it is not possible to remove the wheel until the chain has been removed. True, a knock-out spindle may be provided but where the driven sprocket must be disturbed the filthy chain must be handled.

For most scooters tubeless tyres are available, whether the wheels are split or not. With tubeless tyres a puncture will often be so slow to take effect that home – or a garage – can be reached in safety without changing the wheel. Where the rim is solid these tubeless tyres fit direct on the rim, but for split rims it is necessary to fit a special sealing band and then fit the cover on this.

It is most important to look after tyres properly, especially to keep them inflated to the correct pressures and to examine them from time to time for small defects that might become big ones. Tyre pressures vary between one make and another. Indeed, scooter owners were once startled to learn that one manufacturer was advising tyre pressures very different from those in the scooter maker's handbook. The explanation was that the Bloggs tyres made in Italy are not quite the same thing as the Bloggs tyres made in the British factory. It is difficult to give an estimate of the life of a tyre. Three years at 8,000 miles a year would be good service, two such years being usual, but much depends on the way tyres are treated. The rider who accelerates fiercely and brakes fiercely may get only one quarter of the tyre life his neighbour gets. Tyre pressures vary between front and rear wheel, the latter having the greater load and so the greater portion of the total weight of the scooter.

The front wheel carries a load between 30 and 37 percent according to a table drawn up after accurate weighing of a random selection of scooters.

It is good practice to change front and rear wheel round occasionally to equalise wear and, of course, to use the spare occasionally – this makes it more likely that when you need the spare it will be correctly inflated. A tyre pressure gauge is useful particularly if you are going abroad or on a long tour in Britain. The pressure gauges installed by filling stations and used by all and sundry are rarely accurate. This may not matter for car owners but scooterists are only one wheel from danger and it pays to carry your own pressure gauge and use it.

Many scooterists prefer to buy remoulded tyres when their present pair wear. If the casings are good they can be handed in and the remoulded tyre will give excellent service, especially as most of the remoulding is done under more or less direct supervision from the tyre makers. A casing can only be re-moulded once. It must then be abandoned. A casing will not be accepted unless it is sound. It therefore pays not to run the tyre to the point where the casing is damaged.

Front and rear wheels run on pairs of ball bearings. These are designed to last as long as the scooter and should never require attention. They are packed with grease before the scooter is assembled. Additional grease should never be necessary. If too much grease is packed into these bearings the grease may emulsify and cease to be an effective lubricant, with consequent damage to the balls or the housings. The grease is retained by oil seals, usually of synthetic rubber. Where the final drive gearing is mounted on the rear wheel assembly these gears often run in oil. If the oil seals are damaged this oil may be driven through to the brake lining. When the brake linings were of asbestos fibre an oil leak often meant the lining was permanently ruined. The more recent linings are bonded to the brake shoes, not riveted, and merely call for a wash in petrol to restore their efficiency. These resin-bonded linings were a great improvement all round.

There is a pair of brake shoes to each wheel. Each shoe has a brake lining. To the brake lining manufacturer the scooter is known as the willing horse. Carrying vast loads of luggage, two up, small wheels and small brake drums, with average speeds becoming higher and higher – these were formidable problems. To the commuter, halted in traffic blocks morning and night, town travel is a nightmare at a snail's pace but in fact town traffic gets away from rest quickly and stops quickly, adding every year to these problems.

You can get some idea of the problems if you calculate the kinetic energy of the scooter in motion, say at 30mph. The calculation is:

$$K = \frac{1}{2} \times \frac{W}{G} \times V^2$$

If the scooter has one passenger W = 320; V = 44 ft/sec and G = 32.2

$$K = \frac{1}{2} \times \frac{320}{32.2} \times 1936 = 9,630 \text{ ft/lb}$$

and to emphasise the final figure, remember that it would be sufficient to throw the scooter and passenger thirty feet into the air.

When the scooter is moving at this speed and is then stopped all its energy has to be absorbed in some way. It can be changed into heat, sound or some destructive effect.

Heat. To stop a rotating body involves transferring some of its energy into heat. With a mechanical brake you use a brake lining and a brake drum; almost all the energy is transformed into heat which passes through the brake drum and so to the outside air. Some heat passes to the brake shoes, etc.

285

Sound. Some – not much – of the energy may be expended in the effort to make the brake drum, brake shoe and even the scooter frame vibrate and some of these vibrations will induce sound waves.

Destructive effect. The scooter's energy may be absorbed by hitting something. If the rear wheel has locked solid the effect may be the removal of a lot of rubber from the tyre and a great black streak on the road.

The best of these three methods is to absorb the energy by heating the brake drum and getting rid of the heat before it has done damage. The best brake drums are made of cast iron though some of the earliest scooters had brake drums which were merely pressings. These gave trouble. They had little rigidity and often belled on the open side, reducing the braking effect. In addition, the shapely cowlings over the wheels made cooling more difficult.

The three major qualities of a good brake lining are that the linings are:

1. Noise-free.
2. Kind to the drums.
3. Resistant to temperature changes.

The first, strangely enough, is nearly the most important. Occasionally brakes squeal and it is difficult to locate the trouble. With riveted brake linings it was usual to put the blame on the linings as having worn down until the rivets were scoring the drum but brake squeal is almost always due to vibration being set up in the shoe, the lining and the adjacent parts. Since the drum is the perfect shape for resonance effects the sound is magnified.

The lining must be kind to the drums. The brake shoes pivot outwards from a fixed point, tending to distort the drum. If the linings are harsh they will wear the drum unevenly and excessively. Brake drums are bell-shaped and all bell shapes tend to become oval when whirled at high speed. The application of the brakes increases this tendency and if it becomes noticeable there will be rapid drum wear. For instance, a lining designed for a cast iron drum may be quite unsuitable for use with a brake drum of aluminium.

The linings must also resist temperature changes. Their coefficient of friction varies with temperature and there is a point at which the coefficient will not so much drop as vanish. This has nothing to do with the brake lining burning. The disappearance of a brake lining's holding power is known as fade and the temperature at which any brake lining material will fade is known with some certainty. Therefore, before a brake lining is chosen it is always necessary to know the conditions under which it will work – speed, loading, rate of temperature change, etc. The average scooterist is unlikely ever to have his brakes fade.

Fade is a function of heat, not so much the amount of heat as the rate at which it can be dissipated. The linings themselves are heat insulators but they create a lot of heat which must be got rid of. Almost the only way for the heat to escape is through the drums and that is why brake drums on scooters have fins or ribs – to increase the surface area through which the heat can escape.

The woven linings made from asbestos fibre often had brass wire included. This was originally to make the short fibres easier to handle but it was found that such linings were an improvement and the brass wire was retained even when new methods of weaving made it unnecessary. Today almost all scooter brake linings are moulded. They are homogeneous and it is easier to control their consistency and to make small variations for differing conditions. Some of these moulded linings are jog-drilled for riveting and replace linings can be bought but the current tendency is for the lining to be bonded to the shoe and to offer the complete unit as a replace exchange. The pair of worn brake shoes are handed in and a fresh pair obtained in exchange complete with new linings bonded in position. No other work is then necessary except to fit the fresh brake shoes. The dealer will return the old unit to the factory where a new set of linings will be fitted, ready for another customer. This system of factory replace units, or service exchange, has become very popular. Where design has reached the point of stability it is very satisfactory and economical. Brake shoes should always be exchanged in pairs; replacing a single brake shoe is rarely satisfactory.

Scooterists sometimes compare braking efficiencies by reference to the distance in which a scooter can be stopped from given speeds. This is a popular method. It is rarely accurate. One of the leading brake lining manufacturers after using this system for half a century abandoned it in favour of measuring the time between applying the brake and coming to a halt. A test of this type applied to a highly efficient lining gave a halt from 30mph in 1.7 seconds with a deceleration of 0·6g. The testing of brake linings is a tedious and accurate business. Lining and drum temperatures are recorded continuously through thermo-couples and the aim is to find a lining which will give uniform braking through the widest possible range of temperatures.

To be effective the brake drum must be rigid and this cannot be done without using a machined casting. Drums have become robust and the linings themselves are greatly improved. This has meant an increase in wheel weight but this has to be accepted. Front and rear brake drums are almost always of the same diameter, though there may be small variations. It is often said that the good rider uses the front brake as a general rule. It is often added that the front brake has greater stopping power than the rear brake because when the brake is applied the weight is thrown forward on the front wheel. The advice to use the front brake rather than the rear is probably derived from motor cycle racing where this certainly is the rule. The advice is, however, not reflected in the design of scooter brakes. Front and rear brakes are usually of the same diameter and where there is a difference the rear lining is always bigger. In addition, the manufacturer who fits a brake warning light couples it to the rear brake, a fairly plain hint that he expects it to be used as a general rule.

Scooter bodywork varies according to the layout of the units and the suspension method adopted. It will almost always consist of a tubular steel framework with the engine mounted towards the rear; the steering column, seat, wheels, etc., are anchored to lugs welded to the chassis, which is very rigid and should not require further attention during its life. Spot welding is used to fix the lugs and special welding machines have made it possible to manufacture complicated frames economically. Though most scooters had a flat footboard, others such as the German Zundapp and the British Velocette arranged the main chassis tube so that there was a kind of tunnel. The Velocette broke new ground by, as it were, hanging engine and transmission from the main tube, a very unusual arrangement indeed. A piece of ingenuity never adopted in Britain was seen in one or two Japanese scooters where the air enters through the front windshield, passing through a main chassis member to the carburetter.

In designing the bodywork itself there are three main problems and the variety of solutions offered suggests that none could be recommended without reserve.

Accessibility. Since the owner will want to do routine maintenance at home there must be some way of getting to the engine, giving enough room to work. Lambretta developed the big side panels and Vespa had their removable cowling. Both methods exposed the complete engine and no further dismantling was required even when removing the engine from the chassis. As engines became larger the limits of this system showed in a much reduced degree of accessibility. The other favourite method was to provide small side panels – or none at all – and to make the bodywork as a unit, usually pivoting at the front end. This could then be propped up, exposing the engine; or unbolted and removed in one piece. In both cases there were few fastenings so that accessibility can be called good. Where the bodywork had to be removed it was usually necessary to disconnect one or more lighting wires, and this led to some makers using split wiring with snap connectors. One or two British makers made rather absurd bodywork designs with complicated fastening systems using long threaded screws; while BSA made probably the most absurd of all – a special instruction sheet was issued explaining how the bodywork could be removed and the three dozen nuts and bolts kept safe for further use. Generally, however, the designer concentrates on giving easy and rapid access to plug and carburetter. He feels – perhaps with justice – that the owner will often wish to get at these two pieces of equipment.

Fuel tank. This is a bulky item and although it was usually carried close to the rear wheel some designers moved it to the steering column. Since the fuel feed is by gravity the position of the tank is fixed above the carburetter. This limits the tank's position. On motor cycles the tank was carried between the handlebars and seat but when a definition of the scooter was needed for competition riders it was ruled that this space must be clear. The British DKR and the German Prior had the tank below the handlebars. This enabled a big tank to be fitted – scooters originally had very small fuel tanks and many owners complained of the small cruising range which this imposed. If you fit the engine and tank below the rider's seat the size of the tank has obvious limits. Fuel tanks are usually made of pressed steel halves welded together. Greeves and Maico used tanks of bonded glass-fibre sheet. These were cheaper than sheet steel where small quantities were involved but there have been crashes where the glass fibre tank has shown itself less sturdy than metal, with disastrous fires resulting.

Glass fibre has also been used for the complete bodywork, notably on the Bond and Excelsior scooters. The method is well known and allows flexibility of design. Changes of shape or fastening can be made quickly and easily. Since the units are made by hand the method is not suitable for mass production, but an excellent finish can be obtained and there are plain advantages in having bodywork which is not liable to rust. Careful design is needed, however, since it is not easy to attach hinges, catches, doors and other parts to glass-fibre sheets or moulds. It was used on the Bond scooter because the firm already had suitable facilities as makers of the Bond three-wheeler. In the case of the Excelsior, the prototype was a thing of beauty, but it never went into production and soon afterwards the firm itself disappeared, another case of the scooter seeming to have the evil eye.

The most usual material for the bodywork is sheet steel pressed to shape. These pressings are produced on enormous machines and the dies used are very expensive. Design changes in pressings are therefore costly and not to be lightly made. The system is obviously geared to mass production. Here the outstanding success story is that of Vespa. Strangely, in spite of the success, only Lambretta ever attempted a similar design and even then it had a short and not very happy life.

The enamelled finish is sprayed – sometimes electrostatically – and then baked by means of a conveyor belt carrying the parts through a series of ovens. The general high finish of scooter bodywork helps to make these little machines the most decorative features of the present-day traffic scene.

15 Maintenance: The Scooter on the Road

(a) Easy starting

Getting started is one of the two-stroke's biggest problems. There can hardly be a scooterist who, at some time or another, has not come up against this problem in a practical and sometimes heartbreaking manner.

The beginner is particularly affected. She stalls the engine and cannot get it re-started. The more she kicks the deader the engine sounds. Another scooterist comes along, changes the plug, gives a hefty kick and away goes the engine, leaving the novice feeling that it was all her fault.

Not so. Experts have this trouble too. If you go to any motor cycle meeting you will find two or three riders left at the start. The rest of the field is hurtling round the first corner but one or two experts are left with engines that will not start. A lot of money, a reputation may be at risk – but the luckless expert can only push his machine to the side. For him the race is over before it has begun.

Now your engine needs three things before it will start.

1. Correct mixture in the combustion chamber.
2. A spark at the plug points.
3. Both these together at the right time.

Take the last point first. This is the least likely thing to go wrong. The spark at your plug occurs when the contact breaker points open. It is automatic. It has been checked by your dealer and usually stays set for months without any attention from you. If you look in the "Technical Data" section of your handbook you will see something like this. "Spark advance – 30° before TDC". Some makers give the amount of advance in millimetres. Your dealer is the man to put this right if it is wrong – which is unlikely.

Therefore, you can usually rule out the possibility that difficult starting is due to the timing being out. Even with a secondhand machine it is unlikely. Rather more likely is our first item – the mixture. Is this correct? Have you the right amount of oil, petrol and air? You have an instruction book and this tells you how much oil to use per gallon of petrol. Half a pint of oil in a 16:1. One-third pint in a 24:1 and one-sixth in a 50:1 mixture. It is not very likely that you will have trouble starting even if you have twice as much oil as you should have, but if when filling up you put the oil in first while the fuel tap is open you may have trouble – not very likely, but possible.

What about the air? This may give trouble if the air enters the carburetter through a long curly rubber tube. This tube may be twisted, cutting off the air supply, or it may be punctured, giving you too much air. Finally, the air filter may be blocked with road dust, again cutting off the air supply. These three points should be checked if you have starting difficulty.

An even more likely reason is that your kick is not powerful enough. Your scooter has flywheel magneto ignition – most probably – and unless the flywheel is revolving at a given speed you will not get a spark. As a general rule you must get 200+rpm to give the 7,000 volts needed. Usually there is no bother about this 200rpm, for it is not much, but if you have a new engine and light shoes you may hurt your feet on the kickstart pedal. The scooters made by British firms usually assumed that you were wearing heavy boots. There is an art in using the kickstart. Press down lightly to take up the free movement, then push firmly.

Finally we come to the most likely reason for impossible starting – the current does not reach the plug or, if it does, leaks to earth. In either case, no spark.

If you push and push but get no spark, remove the sparking plug. The points may be perfectly clean – indeed greasy, but a thin whisker bridges them. Remove the whisker – knock it off with a screwdriver or wipe it off with a duster – and the engine will almost certainly start easily, but make a note that you have too weak a mixture and put this right later. Secondly the points may be covered with black carbon deposits – wet or dry – which have bridged the points. You will need a clean plug in its place and you have too rich a mixture – either from running with the choke out, or simply too much oil in your petroil.

All these are simple. Here is something more complicated. If you look at wiring diagrams you will see that the plug is connected to earth, not by a wire but through being screwed into the cylinder. The connection to earth is through the whole machine via the tyres, so if you are told that the plug has shorted to earth you may wonder what the fuss is about since the plug goes to earth anyhow. What the diagram does NOT show is that only the outside of the plug is earthed. The inner electrode is connected via the HT lead to the flywheel magneto (from which it gets the current) but is insulated from the rest of the plug. So if you spray petroil over the end of the plug, shorting the insulation you might just as well have taken the plug out and run the HT lead straight to the earth terminal.

You will have gathered that if the plug points are wetted with oil or water the only solution is to remove the moisture. You cannot do this effectively by brushing. If this happens on the road, the best thing is to remove the wet plug, fit a fresh one from your toolkit and have the wet plug cleaned at a garage as soon as possible. It is difficult to clean a plug yourself.

You may find that the plug points are quite clean, no whisker, but you still cannot start. This may be serious – a faulty condenser, coil or rectifier. It may not be serious – a leak in the HT lead due to the rubber cover cracking and water leaking along these cracks. The cure is to dry the HT lead immediately and either fit a new one when you can or waterproof the present one. This kind of trouble is unlikely but if you get no spark at the plug, locating the trouble may take time; so remove the sparking plug, fit the HT lead again, and rest the plug on the engine. Try the kickstart pedal. If a few pushes gives nice sparks at the points you can replace the plug and start looking for something mechanical wrong. If there is no spark you may have a faulty plug, so remove the HT lead and, holding it very close to the metal of the engine, try the kickstart again. You should get a nice series of sparks from the HT lead to the engine. If you do, the plug was faulty – get a fresh one. If you get no sparks you will have to check back item by item; first the HT lead, then coil, condenser and so on – really a job for the service station. With many HT leads, unfortunately, this method of checking is difficult because the lead ends in a plastic cap. You can fit a short metal rod where the plug usually fits and see if you get a spark between this and the engine but the method needs careful handling. Do not touch the metal rod or you may get a sharp shock.

No hints on starting are complete without some reference to the choke. Your carburetter is set to give you the right proportion of fuel to air. For practical purposes the best ratio is about 1:11 but you need about 1:7 when the engine is cold. The reason for this is simple, but not immediately obvious. If the metal of the carburetter is cold and you spray on it a fuel/air mixture some of the fuel will condense out and the mixture reaching the combustion chamber will be about 1:17, which is too weak to burn. Therefore, if you start with a very rich mixture at the carburetter some of the fuel may condense out but a 1:11 mixture still reaches the combustion chamber and the engine fires. You need this richer mixture until the engine warms up. Then the fuel will no longer condense out and you can go back to your more economical 1:11 mixture again. With some carburetters more fuel is provided; in others less air is allowed through – through the operation of a choke lever. Use the choke only when starting – but remember that some engines always require the choke to be used when starting, while others only need it when the engine is cold. Note that when you pull the choke out to start and then push it back the exhaust continues for a second or two to emit billows of smoke. The mixture at the carburetter has gone back to normal but there was a certain amount of fuel condensed out in this choke tube and this is being picked up even with the choke lever disengaged.

With this in mind you will have no difficulty in seeing how the plug points get wet. If the engine is cold the plug points are cold and fuel in the mixture will tend to condense on them. That is why the experienced scooterist, having tried the kickstart pedal a few times with no result, knows that further kicking will be useless. The plug points will be wet and there will be no spark.

Thus, the first kick or two is very important. They must be brisk and forceful. If not, you will not get your 200rpm and thus no spark. For some years there was a fashion for some kind of automatic choke return – the choke operated only until you opened the throttle, then it automatically returned. With a few scooters you would always have difficult starting if the choke and throttle were used together. All of this emphasizes the importance of getting to know just what should be done with your engine's controls to get the quick starting which some scooterists have now and always have had.

(b) Running in

There is general agreement that a scooter must be run in before you drive it at full power. How the running in should be done is not generally agreed. For the Moto Guzzi Galletto you were told:

"Running in. It is recommended that during the first 500km of running you should not subject the engine to excessive force. In this way you will also obtain the necessary practical knowledge of how to drive it."

While the makers of the Zundapp Bella said:

"During the first 300 miles the engine should not be driven at full load. From then on to 600 miles you can ride it with ever-increasing loads. There are no speed limits to be observed during the first 600 miles."

while Maico said:—

"Running in is largely a matter of instinct. Non-expert riders should take the following speeds as a guide during the first 600 miles:

1st	12mph
2nd	20mph
3rd	32mph
4th	40mph."

These three firms are world-famous. Their ideas of running in do not agree with each other nor do they agree with Vespa (in the first 1,200 miles do not keep the throttle fully open for long periods) or Lambretta (do not exceed these speeds: 1st/12mph, 2nd/30mph, 3rd/40mph, 4th/55mph) nor with many others. Some of these contradictions are real. Others only seem to be different. Many a young wife, after ruining an apple charlotte, has lamented to her mother:

"You told me to put a teaspoonful in" only to hear the indignant retort:

"Yes, but not THAT size teaspoon,"

and when you find contradictory advice given about running in, remember that some teaspoons may be bigger than others.

In your engine, various metal parts slide one on the other; the piston slides up and down the cylinder, steel shafts revolve rapidly inside bronze bearings, gear faces roll on each other and so on. Between all these surfaces is a thin film of oil and in theory the metal faces should never touch each other. You will have been told that to break this film is to do damage – try sharpening a chisel or a pen-knife on an oilstone. If the blade is merely blunt it slides easily, leaving no trace. If the blade is nicked you will leave a nasty scratch on the oilstone.

Exactly the same thing may happen in your engine. Look at the side of the piston, how smooth it is; yet under a microscope it looks like a ploughed field. The ridges and humps depend on the composition of the metal and on the tools which were used to machine it. Fine grain metal and high-speed tools – these give you good surfaces.

However, the bumps are always there, as they are on the steel shafts, the faces of gear teeth, the bronze bushes. The more you have paid for your scooter the smaller these bumps should be.

There are exceptions and these have recently become important. Ball and roller bearings, when they are of first quality, are made to such fine limits and with such skill that they do not require the normal running in process. There are no humps to be ground down, no bumps to be knocked off. This is not the full story, of course, for there is no sliding motion such as you have with pistons, but these bearings are a great improvement on bronze bushes. Running steel shafts in soft metal bearings was always a makeshift and its continued use in engines is a tribute to the tenacity rather than the ingenuity of the designer. Then where are you likely to have trouble?

Gears. The gears roll against each other. They do not slide. It is very, very rare to have gear trouble. There is a small amount of play (backlash) and if you start or stop very suddenly you might just possibly chip a pair of gears but this is unlikely. You will hardly ever have trouble with the gear train, even in British scooters where the gears engage by means of dogs on their faces.

Chain drive. You can have trouble here, and do damage. If the chain is slack you may set up excessive grinding of the chain roller against the sprocket teeth, leading quickly to the need for new chain, new sprockets. Keep the chain tension correct. Keep the chain lubricated.

The connecting rod. There is a bearing at each end. Most scooters have needle rollers at both ends and it is very unlikely these will give trouble. They require no running in.

Piston, piston rings, cylinder barrel. This is where you are most likely to have trouble. The piston does not fit the cylinder exactly. There is a total clearance of perhaps 0·005 ins between them, but the rings do fit closely to the cylinder bore, separated only by the extremely thin film of oil which comes from the petroil. If you looked closely at the surfaces, under high magnification you might think you were looking at a ploughed field or a slice of bread. Even with a thin film of oil between them the piston moving in the cylinder is at first like using a flue brush or a pipe cleaner – a lot of stuff comes away.

You many think the obvious cure is to make both surfaces infinitely smooth but this would be disastrous. Some metal blocks (slip gauges) are made as smooth as this and you can press a pair together by hand so closely that the surfaces interlock and cannot be separated without using enormous pressure. Sometimes, when you manage to separate them, both surfaces are ruined. It is fortunate that you cannot make pistons and cylinders as smooth as this, or every single such engine would be destroyed. No, you must accept these rough surfaces and make use of them.

If your engine seizes you will naturally be alarmed. The

piston breaks through the oil film and the two metal surfaces are touching. Much heat is generated and the area of contact spreads, piston and cylinder sticking together more and more. You can feel this as you ride along, like a brake being applied. Eventually the engine seizes solid and your back wheel skids. This may cause a bad crash. The whole process may take five seconds, or may be dramatically sudden. If you are alert you declutch and halt safely.

Put the scooter on its stand, engine in neutral. Try to depress the kickstart pedal by hand, gently. If it moves, heave a sigh of relief and then wait. The engine will be hot so remove side panels and wait for it to cool down. If you have a squirt-type oilcan, remove the sparking plug and put a couple of squirts of oil in as you press the kickstart pedal down once or twice. As a rule you will then find the machine runs as well as ever. It has been a useful warning that you need to go more carefully.

You have three golden rules for running in:-

1. Avoid low speeds in high gears.
2. Keep varying your speed.
3. Do not run flat out.

The beginner wants to get into top gear as quickly as possible. He wants to stay there as long as he can. Of every hundred scooter engines ruined in the first 500 miles ninety of them are ruined because of this. Manufacturers are not blameless. If they give maximum speeds in the gears they should also give minimum speeds. No general rule can be given, as so much depends on number of gears and engine capacity. However, all the intermediate gears are powerful. They are the pullers. It is in top gear that you can do most damage for usually this is not a working gear. If you are in top gear and have to brake, or if you slow down by as much as 7mph even without breaking, you should change to a lower gear. Try not to accelerate in top after a check. It is an excellent rule.

Keep varying your speed. A notorious engine wrecker is the owner who, having decided to run the scooter in for 600 miles, picks a motorway, sets the throttle for 30mph – or any other speed – and keeps going at that speed. The engine is very, very likely to seize. Why this should be is not easily explained. At first glance it seems to be an excellent way of getting a lot of miles in but please believe that running in should NOT be done at a uniform speed, even if that speed is well within the capacity of the engine. Vary the speed. Change gear frequently. Apply the brake, change down, accelerate. Do not choose the easy way out down the motorway.

Do not run flat out. This applies to all gears, not only top. It is obvious that you must not belt along at top speed in top gear. It is just as important that you should not run at top speed in any gear. Always have something in hand. For the first 300 miles always have a lot in hand, in all gears. The expert does this by instinct. You may need a guiding rule and here is one: – If you open the throttle a little more and you do not go any faster, you are either going too quickly or you are in too high a gear. You must have something in hand. Going up a hill you should apply this rule always. Start with a bit of a run at it in top, but as soon as your speed drops, change to a lower gear. Never hang on in any gear with the speed dropping. You can try this later on, when you know your machine. At first, change gear when the speed drops. Do not wait, hoping for a miracle.

The ideal course for your running-in-period is a series of secondary roads between two major roads. There should be no steep hills, no straights more than a mile long, lots of cross-roads where you must change to a lower gear, lots of places where you must come to a halt. On such a course you would be constantly varying your speed, changing gear, giving engine and transmission different loads. Some scooter clubs have worked out a route of this kind. It is impossible to run your scooter in by getting into top gear and staying there. All the gears require running in. Things to avoid when running in: –

Long hills. These are dangerous either way. Going up them the engine overheats. Going down them there is danger of the engine idling with the throttle closed – very bad.

Straight roads. On these it is almost impossible to vary your speed as you should.

Short runs. Get the running in done with trips of fifty miles or so. A series of one-mile trips, with long halts between, is very harmful, especially on bigger scooters.

Strangely enough there is not the same need for a long running in period with some of the smaller scooters. The new 50cc engines can be run flat out after the first fifty or hundred miles. This was shown when fifty of these machines, taken at random from stock, were driven from London to Paris flat out and with no pretence at running in and without any harm to the engines. Some engines need more oil in the mixture during running in and your instruction book will make this clear.

Above all, do not be afraid of the noise of the engine. It is better to have it ticking over briskly than to have it stalling every time you slow down. Have the tickover speed on the fast side, therefore.

And watch that top gear.

(c) The first checkover

In theory a scooter is in first-class condition when delivered to the dealer. In theory all the controls have been adjusted, oil and grease are just where they should be and all that is needed is a spot of fuel – and then off down the road.

In practice this is not so. Therefore, before you receive the scooter there is carried out a Pre-delivery Check. This covers all major nuts, all controls, all greasing and lubricating.

Particular attention is paid to the adjustment of the controls. This check is so useful that every scooterist should know about it and be able to do it. No mechanical or technical knowledge is called for. The tools you need should be in your own toolkit.

First of all, the major nuts: –

Wheel nuts, usually three types:

(*a*) Those holding the split rims together.

(*b*) Those holding the wheel to the hub.

(*c*) Those securing the spindle.

These are the nuts which you might loosen yourself, and when you repair a puncture they should be tight and kept tight.

Suspension Units. Usually these call for no attention – leave maintenance to the service station, but the securing nuts should be checked for tightness.

Lock Nuts: on all cable controls – for clutch, gearchange, brakes, etc. Adjuster nuts are usually fitted to each cable, with a lock nut to hold the setting. Check that the latter nut is firm.

The above are the most important, but you should go round the scooter with a small spanner, checking all others. Note the handlebar lighting switch, the kickstart pedal, the footbrake pedal and the various bodywork fastenings. There are also several points which you should be familiar with: –

GEARBOX OIL LEVEL. On two-stroke engines this is the only oil level you have to watch. Find out how to drain, flush out and refill.

CLUTCH CABLE. To see that there is slight play on the clutch lever, and that the clutch engages and disengages well within the limits of travel of the lever.

BRAKES. The front brake works from the handlebar. The lever should not come right back to the handlebar when the brake is full on. The footbrake pedal should never hit the footboard. Both pedals should have slight initial play. The amount of free play depends entirely on your own preference.

Some owners like almost no play, but the average owner should have a little.

GEAR CHANGE. With a handlebar gear change control the setting is fairly critical. The gear numbers are marked on a movable sleeve and the numbers should line up with a fixed mark. It is not good practice to work the gearchange unless the engine is running. You can do it, but try not to. If the zero (neutral) does not line up with the fixed mark, adjust the cables until it does. When neutral lines up all the others will. If the engine jumps out of gear it is usually because one of the gear cables is too tight, so slacken it off slightly.

FINAL CHAIN. Very few scooters now have a final chain drive. If one is fitted, check that there is no excessive slack. Find out also, how to adjust it if there is. If you can, try doing so in the dealer's shop so that you know the drill and any snags.

TYRE PRESSURES. Don't leave these to chance. You cannot tell whether a tyre is correctly inflated merely by looking at it – nor even by pressing it with your thumb. Buy a tyre pressure gauge – or persuade someone that it is the ideal gift for you.

FUEL. Find out what proportion of oil is needed with the petrol. It varies between 2% and 5% on average. A few want 6%. Find out for certain how much oil is needed during running in. Don't leave this to chance.

CARBURETTER. Some types are complicated, but you should check three points:

1. How does the choke work? When should it be used? Is it automatic?

2. The slow-running control. This is usually a screw which holds the throttle slide slightly open when the engine is ticking over.

3. The air mixture control. This small screw admits more or less air to the mixture at low speeds.

It will help if you know how the carburetter works, though

it is not necessary, but you should know how to check these three points. The two latter need balancing against each other. When you alter one you usually need to adjust the other to suit. Before you take over the scooter it would help if these settings were disturbed and you have to put them right again. Also find out where the jets are, take them out and replace them, just so you know how.

SPARKING PLUG. Take this out. See it is of the correct type, that the points are clean and set at the correct gap. Find out what the equivalent plug is in at least two other makers' lists and note them down. Check that there is a spare plug of the right type, clean and correctly gapped.

LIGHTS. Check that they all work, including dipped head-lamp beam and stop light. Set the engine going, switch on all lights, including stop light – and winkers if fitted – and change from main beam to dipped. If the engine falters when the lights are switched on the contact breaker setting is probably wrong.

BATTERY. Most scooters today have a battery. The terminals should be clean, the leads firmly connected. The electrolyte level in the cells should be just above the tops of the plates. The battery itself should be firmly fixed in its bracket.

TOOL KIT. See that this is in place and is a toolkit, not a joke. Put in it your spare plug and tyre pressure gauge. Both should be wrapped in a plastic bag.

INSTRUCTION BOOK. Check that you have one before handing over your money for if it is difficult before the sale it will be impossible afterwards. An instruction book is part of the standard equipment of every new scooter.

CONTACT BREAKER GAP. Here it is not a matter of checking that the gap is right. It almost certainly will be, but eventually you may have to adjust it so you should know how it is done. It is a fiddling job. You will need a small screwdriver and a feeler gauge – is there one in the toolkit? The ideal is for you to be shown how – and actually to make the adjustment – before you buy your scooter. Some dealers will be glad to show you how to do it. A wrong gap means difficult starting and misfiring under load or at high speed; also the engine may stall when the lights are switched on.

If you have just taken delivery of your scooter – new or secondhand – these are points you should check before riding it. The dealer may be absolutely reliable and when you do your check you may find every single item correct. Still – these are the things you should know about. If anything goes wrong when you are out on the scooter the responsibility will be yours, so watch these points beforehand. It has happened that a scooter has been handed over to a customer with no oil in the gearbox. It is rare, but it has happened.

(d) Routine maintenance
Except for one or two items which are clearly labelled, all the maintenance work here described can be done by the average scooter owner. No technical knowledge is required and the tools should be in your normal toolkit – except for a scraper and perhaps a feeler gauge.

First of all, go back to The First Checkover because the checks called for there are those which should be made periodically. Those are the places where adjustments become necessary. Follow these checks and repeat them regularly. You will then get excellent service from your scooter. If you neglect them your scooter – and your pocket – will suffer.

For regular maintenance there is no substitute for a really efficient service station. That should be clear from the beginning, for they have the specialised equipment and the trained mechanics. Owners of new scooters often leave all maintenance to a service station but if you wish to do your own there is absolutely no reason against it, as long as you keep within bounds – leaving jobs which are beyond you. Adjusting the clutch control, for instance, is a job you should be able to do perfectly, but dismantling the clutch is something most owners should leave alone.

GEARBOX LEVEL. Very important indeed. Find out where the filler, level and drain plugs are and keep the upper surface of the oil at the correct level. Find out what kind of oil is specified – and use it. You may do serious damage if you put too much oil in, for great pressure may be built up and the oil forced through the oil seal to the brake shoes. Check the level with the scooter upright and engine warm, but allow the oil to drain down before checking. When you drain gear oil out you should flush with light oil – petroil will do, but not paraffin – and then fill to the correct level with the correct grade of oil.

FUEL LINE. A sound precaution – put some fuel in the tank, disconnect the fuel line at the carburetter and turn the fuel tap to the "On" position. Let some fuel run through into a teacup. This may bring down dirt trapped in the tank during assembly. Strain the fuel and put it back into the tank. There may be a filter in the fuel line. Find out where it is and how to clean it. Polythene fuel lines will harden and crack in time, so be ready for this – a length of rubber tubing will make a temporary repair. If fuel is not reaching the carburetter you may clear a blockage by disconnecting the fuel line at the carburetter and blowing up it – but have the fuel tap "On" first. The blockage will probably clear, but plainly the fuel supply needs testing when you have more time.

CARBURETTER. The filters are now so efficient that your carburetter really needs no maintenance for months at a time. Do not alter the settings idly, though you should know where they are and how they work. Know also how to remove and replace the jets, but it is not necessary to disturb them. If you remove and dismantle the carburetter do observe scrupulous cleanliness. It is easy to introduce grit and so do more harm than good because you will have by-passed the filters. There is little point in experimenting with different size jets except for competition work.

CLUTCH. Whatever make of scooter you have, you can test the clutch in the same way. With the engine in neutral and switched off, test that you can move the clutch lever on the handlebar for about one-eighth of an inch, measured at the base of the level. It should move freely for that distance – not more and preferably less. This is the free movement. Now slowly depress the kickstart pedal. You should feel considerable resistance. Continue to depress it slowly time after time and meanwhile squeeze the clutch lever. At about one-third of its travel you should begin to feel the kickstart pedal moving more freely. At two-thirds of its travel the kickstart pedal should move very easily. This means the clutch is fully withdrawn. Without a kickstarter this method does not apply.

If you have to take the clutch lever right back to the handlebar before the kickstart pedal moves easily, or if it moves easily with the clutch lever only half way through its travel, your clutch is either very worn or is seriously out of adjustment. Take it to a service station.

A word about clutch slip. The clutch transmits the entire engine power and depends on two factors, the friction plates themselves and the springs which press them together. If you accelerate you will normally go faster but if you find the engine note rises but you get no extra speed you may have clutch slip. The causes may be: –

(*a*) The clutch plates are faulty – either deformed so that they do not grip over their full area; or the friction pads may be worn.

(*b*) The clutch springs are too weak – you need stronger ones.

The clutch plates may simply have worn in the usual way but the springs may not be strong enough for a curious reason.

The previous owner may have souped-up the engine so that it gives more power than the clutch springs can handle. The cure is simply to fit stronger springs. On a standard machine you rarely get this trouble. Clutch springs do become tired, but very rarely on standard engines.

On some early scooters there was trouble with the clutch housing belling. It was made from a rather feeble steel pressing and the open end belled, allowing the retaining circlip to jump out. If you find this circlip jumping out on your scooter you usually need a new clutch housing. In later models the open end was strengthened.

GEAR-CHANGE CONTROLS. Where gear changing is done through a handlebar lever coupled to the clutch occasional adjustment is necessary. The gear change operates through a pair of Bowden cables working a lever or quadrant or some such control at the engine end. Each cable has a lock nut and an adjuster nut. There is an index mark on the fixed portion of the handlebars and this should line up with the centre of the of the o (marking neutral) on the movable sleeve. If this is not so, slacken off both lock nuts at the engine end of the cables, tighten up one of the adjusters and you will see the movable sleeve move slowly round, When the index mark is exactly opposite the centre of the o you should tighten up both lock nuts on the cables and then test again. Squeeze the clutch lever – try to move the gear shift. It should not move freely either way. You do not need any slack in the lever. At the same time the cables should have equal tension. If one is much tighter than the other you may have the engine jumping out of gear when you are riding along. The adjustment is very easy to make and should be checked each month. Some scooterists like a sloppy gear-change control, but it has no advantage.

BRAKE ADJUSTMENTS. The front brake is operated by a Bowden cable. The rear brake also, but with some scooters by a series of solid jointed rods. In all cases there is an adjuster screw, with a lock nut to hold any given setting. Adjustments are easy to make but some owners neglect them because the fittings are always coated with grease and filth. Put the machine on its stand so that the front wheel spins freely. Tighten the adjuster nut so that the brake begins to rub. Then slacken off perhaps half a turn. Tighten up the lock nut and then check that you have not disturbed the setting. The wheel must revolve freely. This is most important because a rubbing brake will generate a dangerous amount of heat. Repeat the process for the rear wheel – with the scooter on its stand you can usually raise the footboard and jam it so that the rear wheel clears the ground. When you make these adjustments, have handy a small brush and an eggcup full of petroil. Brush the mechanisms clean. You can see a portion of the inner cable – clean this and coat lightly with grease as a protection.

The free movement of the brake lever – the amount the lever moves before it operates the cable – is entirely a personal matter. Some riders like keen brakes. The front brake lever should never come right back to the handlebar, even with the brake full on, nor should the footbrake pedal touch the footboard. The angle made by the brake arm with the brake control should never be more than a right angle. These three symptoms, if present, point to serious maladjustment of the brakes – usually it means that the brake linings are dangerously worn and new brake shoes should be fitted.

New brake linings may be fitted or the complete brake shoes handed in for service exchange parts. The mechanically-minded owner should be able to do the job himself. It is more satisfactory to fit replace shoes than to try fitting new linings alone.

CONTACT BREAKER POINT ADJUSTMENT. This sounds complicated but it is very easy. It is made necessary because as wear takes place on the cam follower the gap tends to alter gradually and this affects the timings – the point at which the spark occurs.

The contact breaker mechanism is placed inside the flywheel. There are the two points, one fixed, the other one a cam-operated arm which moves as the flywheel revolves. When the points are wide open they should be about 0·018 ins. apart (the exact distance varies between engines and is given in your instruction book). Turn the flywheel slowly and watch the points open; there are windows in the flywheel for this viewing. You can turn the flywheel by hand with the engine in neutral or through the rear wheel with a gear engaged; engine off, of course. As the flywheel moves an inch or so you will be able to judge when the points are open at their widest. Check this with a feeler gauge. The fixed contact point is held on a plate and this, being locked by a screw, can be moved if the screw is slackened off. This is how the adjustment is made. Slacken off the screw, check the maximum gap between the points, and lock up the screw again. It is just as simple as that. After locking up, check the adjustment once more to see the gap really is correct. There is all the difference in the world between the engine note when the gap is correctly set. It has a snappier, healthier note, and the engine starts more easily from cold.

The stator plate itself is adjustable. This is set at the factory and should not need alteration during the scooter's life. However, some owners make radical changes to their engines, and if the power is significantly increased some timing adjustment is usually needed at the stator plate. This is beyond the scope of the average owner.

A small job you can do; put a spot of oil on the cam felt. One spot – that's all. More will be harmful. Much trouble is caused through excess oil in the magneto.

CHAIN. In some scooters the final drive is by half-inch roller chain. This should be checked monthly for tension, with machine upright and off the stand, unloaded. The total up-and-down movement of the slack side of the chain measured at the centre is about half an inch. A tight or slack chain will damage itself and its sprockets. If you have to fit a new chain because the old one is worn you should fit new sprockets and this is costly. Where the chain really is enclosed little maintenance is needed.

CABLES. If these are fitted correctly the only attention they need is to keep the free length of inner cable (that outside the sheath) clean and lightly coated with grease. The fitting of cable lubricators is no longer necessary. The more modern cables run in inners of fluon, a special non-stick substance. If a cable breaks or frays you should fit a complete new cable, not just the inner. Most cable trouble is due to faulty fitting, some to fitting the wrong cable.

DECARBONISING. A two-stroke engine runs on a mixture of petrol, oil and air. The oil is not completely burned away when the engine is running – nor is all the sulphur in the air; therefore you will find on cylinder head, piston crown, exhaust unit, etc., a blackish or brownish deposit, usually referred to as "carbon deposits". These become incandescent under pressure – as when you accelerate – and may ignite the mixture when you round a bend or go uphill. You will notice that this noise becomes worse when you open the throttle, though your speed will hardly increase at all. The simple cure is to remove these carbon deposits, particularly from cylinder head and piston crown. It might be useful here to give general directions for the two types of decarbonising, since these general notes are applicable, with detail variations, to scooters of all makes. It used to be said that you should decarbonise a two-stroke engine every 2,000 miles or so, but the more recent engines do not call for decarbonising at intervals of less then 5,000 miles.

THE TOP DECOKE

This is a simple and easy operation which the average owner can carry out at home, thus saving a great deal of money.

Turn the fuel tap off. Disconnect the fuel line at the carburetter. Disconnect the HT lead from the plug. Remove the plug and clean it – your garage will sandblast it, which is the most satisfactory method. Check the gap afterwards. Remove the aluminium cowling from the engine. Usually it is in two portions. Don't remove one screw at a time. Slacken them all in turn as cowlings of sheet metal (some are cast) have a lot of spring in them. Then remove the cylinder head nuts with their washers. Traditional way is to slacken one nut half a turn; then do the same to the nut diagonally opposite; finally do the same with the other two nuts. Repeat this drill until you can slacken the nuts with your fingers. Carefully preserve the washers and if there are two to each nut, replace them the same way round.

Pull off the cylinder head. If there is a gasket, inspect it for damage. If damaged, fit a new one but this replacement should not be necessary. By depressing the kickstart pedal bring the piston to its top position. Get a blunt screwdriver, a stick of solder or a piece of very hard wood and scrape the carbon deposits from piston crown and cylinder head. Do not scratch the aluminium. Get a nice clean, smooth surface. Some people finish off with metal polish. Do NOT use caustic soda on aluminium. Do NOT use emery paper on any part of the engine.

Take the piston down to its lowest position. The holes (ports) in the cylinder may have similar deposits partially blocking them. If so, scrape them clear for at least an inch. For this you will need the screwdriver end bent at a right angle or you can buy one of the excellent ready-made scrapers (though they have fairly sharp edges and must be used carefully). Wipe off the deposits you scrape out, using a slightly oily rag. Wipe the inside of the cylinder. Bring the piston up and then down again. Wipe the bore again.

You have now done the Top Decoke, so called because it is all done from the top. It should have taken you about forty minutes at most, including getting everything put back again. Second time you will do it in half an hour. It is not in the least a dirty job. It is the average owner's decoke.

THE FULL DECOKE

The second type of decoke is more thorough. The average owner can do it, but it is a dirtier job. It includes removing the exhaust system and silencer, cleaning them and cleaning the exhaust port from outside the cylinder. The inlet ports rarely need cleaning.

Methods of cleaning the exhaust vary. Here is the caustic soda method. It does not apply to all exhaust systems, so make inquiries beforehand, because some exhaust systems simply cannot be cleaned out. The cylinder barrel is usually of cast iron and the caustic soda method can be used for that. Take a bucket of cold water – a plastic bucket is best. Add one lb. of caustic soda crystals. The water will become very hot and will bubble as though boiling. Put the metal parts gently into the solution. They should be totally immersed. Leave them overnight. Next morning hook them out with a stiff wire, rinse them in cold running water. All carbon deposits can then be easily brushed off. When the parts are cleaned, coat the cylinder barrel with light oil as a protection. On no account handle the crystals. Do not allow any of the solution to touch your skin, clothes, linoleum or paintwork. The job is best done outside on a stone or concrete surface.

Between the exhaust pipe and the cylinder is a stout gasket. It is rarely damaged but should be examined and a new one fitted in case of doubt.

FOR THE MECHANIC

The third and most thorough decoke requires that the cylinder barrel should be removed. Usually this merely means disconnecting the exhaust system and pulling the barrel up over the studs. The piston should be brought to its lowest position first. The cylinder base gasket is almost always damaged at this point and a new one should always be fitted. The barrel can be removed to a bench for cleaning, or soaked in a caustic soda solution (see above). Clean the piston crown before you do this.

Having gone thus far it is usual to check the big-end and small-end bearings. Wear in the former can be detected by holding the connecting rod and trying to move it vertically relative to the piston; wear in the latter by movement relative to the crankshaft with the crankshaft, of course, stationary. Any perceptible movement calls for investigation. You are unlikely to have the big-end bearing fail, but on some scooters the little-end is a bronze bush (old scooters) and this may become oval. In this case you need a new small-end bush and since the design of these bushes changed from one model to another, make sure you get the correct replacement from the service station.

This is also an opportunity for checking piston rings. They should be carefully removed, being brittle, and fitted into the cylinder barrel. Check the gap between the ring ends and if the gap is too big (consult the handbook for tolerances) fit a complete set of new rings. Do not replace one ring only. Clean out the ring grooves – the usual tool is a piece of broken piston ring.

Do not remove the gudgeon pin unless it is necessary, usually held by two circlips. The average owner should not remove the piston. It is possible to fit it the wrong way round. This is the most thorough and complete decoke. The majority of scooterists should not attempt it. The mechanically minded will take it in their stride.

JOBS TO AVOID. The average owner is advised to avoid the following jobs: –

Cleaning hub bearings and packing them with grease.

Dismantling the steering head or adjusting it.

Timing the engine.

Filing contact breaker points.

Filing down pistons.

Removing the engine.

Fitting main bearings and oil seals.

Glossary of Technical Terms

Acceleration: Increases of speed from one moment to another. Speed may not convey any sensation but you can always feel acceleration.

Alternating current (AC): This is generated by the flywheel magneto and may be fed direct to the headlights (hence direct lighting) or may go to a rectifier and so be used to charge an accumulator.

Ammeter: An instrument for measuring in amperes the current passing through a circuit.

Battery lighting: A system in which the lights obtain their current from an accumulator, the latter being charged from a flywheel magneto or dynamo. Battery current is direct current.

Bearings: Properly these are either ball or roller. Solid so-called bearings are bushes or journals. A ball bearing consists of the outer housing, the balls and the inner race, though double-row ball bearings also have a cage. Roller bearings consist of an outer housing, the rollers and the inner race. In a special type, needle roller bearings the rollers are of very small diameter.

Bevel gears: These have their shafts at right angles as a rule. The junction lines produced from the two gears meet on the shaft centre lines produced.

Big-end: Usually a ball bearing at the bottom end of the connecting rod. It carries a spindle force-fitted into the crank-shaft webs.

Brake shoes: Sturdy aluminium castings mounted in pairs on the back plate, having on their outer surfaces a pair of brake linings, usually bonded to the shoes. One end of the shoe is fixed. The other moves outwards as the brake is applied.

Carburetter: A device for mixing air with a measured quantity of fuel and delivering it to the engine. According to the direction of the air stream a carburetter is horizontal, vertical (or down-draught) or inverted.

Choke: A device on the carburetter which closes off most of the air supply and so allows a very rich mixture to pass to the engine.

Clutch: By pressing together two sets of plates revolving about a common axis the engine motion is transmitted to the gears. By separating the two sets of plates they spin independently and so the engine continues to revolve without moving the scooter. The device is known as a clutch and may be single-plate or multi-plate.

Condenser: Two sets of insulated plates, sandwiched and sealed to store current and protect the contact-breaker points.

Connecting rod: A steel forging, one end of which carries the piston, the other end being connected to the crankshaft. It transmits the vertical motion of the piston to the crankshaft, causing the latter to rotate.

Contact breaker: A cam-operated switch in the HT circuit which, when it opens, passes the HT current to the sparking plug.

Crankshaft: The connecting rod is connected to the offset web of the crankshaft and the rotating shaft turns the flywheel on one side and the gears on the other through a clutch.

Decarbonisation: The process of removing carbon deposits from cylinder head, piston crown and ports. Also known as decoke.

DC: Direct current; continuous, as opposed to alternating current (AC). Direct current is obtained from a battery or accumulator.

Deflector piston: A piston with a shaped crown which deflects the incoming stream of mixture as it enters the combustion chamber. Scavenging by means of a deflector piston is a fairly unsophisticated system though it was used by Vespa for many years.

Detonation: Too-rapid burning of the mixture in the combustion chamber, usually through ignition occurring in two places simultaneously. Also known as knock. It should not be confused with pre-ignition.

Direct lighting: A system in which electrical current is supplied to horn, light, etc., direct from the flywheel magneto, not from a battery.

Dog: A projection on the face of a gear or clutch member by means of which drive is transmitted to another gear or clutch member.

Fade: When a brake lining reaches a certain temperature its coefficient of friction drops rapidly and it will no longer provide an effective braking power. This is known as brake fade. The lining usually recovers completely when it cools down.

Flywheel magneto: A flywheel carrying magnets revolves round coils mounted on a stator plate and thus creates an electric current which can be fed to a battery or can be fed direct to lights, horn, etc.

Four-stroking: When the combustion chamber contains only a weak mixture or one fouled by burnt gases the engine will not fire at every stroke. This may also happen in high gear with closed throttle because the incoming mixture does not travel quickly enough. The resultant intermittent firing is called four-stroking.

Gap: The distance between spark plug or contact-breaker points.

Glossary of Technical Terms

Gasket: A thin, shaped membrane between metal surfaces to prevent gas or liquid leaking.

Gudgeon pin: A machined steel bar holding piston to connecting rod.

Heat range: An index of the temperature at which a sparking plug will work satisfactorily. The Bosch Heat Scale is widely used, but British plug manufacturers use – as a rule – a different scale in addition.

Heel-and-toe-pedal: As foot gear changes require a forward and backward movement (or up and down movement) two levers are linked to the pivot so that both motions may be obtained by pressing down with the heel or the toe on one or other of the pedals.

HT: High-tension current of about 10,000 volts (10kV) is passed to the sparking plug from the HT coil.

Ignition: The electrical circuit which provides a spark at the sparking plug. In flywheel magneto ignition the magnets which revolve round the coils are contained in the flywheel.

Jet: A drilled plug, the diameter of the hole allowing a known quantity of fuel to pass in the carburetter. The principal jets are main, choke and pilot jets.

Knock: For engine knock see DETONATION and PINKING.

Leading link: A suspension system in which the front fork is set forward relative to the hub.

Little end: The bearing or bush at the top end of the connecting rod. In the earlier scooters a bronze bush was fitted, but later scooters almost always had needle rollers.

Magneto: By making magnets revolve round a series of wire coils an electric current is produced which can be used for lighting, charging a battery or feeding an HT coil. If the magnets are contained in a flywheel the device is known as a flywheel magneto and this system became almost universally adopted in scooter engines where a 6-volt circuit was fitted.

Mainshaft: A shaft carrying gear pinions. There is much confusion in the names of these gear-carrying shafts. There are two such shafts. The rearward one may be called the primary (Moby, Iso Milano), layshaft (Lambretta) or mainshaft (Villiers). Since the gear-shift systems are not uniform the rear shafts are not strictly comparable.

Manifold: A pipe or short tube. In two-stroke engines the inlet manifold leads mixture to the crankcase; the exhaust manifold leads burnt gases to the exhaust. The name is derived from the multi-cylinder engines, where the inlet manifold branches to each cylinder and the exhaust manifold branched from each cylinder to the exhaust system.

Needle bearing: A bearing consisting of a housing with a series of small needle rollers held in an integral cage. The spindle fits direct on to the needle rollers. It has replaced the solid bronze bush in many applications, such as the little end.

Needle jet: A misleading way of referring to the taper needle which fits in the main jet centrepiece and allows more fuel to pass through the main jet as the throttle is opened.

Neutral selector: A lever which will select neutral gear. It was fitted to some German scooters having foot gear changes. A neutral selector could operate from the handlebar or from a foot control such as the kickstart pedal.

Octane: A measure of the anti-knock rating of a fuel.

Otto cycle: The four operations of Induction, Compression, Ignition and Exhaust; named after Dr. N. A. Otto.

Petroil: A mixture of petrol and oil. A petroiler is a pump which delivers petrol and oil ready mixed in the required proportion.

Pilot jet: A small auxiliary jet in the carburetter with its own air supply. It functions when the throttle is closed to allow the engine to tick over at a low speed.

Pinking: When the mixture in the combustion chamber burns at two separate points simultaneously the second ignition causes a sound wave to oscillate. This strikes the cylinder wall and makes a tinkling sound which becomes more noticeable as load increases and is known as pinking. It may mean that too high a compression ratio is being used for the fuel; but is more often caused through carbon build-up in the combustion chamber.

Piston slap: A hollow, bell-like sound made by the piston hitting the cylinder wall. It may be due to a worn piston, though in some scooter engines there is piston slap until the engine has warmed up.

Play: Movement, other than circular, between one part and the part in or around which it is fitted.

Ports: In a two-stroke engine, holes in the cylinder wall to admit mixture (transfer ports) and to allow burnt gases to make their exit (exhaust port).

Power stroke: The downward stroke of the piston.

Primary drive: The drive from the crankshaft to the clutch or gearbox; usually by roller chain or gears.

Rectifier: Inserted between flywheel magneto and battery this transforms alternating current into direct current (and so feeds the battery) by sending appropriate impulses to one (half-wave) or both (full-wave) terminals.

Regulator: A type of switch which cuts off incoming current from the battery when the latter is fully charged. As the switch is operated by a spring the regulator is apt to stick in which case the battery may not be charged, or may be over-charged. Mechanical regulators are often replaced by diodes.

SAE: The Society of Automotive Engineers, a leading American authority. It is widely known in Britain because of the SAE system of viscosity classification of oils, which has replaced the Redwood and other systems. Viscosity today is almost always quoted by an SAE number. Oils used in scooters may be 20, 30, 40 or 50 SAE. A more recent tendency is to market a single oil to cover a wide variety of SAE numbers.

Glossary of Technical Terms

Scavenging: The process of driving out the burnt gases from the combustion chamber. The two principal systems are Loop Scavenging and Reverse Flow scavenging.

Scraper Ring: The piston ring which scrapes oil and carbon from the cylinder wall.

Seize: When the oil film between piston and cylinder breaks down the piston is said to seize; the cause may be lack of lubricant or overheating. Also applies to bearings.

Silencer: A device for reducing engine noise by smoothing out the pressure variations in the exhaust gases.

Small-end: See Little-end.

Spitting back: Due to weak mixture, incorrect timing or faulty plug. In four-stroke engines the mixture spitting back into the carburetter may carry a flame.

Sprocket: A toothed wheel for use with chain drive.

Stroke: The distance through which a piston moves vertically. It is usually given in millimetres. Stroke multiplied by cylinder cross-section gives engine capacity.

Stud: A headless bolt, threaded at each end.

T.D.C.: Top dead centre. The uppermost point reached by the piston.

Telescopic: Applied to shock absorbers. One tube fits into another but is free to slide, movement being limited by springs, oil or air.

Timing: Arranging that the spark in a two-stroke engine occurs just before the piston reaches tdc. In a four-stroke engine, additionally arranging that the valves open and shut at appropriate points of piston travel.

Top up: Add distilled water to a battery to maintain the correct level; also applied to oil levels.

Torque: The force which tends to twist or bend a part, or cause it to rotate.

Torsion bar: A shock-absorbing shaft which twists under load in the same way that a coil spring compresses under load.

Glossary of Technical Terms

Turbulence: The swirling of a fuel mixture to give more even, more rapid flame spread.

Two-stroke cycle: An internal combustion engine arrangement whereby each downstroke of the piston is a power stroke; a development of the four-stroke cycle.

Vapour lock: Interruption of the fuel flow, usually due to great heat and poor routing of the fuel line. It was common in early motor cars, but is rarely met with today.

Venturi: A tube which serves as an air passage and has a restriction of bore at one point is known as a Venturi Tube. As air speed at that point increases the pressure is lowered.

Wheelbase: The horizontal distance between hub centres.

Index

Index

Index

Index

Index